Portland Community College

Arduino in Action

Arduino in Action

MARTIN EVANS
JOSHUA NOBLE
JORDAN HOCHENBAUM

MANNING

SHELTER ISLAND

Photographs in this book were created by Martin Evans and Jordan Hochenbaum, unless
otherwise noted. Illustrations were created by Martin Evans, Joshua Noble, and Jordan
Hochenbaum. Fritzing (fritzing.org) was used to create some of the circuit diagrams.

Many of the designations used by manufacturers and sellers to distinguish their products are
claimed as trademarks. Where those designations appear in the book, and Manning
Publications was aware of a trademark claim, the designations have been printed in initial caps
or all caps.

Manning Publications Co.
20 Baldwin Road
PO Box 261
Shelter Island, NY 11964

Development editor: Cynthia Kane
Copyeditor: Andy Carroll
Proofreader: Katie Tennant
Typesetter: Dennis Dalinnik
Cover designer: Marija Tudor

ISBN: 9781617290244
Printed in the United States of America
1 2 3 4 5 6 7 8 9 10 – MAL – 19 18 17 16 15 14 13

brief contents

v

contents

preface

My Arduino journey started after watching Elise Huard present her talk, "The internet of things," at Rails Underground in the summer of 2009. Following the conference, I immediately purchased a copy of Massimo Banzi's *Getting Started with Arduino* (O'Reilly, 2008), which I read from cover to cover on the train back to where I was staying.

Shortly afterwards, I purchased my first Arduino and started playing, experimenting, and building small projects. My first major project was an obstacle-avoidance robot, which I presented at the 2010 Scottish Ruby conference in Edinburgh, Scotland.

I've had a lifelong interest in underwater vehicles and the marine environment, and following the conference I started work on an Arduino-controlled underwater remote-operated vehicle (ROV), which I duly presented at the 2011 Scottish Ruby conference.

Since then, I've toured the UK and Ireland displaying my ROV at a number of Maker Faires, where it has generated much interested and discussion.

I'm one of the founding members of Aberduino, a hack space based in Aberdeen, Scotland, where we produce installations for various events.

Other Arduino-based projects I've worked on include the development of a medical training aid and helping with the Wikispeed project, an open source car.

I continue to work with underwater vehicles and am actively developing a new Arduino-based underwater ROV that can be distributed as a kit.

MARTIN EVANS

I first started working with microcontrollers with the same introduction that a lot of artists and designers had ten years ago: PIC controllers. I found them difficult to understand, finicky, slow to build with, and yet they were the only option. Later I discovered Teleo controllers and then Wiring boards, but when the Arduino arrived in my world, I was hooked.

I've used Arduinos for everything from prototyping smart spray-paint cans to building interactive exhibits for museums to creating tools for science experiments. I'm in love with the boards, the environment, and, most especially, the community that has grown up around the Arduino and that's so willing to teach, experiment, explore, and share.

JOSHUA NOBLE

My interest in music technology led me to discover the Arduino as a platform for rapid development and physical computing sometime around 2008. I was originally introduced to the Arduino as a tool for designing musical interfaces for live performance. This led to the Arduinome project, an open source port of the popular Monome USB MIDI controller, which I worked on with longtime collaborator Owen Vallis. The success of the Arduinome project was a true testament to the uniqueness of the Arduino itself—a device that empowers musicians and artists of all technical backgrounds to create unique and powerful tools for expression. Around the same time, I was taking a course in musical robotics and kinetic sculpture, and we used the Arduino to drive a collaborative musical robotic instrument.

Since then, the Arduino has been at the heart of my work. In 2009 I began pursuing my PhD, which investigated the affordances of multimodal sensor systems for musical performance and pedagogy. Using the Arduino, I've built numerous interfaces and hyperinstruments for capturing data and metrics from musical performance. I built the SmartFiducial, which added z-depth (in-air proximity) and pressure sensing to tangible tabletop surfaces. Embedding multimodal sensing systems within instruments or placing them on human performers, I've investigated a wide variety of machine learning tasks, such as performer recognition and drum-hand recognition. I completed my PhD and became a professor in Music Technology: Interaction, Intelligence, and Design at California Institute of the Arts in 2012, and the Arduino continues to be an important part of my artistic and academic practice. My work with the Arduino has been featured online and in print, including in WIRED and Computer Arts magazine, and my current Arduino-based projects range from kinetic surfaces for live projection mapping and visuals to wireless sensing systems for interactive dance performance.

JORDAN HOCHENBAUM

acknowledgments

We would like to thank the following people at Manning: Sebastian Stirling for his endless patience and support; Cynthia Kane for guiding us and giving gentle prods over the final review stages to bring the manuscript to publication; Troy Mott who handled the preproduction stages; technical editors Sharon Cichelli and Daniel Soltis who offered help and advice on how to improve the final manuscript; and copyeditor Andy Carroll who carefully combed through the manuscript, removing unnecessary words and tidying everything up.

We also want to thank our reviewers who helped clarify parts of the book that needed further explanation and who pointed out inconsistencies. Thanks to Alan Burlison, Andrew Davidson, Bill Westfield, Daniel Soltis, George Entenman, Howard R. Hansen, Jeroen Benckhuijsen, John Raines, Margriet Bruggeman, Matt Scarpino, Nikander Bruggeman, P. David Pull, Philipp K. Janert, Scott Couprie, Scott Howard, Steve Prior, and Ursin Stauss.

MARTIN EVANS would like to thank his wife Henrietta and children Leanne, Heather, and Luke, who all in one way or another encouraged him to keep on working on this book. He would also like to thank Paul and the team at Symposium Coffee House, Peterhead, who kept him fueled with coffee when most needed.

JOSHUA NOBLE would like to acknowledge a huge debt of gratitude to Simona Maschi, David Gauthier, and everyone at CIID who let him slack off a little on his thesis project so he could finish his chapters for this book, his lovely girlfriend Rachel Buker, and of course the man who originally taught him to program in his first halting steps, Morgan Schwartz.

JORDAN HOCHENBAUM would like acknowledge his friend and mentor Ajay Kapur for introducing him to the Arduino and to systematically thinking about musical interface design. He'd also like to thank longtime friend and collaborator Owen Vallis for his help as they stumbled through their first Arduino sketches together and delved deeper into the world of the AVR.

about this book

This book is organized into two parts. Part 1 discusses the Arduino in general and includes a tutorial that introduces you to your first project before looking at a couple of simple projects that use the Arduino inputs and outputs. Part 2 looks at the Arduino in more depth, and this is where we really start to put the Arduino to work with a number of advanced techniques that you can use in your own projects.

Code for the sketches covered in each chapter is available online via the book's website: www.manning.com/ArduinoinAction. We suggest trying to follow along with the projects in the book as much as you can. Typing in the individual code listings will help to fix concepts and ideas into your mind.

This book is suitable for both beginners and intermediate Arduino users. It starts from a very basic level and assumes no prior knowledge, but we think even expert users will gain things from the second part of the book, which covers a wide variety of subjects, many of which can be combined into your own projects. A basic understanding of electronics will help with some project circuits, although we endeavor to explain them as much as we can.

Roadmap

Part 1 of the book discusses the Arduino in general.

Chapter 1 explains how to get started by setting up your development environment and a basic software and hardware toolbox. It shows you how to blink your first LED and walks you through the anatomy of an Arduino sketch.

Chapter 2 takes the form of a tutorial that introduces your first project and covers a number of key concepts.

Chapter 3 builds on the knowledge gained in chapter 2 by looking at a couple of simple projects that use the Arduino inputs and outputs.

Part 2 of the book looks at the Arduino in more depth. This is where we put the Arduino to work.

Chapter 4 covers software libraries that extend the Arduino's functionality.

Chapter 5 gets the Arduino into motion by showing how an Arduino can be used to control a range of motors.

Object detection is covered in chapter 6 with a section on how ultrasound and ultrasonic sensors can be interfaced.

Chapter 7 is all about outputting data to LCD displays. It covers communication with the Hitachi HD44780 parallel LCD as well as the KS0108 graphic LCD that can also display graphics.

In chapter 8 we cover communication with the external world. We start by using an Ethernet Shield to create a web server and then move on to tweeting messages from an Arduino to Twitter, using a Wi-Fi network and Bluetooth communication, logging data to an SD card and the internet using the Cosm service, and communicating with other devices over the serial peripheral interface (SPI).

Chapter 9 details connecting an Arduino to game controllers, starting with the widely available Wii Nunchuk over I2C. Then we take a detailed look at using a USB shield to interface with a USB Xbox controller.

Chapter 10 covers integration with iOS devices like the iPhone and iPad using the Redpark serial cable.

In chapter 11 we look at two alternative forms of the Arduino that can be used as wearables: the LilyPad that can be sewn into clothing, and the Arduino Mini Pro, which is a special customized version of the Arduino notable for its small size.

Chapter 12 looks at shields, which provide a simple method of extending or enhancing the Arduino hardware. This chapter includes instructions for creating your own shields.

Finally, chapter 13 is on software integration, and it covers communicating with the Arduino from other software programs.

There are also several appendices.

Appendix A is about installing the Arduino software on Windows, Mac OS X, and Linux operating systems.

Appendix B is a coding primer for the Arduino language.

Appendix C is about Arduino software libraries and their structure.

Appendix D provides a listing of all the components required to complete the individual projects in each chapter.

Appendix E is a list of useful links.

Code conventions and downloads

There are many code examples in this book, edited using the Arduino integrated development environment (IDE). Source code in listings and text is in a `fixed-width font like this`, to separate it from ordinary text, and code annotations accompany many of the listings.

You'll find the source code for the examples in this book available from the publisher's website at www.manning.com/ArduinoinAction.

Author Online

The purchase of *Arduino in Action* includes free access to a private web forum run by Manning Publications, where you can make comments about the book, ask technical questions, and receive help from the authors and from other users. To access the forum and subscribe to it, point your web browser to www.manning.com/ArduinoinAction. This page provides information on how to get on the forum once you are registered, what kind of help is available, and the rules of conduct on the forum.

Manning's commitment to our readers is to provide a venue where a meaningful dialogue between individual readers and between readers and the authors can take place. It is not a commitment to any specific amount of participation on the part of the authors, whose contribution to the forum remains voluntary (and unpaid). We suggest you try asking the authors some challenging questions lest their interest stray!

The Author Online forum and the archives of previous discussions will be accessible from the publisher's website as long as the book is in print.

about the cover illustration

The figure on the cover of *Arduino in Action* is captioned "Travailleur de déplacement," which means an itinerant laborer. The illustration is taken from a 19th-century edition of Sylvain Maréchal's four-volume compendium of regional dress customs published in France. Each illustration is finely drawn and colored by hand. The rich variety of Maréchal's collection reminds us vividly of how culturally apart the world's towns and regions were just 200 years ago. Isolated from each other, people spoke different dialects and languages. In the streets or in the countryside, it was easy to identify where they lived and what their trade or station in life was just by their dress.

Dress codes have changed since then and the diversity by region, so rich at the time, has faded away. It is now hard to tell apart the inhabitants of different continents, let alone different towns or regions. Perhaps we have traded cultural diversity for a more varied personal life—certainly for a more varied and fast-paced technological life.

At a time when it is hard to tell one computer book from another, Manning celebrates the inventiveness and initiative of the computer business with book covers based on the rich diversity of regional life of two centuries ago, brought back to life by Maréchal's pictures.

Part 1

Getting started

Part 1 of this book (chapters 1 to 3) is a discussion of the Arduino in general. You'll start by learning your way around the Arduino and its development environment and completing a tutorial that introduces you to your first project. Then you'll look at a couple of simple projects that use the Arduino inputs and outputs.

Hello Arduino

This chapter covers
- The history of the Arduino
- Arduino hardware
- Hardware and software setup
- The first blinking LED

What can the Arduino be used for? The answers are surprisingly diverse. The Arduino has been used in a wide variety of projects:

- Video games such as Pong and Space Invaders that will remind some readers of their childhood and introduce others to the games their parents played when they were young, complete with monochrome graphics and simple sound effects
- Line-following robots that introduce robotics principles but are also used in factories and warehouses to deliver components along predetermined paths
- Light harps that produce music with a wave of your hands, as used internationally by the performer Little Boots
- MIDI controllers that control a series of instruments
- Self-balancing robots that mimic the Segway

These are all examples of projects built using the Arduino, a microcontroller so small that it fits in the palm of your hand. Originally designed to be used as a tool for physical computing projects by design and art students, the Arduino has been adopted as the tool of choice by communities of tinkerers and makers interested in building and prototyping their own projects.

In this chapter, we'll start with a look at the history of Arduino and how it became the tool that many makers reach for when starting a new project. This background includes its origins at the Interaction Design Institute Ivrea and explains why it was so desperately needed. We'll then review the different types of Arduinos available and the advantages and disadvantages of each. We'll also look at what you need to get started: tools, equipment, and suggested electronic components. Finally, we'll round this opening chapter out with a look at the Arduino integrated development environment (IDE) before making our first project: an LED that blinks on and off.

Let's start by learning where the Arduino comes from.

1.1   *A brief history of the Arduino*

The Arduino got its start at the Interaction Design Institute in the city of Ivrea, Italy, in 2005. Professor Massimo Banzi was looking for a low-cost way to make it easier for the design students there to work with technology. He discussed his problem with David Cuartielles, a researcher visiting from Malmö University in Sweden who was looking for a similar solution, and Arduino was born.

Existing products on the market were expensive and relatively difficult to use. Banzi and Cuartielles decided to make a microcontroller that could be used by their art and design students in their projects. The main requirements were that it be inexpensive—the target price was to be no more than a student would spend going out for a pizza—and be a platform that anyone could use. David Cuartielles designed the board, and a student of Massimo's, David Mellis, programmed the software to run the board. Massimo contacted a local engineer, Gianluca Martino, who also worked at the Design Institute helping students with their projects. Gianluca agreed to produce an initial run of 200 boards.

The new board was named Arduino after a local bar frequented by faculty members and students from the institute. The boards were sold in kit form for students to build themselves. The initial run was soon sold out, and more were produced to keep up with demand. Designers and artists from other areas heard about the Arduino and wanted to use it in their projects. Its popularity soon grew when the wider maker audience realized that the Arduino was an easy-to-use, low-cost system that could be used in their own projects, as well as a great introduction to programming microcontrollers. The original design was improved upon and new versions were introduced. Sales of official Arduinos have now reached over 300,000 units, and they're sold all over the world through a range of distributors.

There are now a number of different versions of Arduino boards, so we'll take a look at them in the next section.

1.2   The Arduino hardware

There have been a number of Arduino versions, all based on an 8-bit Atmel AVR reduced instruction set computer (RISC) microprocessor. The first board was based on the ATmega8 running at a clock speed of 16 MHz with 8 KB flash memory; later boards such as the Arduino NG plus and the Diecimila (Italian for 10,000) used the ATmega168 with 16 KB flash memory. The most recent Arduino versions, Duemilanove and Uno, use the ATmega328 with 32 KB flash memory and can switch automatically between USB and DC power. For projects requiring more I/O and memory, there's the Arduino Mega1280 with 128 KB memory or the more recent Arduino Mega2560 with 256 KB memory.

The boards have 14 digital pins, each of which can be set as either an input or output, and six analog inputs. In addition, six of the digital pins can be programmed to provide a pulse width modulation (PWM) analog output. A variety of communication protocols are available, including serial, serial peripheral interface bus (SPI), and I2C/TWI. Included on each board as standard features are an in-circuit serial programming (ICSP) header and reset button.

NOTE Specialist boards called *shields* can expand the basic functionality of the Arduino; these can be stacked on top of each other to add even more functionality.

We're now going to look at the more commonly available Arduino models, starting with the Arduino Uno.

1.2.1   Arduino Uno

"Dinner is Served" was the blog title announcing on September 25, 2010, the arrival of the Arduino Uno (meaning *one* in Italian), and its bigger brother, the Mega2560. The Arduino Uno is pin-compatible with previous Arduinos, including the Duemilanove and its predecessor the Diecimila.

The major difference between the Uno and its predecessors is the inclusion of an ATmega8U2 microcontroller programmed as a USB-to-serial converter, replacing the ageing FTDI chipset used by previous versions. The ATmega8U2 can be reprogrammed to make the Arduino look like another USB device, such as a mouse, keyboard, or joystick. Another difference is that it has a more reliable onboard 3.3 volts, which helps with the stability of some shields that have caused problems in the past. See appendix C for the full technical specifications.

Figure 1.1 shows the board layout and pins of the Arduino Uno.

The Uno is a good all-purpose Arduino and is your best bet for a starter board with its auto-switching power supply and regulated onboard 3.3 volts.

1.2.2   Arduino Duemilanove

The Duemilanove (which means *2009* in Italian) is one of the most popular Arduino boards produced, having replaced its predecessor, the Arduino Diecimila. But it, in turn,

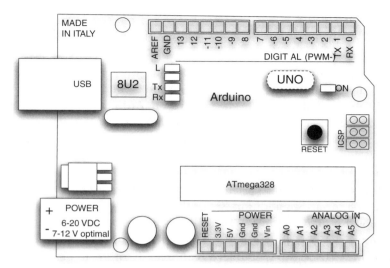

Figure 1.1   Board layout and pins of the Arduino Uno

has been superseded by the newer, more up-to-date Arduino Uno. The Duemilanove features auto-switching power selection between the external and USB, and it uses the ATmega328 processor, although models prior to March 2009 used the ATmega168. Its pin layout and capabilities are identical to the Uno, and it uses the FTDI chipset for USB-to-serial communication.

If you're purchasing a new Arduino, you should get the Arduino Uno. If you already have a Duemilanove, consider upgrading to the Uno if you need the more stable 3.3 volts or want to do some advanced programming with the ATmega8U2.

1.2.3   Arduino Ethernet

The Arduino Ethernet is a low-power version of the Arduino announced at the same time as the Uno. The main differences between it and other Arduino versions are that it has an onboard RJ45 connector for an Ethernet connection and a microSD card reader. The Arduino Ethernet doesn't have an onboard USB-to-serial driver chip, but it does have a six-pin header that can be connected to an FTDI cable or USB serial board to provide a communication link so that the board can be programmed. It can also be powered by an optional Power over Ethernet (POE) module, which enables the Arduino Ethernet to source its power from a connected twisted-pair Category 5 Ethernet cable.

The Arduino Ethernet is ideally suited for use in remote monitoring and data logging stations with the onboard microSD card reader and a connection to a wired Ethernet network for power.

1.2.4   Arduino Mega

The big brother of the Arduino family, the Mega, uses a larger surface-mount microprocessor. The ATmega1280, the Mega, was updated at the same time as the Uno, and

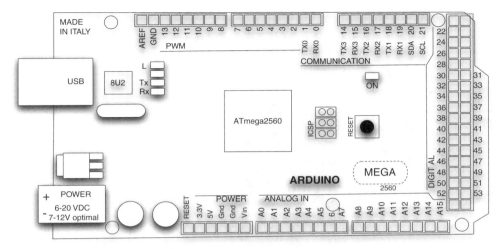

Figure 1.2   The Arduino Mega pins and layout; note the additional input-output pins and the extra serial ports compared to the Arduino Uno.

the microprocessor now used is the ATmega2560. The new version has 256 KB of flash memory compared to the 128 KB of the original.

The Mega provides significantly increased input-output functionality compared to the standard Arduino, so with the increased memory, it's ideal for those larger projects that control lots of LEDs, have a large number of inputs and outputs, or need more than one hardware serial port—the Arduino Mega has four. The boards have 54 digital input-output pins, 14 of which can provide PWM analog output, and 16 analog input pins. Communication is handled with up to four hardware serial ports. SPI communication and support for I2C/TWI devices is also available. The board also includes an ICSP header and reset button. An ATmega8U2 replaces the FTDI chipset used by its predecessor and handles USB serial communication.

The Mega works with the majority of the shields available, but it's a good idea to check that a shield will be compatible with your Mega before purchasing it. Purchase the Mega when you have a clear need for the additional input-output pins and larger memory. See appendix C for the full technical specifications.

Figure 1.2 shows the pin and board layout.

Now let's take a look at a few more specialized Arduino options.

1.2.5   *Other Arduino boards*

The original Arduino has spawned a number of variations that package the design in different ways, usually in response to a need. Let's take a look at two of them: the Lily-Pad and the Nano.

LILYPAD ARDUINO

Designed by SparkFun Electronics and Leah Buechley, the LilyPad Arduino is great for textile projects and for strutting your stuff on the catwalk. It's designed with large

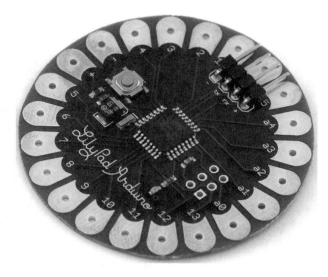

Figure 1.3   The LilyPad Arduino is suitable for sewing onto fabric, and there's a range of sewable accessories available.

connecting pads that can be sewn to fabric, and there's a range of sewable accessories available, including light sensors, buzzers, tri-color LEDs, temperature sensors, E-sewing kits, and accelerometers. This low-power version is even washable; just don't forget to take out the batteries first.

The main difference between the LilyPad and other Arduinos is a slower processing speed of 8 MHz, as opposed to the normal 16 MHz. One thing to watch out for: the input voltage must not exceed 5.5 volts. See figure 1.3 for a picture of the LilyPad Arduino.

ARDUINO NANO

If your project has limited space, the Arduino Nano is the right choice. Designed and produced by Gravitech, version 3.0 of the Nano (with the ATmega328 processor) has a mini USB onboard, a compact format for use on breadboards.

The Nano has similar functionality to the Duemilanove, but it has two additional analog input pins. Power to the board is supplied either by USB or two separate pins: pin 30 can accept an unregulated supply between 6 and 20 volts, or pin 27 can accept a regulated supply of 5.5 volts. The board selects whichever voltage is the highest.

The small size of the board makes it ideal for projects with limited space.

1.2.6   *Attack of the clones*

From the beginning, Arduino was conceived as open-source hardware. Users were free to take the design, download the published computer-aided design (CAD) files, and produce and sell hardware based on them. This has led to the production of a number of clones or copies of Arduino, with many of the clone manufacturers taking the original specification and making their own changes.

The Arduino name is trademarked, preventing derivatives from using the Arduino name in their products unless permission is given by the Arduino team.

SEEEDUINO (YES, 3 E'S)

If you like the color red, this is the board to get. Designed and produced by Seeed Studio, in Shenzhen, China, the Seeeduino is based on the Diecimila design, one of the early Arduino boards, and can be purchased with either an ATmega168 or ATmega328 microprocessor. It uses low-profile surface-mount components and has a distinctive red color.

The board is compatible with the Diecimila's pin layout and dimensions. Improvements include auto-sensing between USB and external power, and better onboard power supplies.

SEEEDUINO FILM

The Seeeduino Film is a different take on wearables than the LilyPad's fabric-based architecture. This flexible Arduino clone, which can also be used in data-logging projects, has a surface-mount ATmega168 on a flexible printed circuit board. Instead of shields, expansion is achieved by what the manufacturer calls *frames*. One frame has been produced so far, consisting of a barometer, 32 MB of flash memory, and a three-axis accelerometer, which should be more than enough to get you going.

BOARDUINO

The Boarduino is a small board similar to the Nano 3.0, but available as a kit only, so soldering skills will be required. Produced by Adafruit Industries, the Boarduino is designed to plug directly into a solderless breadboard. The kit is available in two versions, one with USB and the other with a serial connection for which an additional cable is required. It uses the ATmega328.

SIPPINO

The Sippino is a miniature Arduino-compatible clone from SpikenzieLabs sold in kit form, so like the Boarduino, it requires soldering skills. The Sippino uses the ATmega328, but it can also use the ATmega168. All the digital and analog input-output pins are brought out into a single line so it can be plugged directly into a solderless breadboard. A FTDI-USB serial cable is required to program the board.

EBAY

A number of clone boards are sold on eBay, many of them copies of the Duemilanove. Here are some things to look out for in any clone: make sure it has an ATmega328 microprocessor, and that the headers are suitable for adding shields.

The first Arduino we purchased from eBay had male instead of female headers, which made it difficult to add shields. We also had to buy some special jumpers to connect to a breadboard. It was enough to get us started, but it's better to avoid such mistakes and check that you're buying what you really want.

1.2.7 *Getting an Arduino*

If you're looking to get started with Arduinos, we recommend getting the Uno, with its superior USB connection and better regulated onboard power supply.

The Arduino Uno is available from a number of online retailers. The three most prominent in the USA are SparkFun Electronics (www.sparkfun.com), Adafruit

Industries (http://adafruit.com), and Maker Shed (http://makershed.com/). In the UK, there are SK Pang Electronics (http://skpang.co.uk) and oomlout (http://oomlout.co.uk). A full list of worldwide distributors is available at the main Arduino website (http://arduino.cc/en/Main/Buy).

Once you have an Arduino, you can move on to connecting it to your system and setting up your working environment.

1.3   Setting up your working environment

Once you receive a shiny new Arduino, you'll probably be itching to get started. This section should help scratch that itch, as we'll look at connecting your Arduino to your computer for the first time, and you'll learn what's required to set up your working environment.

To get started, you'll need an Arduino. As mentioned in the previous section, a Duemilanove or a Uno is a good place to start. You'll also need a USB cable to connect the Arduino to your computer.

1.3.1   Software for Arduino

At the moment, your Arduino is just a board with some electronic components on it. To make it do some useful work, you need to give it instructions, which is why you need the Arduino software IDE. The Arduino software IDE provides everything required for programming the Arduino, including a number of example programs or sketches that demonstrate how to connect it to and communicate with some common devices, such as LEDs, LCDs, and some sensors.

You'll be glad to know that, just like the hardware, the software for Arduino is open source and can be freely downloaded from http://arduino.cc/en/Main/Software. Just make sure you download the correct version for your system. Versions of the IDE are available for Windows, Mac OS X, and Linux. For full installation instructions for each platform see appendix A.

It's important to familiarize yourself with the IDE because it's where you'll write all your code. In the world of Arduino, a block of code is called a *sketch*. A sketch gives an Arduino a list of instructions and the Arduino goes off and sketches out your idea. The IDE helps to hide much of the complexity of the Arduino, making it much easier to develop projects.

> **NOTE**   The term *sketch* comes from Processing, a language often taught to design and art students, and on which the Arduino IDE is based. Those already familiar with programming should think of a sketch as being like a software program.

1.3.2   Basic hardware setup

The Arduino board connects to your computer via USB. The USB cable provides the 5 volts required to power the Arduino, and it provides enough power to light up a couple of LEDs and allow for some basic experimentation.

1.3.3 Your Arduino toolbox

Here's a shopping list we recommend to someone just starting with Arduino:

- Arduino (Uno or Duemilanove)
- Mini breadboard and jumpers (used to build small circuits)
- Selection of LEDs
- Selection of resistors
- 9 volt battery
- Battery connector
- Light-dependent resistor
- Small DC motor or servo
- Piezo buzzer (a type of small loudspeaker, like those found in musical cards)
- Potentiometer (a type of variable resistor)

Typical projects you could build with these components include flashing LEDs, model traffic lights, a musical buzzer, and a light-activated switch.

If you're feeling a little more adventurous, you could add the following components:

- Adafruit GPS and data logging shield for recording sensor data, time, and position
- Adafruit Wave shield for playing audio from an SD memory card for special effects
- Motor shield for driving a couple of motors, possibly the beginnings of robot motion

A kit of basic components, including an Arduino and a selection of components, can be purchased from a number of sellers, who often offer a discount when you purchase a kit.

Now that your working environment is set up, it's time to write your first sketch and perform the hardware equivalent of "Hello World."

1.4 Make something happen!

Before you rush out to pick up all those exciting attachments, all you need for your first example is an Arduino, because all of them have an onboard LED connected to digital pin 13. For this first example, you're going to make an LED blink on and off repeatedly.

NOTE In case you want to be a little more adventurous, we've also included instructions for adding an external LED in section 1.4.3.

1.4.1 Your first blinking LED

LEDs are available in a range of colors, but the LED connected to pin 13 on the Arduino is normally green. The LED lights up when a current is applied to it, so you can use pin 13 like a switch. When you switch it on, it will light up the LED, and when you switch it off, it will turn off the LED.

Let's start by writing the sketch.

1.4.2   *Sketch to make an LED blink*

Start up the Arduino IDE and copy the following code. It might look a little overwhelming at first, but don't worry. We'll go into more detail about what this all means later in the chapter.

> **Listing 1.1   Code required to make an LED blink**

```
void setup(){
    pinMode(13, OUTPUT);
}

void loop(){
    digitalWrite(13, HIGH);
    delay(1000);
    digitalWrite(13, LOW);
    delay(1000);
}
```

The code is straightforward. You're assigning digital pin 13 as an output, and then you're looping through some code that switches pin 13 on to HIGH or LOW for 1 second. The delay value is given in milliseconds, so 1000 milliseconds give you a delay time of 1 second.

NOTE   Make sure that you copy the listing exactly. Watch out for the semicolon (;) at the end of some lines and the correct use of capital letters. As far as Arduino is concerned, digitalwrite isn't the same as digitalWrite.

1.4.3   *Connecting everything*

If you connect your Arduino to your computer via the USB cable, this sketch will control the onboard LED next to pin 13.

You can also control an external LED by connecting it between pin 13 and GND. The connection is shown in figure 1.4. Note that the LED must be connected the

Figure 1.4   LED inserted between pin 13 and GND. Note that the shorter leg is connected to GND.

correct way around—the shorter leg is the cathode or –, and the longer is the anode or +, so push the longer lead into pin 13 and the shorter into GND. If you're struggling with some of the electronics terms, a good primer can be found at www.kpsec.freeuk.com/compon.htm.

NOTE A current-limiting resistor would normally be required to prevent the LED from burning out, and we'll cover that in chapter 2. For now, let's just use the existing onboard LED.

Once the LED has been inserted, you can move on to the next section to test the sketch.

1.4.4 *Uploading and testing*

Time to see if your sketch works! First, connect the Arduino to your computer via a USB cable. You now have a couple of settings to make between the software and the Arduino.

First you need to set the board type. Select Tools > Board and then select the type of Arduino you're using. See figure 1.5.

Next, you need to set the serial port because the USB sees the Arduino as a serial connection. Select Tools > Serial Port and then choose your serial port (see figure 1.6). On a system using Mac OS X for an Arduino Uno, the port will be something like /dev/tty.usbmodem; for older boards like the Duemilanove or Diecimila, it will be something like /dev/tty.usbserial. On a Windows system, the port will be identified as something like COM3.

NOTE Figure 1.6 shows the selection for a system using Mac OS X. The port on a Windows system will be different and will be something like COM3.

The next step is to click the Upload button in the IDE. See figure 1.7.

Wait a few seconds, and the LED should start blinking at the rate of about once a second.

Figure 1.5   In this example, the Duemilanove has been selected, but you can see there's quite a list to choose from.

Figure 1.6   Select the correct serial board from the list.

NOTE   The Arduino retains the program in its memory even if it's switched off until you upload another sketch.

It's always exciting when you see that first LED blinking and know everything is working properly, but that's not all you can do with your Arduino. You're now going to get a more detailed look at the IDE and take a tour of the main coding editor screen.

1.5   *Touring the IDE*

As stated earlier, the IDE is based on Processing, which was designed for ease of use and ease of learning. The IDE provides everything you need to write and upload sketches (programs) to the Arduino.

1.5.1   *The main editor*

When the IDE is first loaded, it opens with a blank sketch; the sketch is automatically given a temporary name with a date reference. The name can be changed later to something more appropriate when you save the sketch.

Figure 1.8 shows the IDE containing a sketch, with annotations for the various buttons and windows. The toolbar along the top of the main editor has the following functions:

- *Verify*—Checks sketches for errors. Errors are reported at the bottom of the screen.
- *New*—Opens a new sketch.
- *Open*—Opens up a list of previously-saved sketches and example sketches.
- *Save*—Saves the sketch and prompts for a name if this is the first save.
- *Upload*—Checks the code for errors before uploading the sketch to Arduino.
- *Serial monitor*—Opens the serial monitor in a new window (see figure 1.9 in the next section).

Figure 1.7   Click the upload button to upload the sketch to the Arduino.

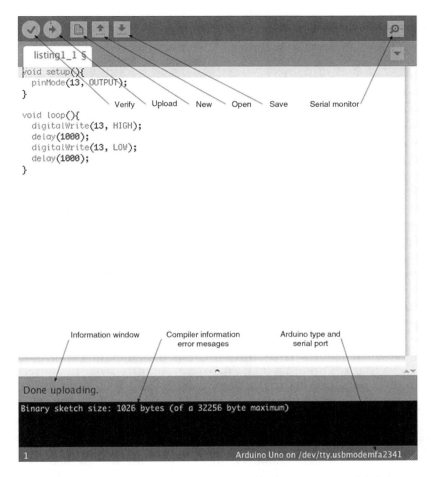

```
listing1_1 §
void setup(){
    pinMode(13, OUTPUT);
}

void loop(){
    digitalWrite(13, HIGH);
    delay(1000);
    digitalWrite(13, LOW);
    delay(1000);
}
```

Verify   Upload   New   Open   Save   Serial monitor

Information window   Compiler information   Arduino type and
                      error mesages   serial port

Done uploading.

Binary sketch size: 1026 bytes (of a 32256 byte maximum)

1   Arduino Uno on /dev/tty.usbmodemfa2341

Figure 1.8   A typical sketch with the buttons and areas of the screen labeled

At the bottom of the main screen are two windows. The first provides status information and feedback; the second provides information when you're verifying and uploading sketches. Any coding errors will also be reported here.

The code editor additionally matches the curly braces, { }, used to denote blocks of code, and it performs syntax highlighting and automatically indents your code for readability.

1.5.2   *Serial monitor*

The serial monitor mentioned in the previous section monitors data between the Arduino and the host computer system over the connected USB cable. The Arduino can send information using code, and it can also receive it. You can see this in figure 1.9.

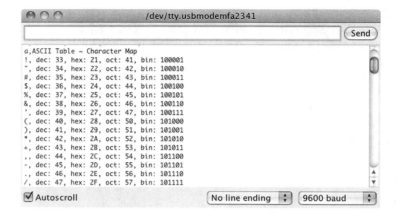

```
/dev/tty.usbmodemfa2341                                    Send

a,ASCII Table ~ Character Map
!, dec: 33, hex: 21, oct: 41, bin: 100001
", dec: 34, hex: 22, oct: 42, bin: 100010
#, dec: 35, hex: 23, oct: 43, bin: 100011
$, dec: 36, hex: 24, oct: 44, bin: 100100
%, dec: 37, hex: 25, oct: 45, bin: 100101
&, dec: 38, hex: 26, oct: 46, bin: 100110
', dec: 39, hex: 27, oct: 47, bin: 100111
(, dec: 40, hex: 28, oct: 50, bin: 101000
), dec: 41, hex: 29, oct: 51, bin: 101001
*, dec: 42, hex: 2A, oct: 52, bin: 101010
+, dec: 43, hex: 2B, oct: 53, bin: 101011
,, dec: 44, hex: 2C, oct: 54, bin: 101100
-, dec: 45, hex: 2D, oct: 55, bin: 101101
., dec: 46, hex: 2E, oct: 56, bin: 101110
/, dec: 47, hex: 2F, oct: 57, bin: 101111

Autoscroll              No line ending    9600 baud
```

Figure 1.9 **The serial monitor showing the output from an Arduino printing out an ASCII table**

The top part of the serial monitor window is used for sending data to the Arduino. You could, for example, use it to send control commands to the Arduino to turn a servomotor a varying number of degrees, or to open or close a switch. The main part of the window displays data output from the Arduino. This could be used to check the output from a GPS or to perform other signal monitoring.

The serial monitor is very useful for debugging code when linking the Arduino to a computer system running software that interacts in some way with the Arduino; you can use the serial monitor to check that the Arduino is outputting the correct data in the format expected. In the serial monitor, you can also set the baud rate used for communication, autoscroll of text, and the form of line ending that is appended to data sent to the Arduino.

1.5.3   *Catching errors*

Now let's return to the main editor. The main area of the screen is the code editor where you type your code. Once you've finished inputting code, you have the option to either verify or upload your sketch to the Arduino.

Any code errors are reported in the bottom window. In figure 1.10 we've introduced an error by omitting a semicolon (;) at the end of one of the lines of code.

Details of the error are provided, as well as the line on which the error occurs. Hopefully the code checker can provide enough information to point you in the right direction if it doesn't point out exactly what's wrong. As you can see in figure 1.10, the code checker has correctly identified the missing ; and where the error occurred.

1.5.4   *Process*

What does the IDE actually do with your code? When you press the upload button, it checks the code for errors and performs some minor translations to convert the sketch to valid C++. The code is then compiled, which means it's converted to a form that can be understood by the Arduino. The resulting file is then combined with the standard Arduino libraries before being uploaded to the Arduino hardware.

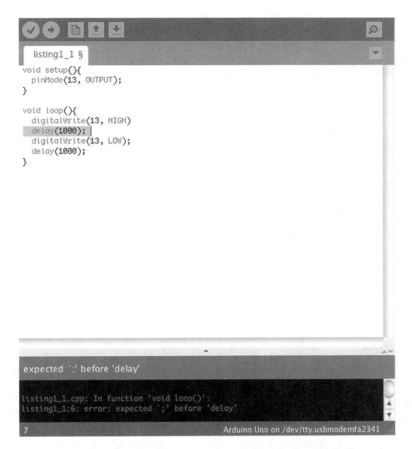

Figure 1.10   The code editor reports an error we've introduced into the code. The code checker indicates which line it thinks the error is on, as well as what it expected.

Now that you've had a tour of the IDE, it's time to get a better sense of Arduino sketches.

1.6   Anatomy of a sketch

A typical sketch consists of two parts or routines: the first is the initialization routine called *setup*, and the second is a routine called *loop*, usually containing the main body of code. We'll take a more detailed look at these two routines next.

1.6.1   A routine called setup

When you want to go out for a jog, there are things you must do before you can go: put on your shoes or trainers, get a bottle of water, and stretch. It's the same with an Arduino. It must be prepared or set up before it can go to work.

This setup is contained within an initialization routine or function appropriately called `setup` (see the following listing). Typical things you would do in `setup` include initializing digital pins—setting them as INPUT or OUTPUT—and setting the baud rate for serial communication.

```
void setup()
{
pinMode(13,OUTPUT);
Serial.begin(9600);
}
```

The setup code in listing 1.2 sets digital pin 13 as an output and configures serial communication at baud rate 9600. The void in front of setup just means the function doesn't return a value.

Even if you don't have anything to set up, the routine is still required or an error will be generated when verifying or uploading a sketch. Just type an empty function with a code comment:

```
void setup(){
      // nothing to setup
{
```

Now let's look at the other required function, loop.

1.6.2   *The endless loop*

When you go for a jog, you keep running until you're done (however you define *done*). It's the same with an Arduino; it runs continually in a looping routine or function called loop until some condition is met or the Arduino is powered down. The following listing shows the loop for the blinking LED from listing 1.1.

```
void loop()
{
digitalWrite(13, HIGH);
delay(1000);
digitalWrite(13,LOW);
delay(1000);
}
```

In this case, the Arduino loops repeatedly, turning the LED on for a second and then off for a second, continuing until the Arduino is powered down.

Now that you know the basics of writing a sketch, it's time to close out the chapter with an important reminder.

1.7   *Commenting code*

You've written a great piece of code that you're really proud of. Now imagine that six months later, someone else is browsing through your past work and comes upon the same sketch, but they can't quite figure out what it does or how it works.

A simple description would help enormously. This is where commenting your code becomes invaluable.

There are two main ways to place comments in a sketch: either as a single line or as a block. A single line comment has a double slash (//) at the start of the line. This tells the compiler that it's just a comment and can be ignored. When you want to add a block of code as a comment, start the block with /* and end with */.

Both methods are demonstrated here:

```
// This is a single-line comment

/* And this is a block carried over
a couple of lines
*/
```

Where should you put comments? Each sketch should have a comment block at the top or header of the sketch, giving a description of what the sketch does, who wrote it, the date, and the version number. The next listing shows an example header.

Listing 1.4 Example header code

```
/*
Code to blink LED
Author: Martin Evans
Date created : 1st September 2009
Version 1.0
*/
```

Single-line comments spread throughout the sketch will quickly allow you to see what the individual pieces of code do. You don't need to comment every piece of code, just places where you think it would help you or someone else understand the code at a later date. It's probably better to have too many comments than too few. The following listing shows some typical code comments.

Listing 1.5 Example code comments

```
void setup()
{
  Serial.begin(9600);

  // prints title with ending line break
  Serial.println("ASCII Table ~ Character Map");
}

// first visible ASCIIcharacter '!' is number 33:
int thisByte = 33;
/* you can also write ASCII characters in single quotes.
for example. '!' is the same as 33, so you could also use this:
int thisByte = '!'; */
```

We've looked at the code editor and the IDE, seen how a sketch is formed with the setup and loop functions, and discussed the importance of code comments.

1.8   *Summary*

This has been a busy chapter, and we've covered a lot of ground. We started by learning a little of the history of Arduino and its beginnings at the Interaction Design Institute in Italy. We saw the layout of the pins and main components of the Arduino Uno and Mega. We caught a glimpse of some other Arduino versions, including the Lily-Pad and the Seeeduino Film, and what they offer. You set up a working environment and wrote your first sketch, getting to see your Arduino come to life.

We looked in detail at the Arduino software IDE and the components of a sketch, with the `setup` and `loop` routines, we looked at using the serial monitor, and we saw the importance of commenting your code.

The next chapter is a tutorial that covers the gradual development of a project and the steps involved in completing it.

Digital input and output

2

Now that you have a sense of what an Arduino can do and have completed your first test run, it's time to delve deeper. You're going to build on what you learned in chapter 1 and build your first complete project, a reactometer that uses LEDs, a push button, and a timer to record reaction times.

Let's get started.

2.1 Getting started

To complete your reactometer, you need a handful of components:

- A breadboard on which to assemble the project
- A selection of jumpers to connect components together
- Six red LEDs; you can use other colors if you want

- One green LED
- One momentary-contact push button
- Seven resistors, each around 180 ohms or slightly greater in value
- One 10k ohm resistor

You can see these components in figure 2.1.

Next, you'll assemble the circuit on a breadboard.

2.1.1 *Using a breadboard*

Breadboards are great for assembling circuits, particularly during the development phase of a project, because they make it easy to move components around or add new ones.

A typical breadboard layout is shown in figure 2.2. The breadboard is made up of a number of sockets. In the central part of the board, the sockets are connected vertically with a break in the center, and they're connected horizontally at the top and bottom. The top and bottom areas are used to provide the power supplies to the circuit being built. Connections between components are made using jumpers of varying lengths.

It's now time to start populating the breadboard by adding your first batch of LEDs and resistors.

2.1.2 *Circuit diagram*

For the first part of the project, you're going to add five LEDs to the breadboard. Figure 2.3 shows a diagram, or *schematic*, of the circuit you're going to build. Don't worry if you don't understand it at the moment—you'll soon get the hang of reading a circuit diagram and translating it to use on a breadboard.

In the circuit diagram, digital pins D8 to D12 of the Arduino each connect to an LED (LED1 through LED5); a current-limiting resistor is connected to each LED (R1 through

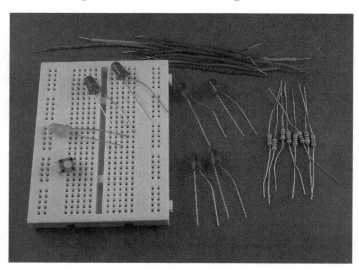

Figure 2.1   The components required to complete this tutorial

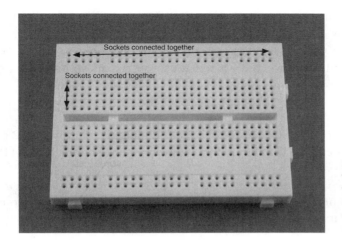

Figure 2.2   Breadboard layout: the sockets in the top and bottom two rows are connected horizontally; the other sockets are connected vertically with a break in the center of the breadboard.

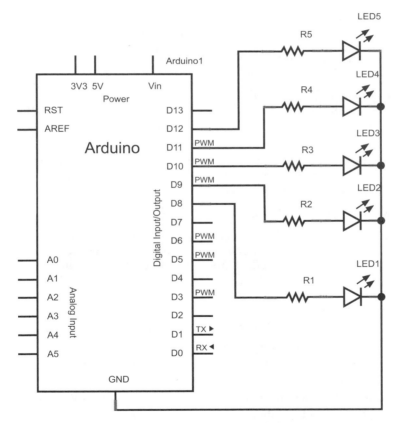

Figure 2.3   Schematic diagram showing Arduino connected to five LEDs

R5). The cathode, normally the shorter leg of each LED, is connected to GND on the Arduino. Power for the circuit is provided by the USB connection to your computer.

When you've made yourself familiar with the circuit diagram and have seen how the LEDs, resistors, and Arduino connect together, you can move onto placing the components into the breadboard.

2.1.3 Adding the LEDs

In figure 2.3, LED1 through LED5 are connected to digital pins 8 through 12 on the Arduino, which are labeled D8 through D12 on the schematic diagram. Each LED goes to a separate pin.

A resistor is connected in series with each LED; these are *current-limiting resistors*, and they act to limit the amount of current that flows through the LEDs, protecting them from burning out.

Calculating resistor values

The resistor value is calculated using the following formula:

(Operating voltage – LED forward voltage) / current in amperes
= resistor value in ohms

As a rule of thumb, most LEDs can take a maximum of 20 mA of current before suffering damage; mA stands for milliamperes, usually called milliamps. Forward operating voltage for red, yellow, and orange LEDs is 1.5V, for green LEDs 2.0V, and for blue and white LEDs 3.0V.

You're going to use the USB connection for power, which is 5V. If you're using red LEDs, which have a forward voltage value of 1.5V, and a current of 20 mA, you can calculate the needed resistance as follows:

(5V – 1.5V) / 0.02 A = 175 ohms

The nearest available resistor is 180 ohms, so to safely protect the LED, you need to use a resistor of 180 ohms or greater. We used 270 ohm resistors because we had plenty of them available, and the LEDs still light up when using them.

2.1.4 Connecting the hardware

Make sure the Arduino isn't connected to your computer yet; you don't want to have it powered up while you're connecting the hardware.

Figure 2.4 shows how to make the first connection to the first LED by connecting a jumper from pin 12 on the Arduino to the first resistor. Note that the resistor jumps over the break in the breadboard; make sure that the longer leg, or *anode*, of the LED connects to the resistor, and the shorter leg, or *cathode*, to GND on the top power rail.

Now connect the other four LEDs as shown in figure 2.5, following the same pattern as for the first LED.

Figure 2.4 Making connections to the first LED with a current-limiting resistor and pin 12 of the Arduino

Figure 2.6 shows the completed circuit. Note the connection of the long jumper from GND on the Arduino to the common rail on the breadboard. You can use the USB connection to provide the power for this project because the LEDs only require a small amount of current.

Now that you've finished assembling the circuit, you can move on to develop your code sketch to make the LEDs flash.

2.1.5 Sketch to flash five LEDs

With the connection of the hardware complete, you can now start to program your code sketch. Launch the Arduino IDE and start a new sketch. Carefully type the following code into the editor window.

Figure 2.5 Connections of the five resistors to pins 8 through 12 on the Arduino

Figure 2.6   The completed circuit with power being provided by the USB connection

Listing 2.1   Five flashing LEDs, flashing after each other

```
int ledArray[] = {8, 9, 10, 11, 12};        ◁⎤  LED array
int count = 0;
int timer = 75;

void setup(){
  for (count=0;count<5;count++){           ◁⎤
    pinMode(ledArray[count], OUTPUT);
  }
}                                              A for loop

void loop(){
  for (count=0;count<5;count++){           ◁⎦
    digitalWrite(ledArray[count], HIGH);   ◁⎤  digitalWrite writes
    delay(timer);
    digitalWrite(ledArray[count], LOW);    ◁⎦  LOW or HIGH
    delay(timer);
  }
}
```

In the first part of the sketch, the sketch variables are declared. An array, ledArray, is used to set the digital pin numbers you're going to use.

You could have used direct pin assignment, as shown here:

```
int ledPin1 = 8;
int ledPin2 = 9;
int ledPin3 = 10;
int ledPin4 = 11;
int ledPin5 = 12;
```

But it's more efficient to use an array when you have a collection of pin numbers that you'll treat similarly.

During the setup routine, you use a for loop so that each pin from 8 through 12 is set as an output.

In the sketch's main loop, you use another `for` loop to set each pin in turn to `HIGH`, turning the LED on with a `digitalWrite` function that accesses the LED to be written to from the `ledArray` array by its index value, `count`. Then, after a delay of 75 milliseconds, the pin is set to `LOW` and the LED is turned off again using `digitalWrite`.

The loop continues to run, turning each LED on and off in turn, with a slight delay in between. You could alter the delay time by changing the value of the `timer` variable.

> **NOTE** The `digitalWrite` function works by writing either a `HIGH` or a `LOW` value to the pin. If the pin is set to `HIGH`, `digitalWrite` sets the pin at 5V, which is enough to power an LED; if the pin is set to `LOW`, `digitalWrite` sets the pin at 0V, which turns the LED off.

Now that you've built your circuit and written your sketch, let's move on and test it.

2.1.6 Upload and test

Connect the USB cable between your computer and the Arduino and then verify that the sketch will compile. If any errors are generated, check that you've typed the code exactly as shown in listing 2.1. Pay careful attention to opening and closing braces, { }, and to the semicolons (;). Once the sketch compiles correctly, upload it to the Arduino. If you see any error messages, check that the correct Arduino type and serial port have been selected.

Once the sketch has been uploaded to the Arduino, and after a short delay, the LEDs should start to flash in turn. If no errors are generated and the sketch uploads correctly to the Arduino, but the LEDs don't flash, disconnect the Arduino from the USB cable and carefully check your connections. Check that the LEDs are plugged in correctly, with the cathodes connected to ground, and then try connecting the USB cable again.

> **NOTE** You shouldn't need to re-upload the sketch because the Arduino should retain the code in its onboard memory.

Your LEDs are now flashing, so it's time to make things more complex. In the next part of the tutorial, you're going to add a push button to the circuit.

2.2 Gaining control

Now that your sketch is working, with the LEDs flashing on and off in turn, it's time to add some control to the circuit by adding a push button. This will be used to start and stop the LEDs' flashing sequence.

2.2.1 Circuit diagram

The circuit diagram is shown in figure 2.7. You'll keep the same components that you used for the first version and add a push button (S1) and a resistor (R6) with a value of 10k ohms.

Once you've had a chance to study the updated circuit diagram, you can add the new components to the breadboard.

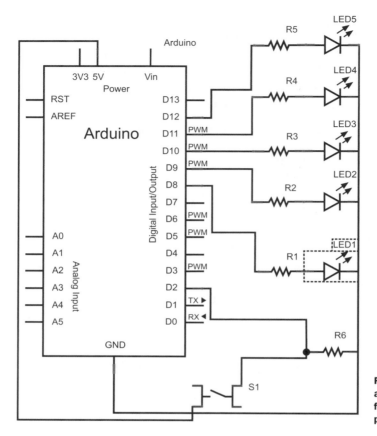

Figure 2.7   Schematic of an Arduino connected to five LEDs controlled by a push button

2.2.2   Connections

First, disconnect the Arduino from the USB cable, and then mount the push button onto the breadboard, as shown in figure 2.8. Note how it straddles the center of the breadboard. The resistor R6 is used as a pull-down resistor, which prevents the input to D2 from floating and ties the input D2 to ground (GND), LOW, when the switch isn't being pressed. When the switch is pressed, the input to D2 switches to 5V or HIGH.

Figure 2.9 shows an overview of the completed circuit laid out on the breadboard; the Arduino's power is provided by the USB cable connected to the computer.

Pull-up and pull-down resistors

It's common in a circuit using switched inputs to use either a pull-up or a pull-down resistor to prevent false positives that are caused by electrical noise or interference. The resistor holds the input at the opposite state to that which the sketch is programmed to detect. A pull-up resistor pulls the voltage up to 5 volts, and a pull-down resistor pulls it down to ground.

Figure 2.8 Connecting the push
button to the breadboard

Once you've connected the push button and additional resistor, it's time to look at the code side of things. In this sketch, you're going to use a special feature of the Arduino called an *interrupt.*

2.2.3 *Interrupts butting in*

Interrupts on the Arduino are very powerful; they can interrupt the sketch or program flow at any time. An interrupt is like someone ringing the doorbell when you're just about to step into the shower—you have to deal with it immediately. The Arduino is exactly the same; when an interrupt is signaled, your sketch must go and deal with it.

The standard Arduino can use a maximum of two interrupts, but for this project you're going to use just one. The interrupt will detect when the push button has been pressed; pressing the push button the first time stops the lighting up sequence of the LEDs, pressing it again restarts the sequence, and so on.

Figure 2.9 The completed
circuit connected to the USB
for power

2.2.4 *Sketch to control the LEDs with a push button*

The following listing shows the new sketch. You can either amend your existing sketch or start a new one.

Listing 2.2   Start-stop display

```
volatile int state = LOW;
int ledArray[] = {8, 9, 10, 11, 12};                    ❶ Sets up volatile
int count = 0;                                              variable
int timer = 75;
int pause = 500;

void setup(){
  for (count=0;count<5;count++){
    pinMode(ledArray[count], OUTPUT);
  }
  attachInterrupt(0, ledOnOff, RISING);                 ❷ Initializes
}                                                          interrupt

void loop(){
  if (state) {
    for (count=0;count<5;count++){
      digitalWrite(ledArray[count], HIGH);
      delay(timer);
    }
    delay(pause);
                                                        ❸ Pauses code
    for (count=0;count<5;count++){                         operation
      digitalWrite(ledArray[count], LOW);
      delay(timer);
    }
    delay(pause);
  }
}

void ledOnOff() {
  static unsigned long lastMillis = 0;                  ❹ Uses static
  unsigned long newMillis = millis();                      variable
  if (newMillis - lastMillis < 50){
  }
  else {                                                ❺ Performs
    state = !state;                                        debounce check
    lastMillis = newMillis;
  }
}
```

At the beginning of this code, you declare the state variable as volatile ❶. The volatile keyword is used for variables that can be altered by something outside the part of the sketch where it appears; one of the main uses of volatile is when using interrupts, as we're doing here.

The standard Arduino has two interrupts: interrupt 0 is attached to digital pin 2, and interrupt 1 is attached to digital pin 3. The Arduino Mega has an additional four interrupts: interrupt 2 is attached to digital pin 21, interrupt 3 is attached to digital pin 20, interrupt 4 is attached to digital pin 19, and interrupt 5 is attached to digital pin 18.

> **NOTE** The function attachInterrupt(interrupt, function, mode) takes three arguments. The first is interrupt, which can be set to 0 or 1; the second is the function to call, which must have no arguments and return nothing; and the third is the mode that generates the interrupt. This mode can have one of four values: LOW triggers whenever the pin is low; CHANGE triggers whenever the pin changes value; RISING triggers whenever the pin changes from LOW to HIGH; and FALLING triggers whenever the pin changes from HIGH to LOW.

In this sketch, you set the interrupt to RISING ❷. The interrupt will be triggered when the push button is pressed and the pin switches from LOW to HIGH. Another change in this sketch is that now the LEDs light up one after the other with a slight delay between each; then, when all the LEDs are lit, there is a slight pause ❸ and all the LEDs are switched off. The sequence then repeats. Pressing the push button stops the sequence; pressing it again restarts it.

Debounce

In the interrupt-service routine, the ledOnOff() function, we've also included some code to help with a problem found in mechanical switches called *bounce*. When a switch is pressed and moves from an open to a closed position, the contact often isn't perfect and produces a number of spurious signals called bounces, causing the connected pin to switch from LOW to HIGH a number of times until it settles to a constant state. It normally takes between 10 and 50 milliseconds to settle, but you can try longer values if you're getting strange results that you suspect are caused by bounce.

In this sketch, you counter the effect of the switch bouncing by using a static variable called lastMillis ❹. Static variables keep their values between calls to a function. The millis() function returns the number of milliseconds since the program started, and each time the interrupt-service routine is called, you assign the value of millis() to the variable newMillis. You then compare the value of newMillis to lastMillis ❺; if the result is less than 50 milliseconds (the bounce period), you do nothing and return to the main sketch loop. If the value is greater than or equal to 50 milliseconds, you're outside the bounce period, meaning that the button has really been pressed again. In that case, you update the state variable and assign the value of newMillis to lastMillis before returning to the main sketch loop.

> **CAUTION** Many people consider interrupts an advanced technique, but if you're careful, you should have no problem using them. During interrupt-service routines, keep your sketch code as small as possible; this will help you avoid unexpected things happening in the rest of your sketch. Another caveat is that you can't use the delay function inside an interrupt-service routine.

Let's move on now and test our newest sketch.

2.2.5   *Upload and test*

Connect the Arduino to your computer with the USB cable. Verify that the sketch compiles correctly, and then upload it to the Arduino. When the sketch has completed uploading, no LEDs will be lit until you press the push button. Try pressing the push button a few times to see how the LED sequence starts and stops.

2.2.6   *Time for a break*

Keeping the same circuit, you're now going to add a statement called a break to your sketch; the break command is used to break out of a loop or switch statement. You're going to use it stop the LED sequence and leave the LED lights lit until the button is pressed again, so if three LEDs are lit when the button is pressed, three will stay lit until the button is pressed again and the sequence starts over.

The following listing shows the new sketch with the break command.

Listing 2.3   Adding a break

```
volatile int state = LOW;
int ledArray[] = {8, 9, 10, 11, 12};
int count = 0;
int timer = 75;
int pause = 500;

void setup(){
  for (count=0;count<5;count++){
    pinMode(ledArray[count], OUTPUT);
  }
  attachInterrupt(0, ledOnOff, RISING);
}

void loop(){
  if (state) {
    for (count=0;count<5;count++){
      digitalWrite(ledArray[count], HIGH);      ❶ Checks state
      delay(timer);                                 variable
      if (!state) {
        break;                                  ❷ Breaks
      }
    }
    delay(pause);
    if (state){                                 Checks value
      for (count=0;count<5;count++){            of state
        digitalWrite(ledArray[count], LOW);
      }                                         Function delay(timer)
      delay(pause);                             removed from for loop
    }
  }
}

void ledOnOff() {
  static unsigned long lastMillis = 0;
  unsigned long newMillis = millis();
```

```
    if (newMillis - lastMillis < 50){
    }
    else {
      state = !state;
      lastMillis = newMillis;
    }
  }
}
```

After each LED lights up, you check the status of the `state` variable to see if the push button has been pressed ❶. If the button has been pressed, the `break` statement is called and the sketch exits from the loop ❷. When the button is pressed again, the sequence restarts.

It's now time to check that your sketch functions correctly.

2.2.7 Upload and test

Verify that the sketch compiles correctly, and then upload and test it. When the button is pressed the sequence of flashing LEDs should halt; pressing it again should restart the sequence.

It's now time to move on to the next stage of your project. You're going to make a reaction tester.

2.3 Reaction tester

This is the last circuit change you're going to make in this chapter. You're going to add two LEDs to the circuit, preferably a green one and a red one, to be used as start and stop indicators. The red LED will initially be lit; when it goes out and the green LED lights up, you'll have to press the push button as quickly as you can to halt the light sequence you set up in the previous section. Someone with an average reaction time should be able to stop the sequence when two or three LEDs are lit.

2.3.1 Circuit diagram

Look at the circuit diagram in figure 2.10 and note how the two new LEDs connect to the Arduino. Green LED6 and red LED7 have been added to the circuit, along with two 220 ohm current-limiting resistors, R7 and R8.

2.3.2 Connections

Figure 2.11 shows the completed connections between the Arduino and breadboard, with the two additional LEDs and resistors added to the existing circuit.

That's the circuit completed for this chapter. It's now time to look at your penultimate sketch for this chapter.

2.3.3 Sketch to test reaction speed

The next listing shows the sketch for the reaction meter; type it carefully into a new sketch.

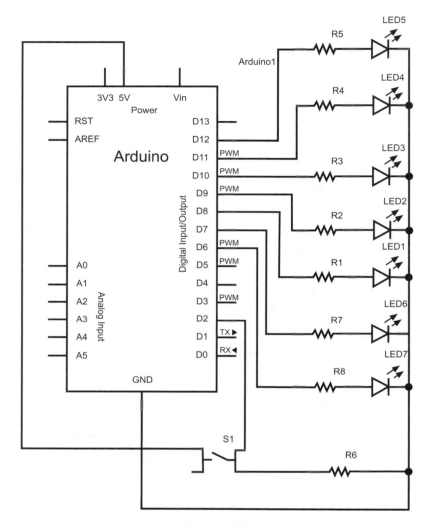

Figure 2.10   Schematic of Arduino with a push button and seven LEDs: two of them are used as start/stop indicators.

Listing 2.4   Reaction tester

```
volatile int state = 0;
int ledArray[] = {8, 9, 10, 11, 12};
int count = 0;
int timer = 50;
int stopLed = 6;
int goLed = 7;
int randMin = 250;
int randMax = 750;
int startDelay;
```

❶ Minimum value for random function

❷ Maximum value for random function

```
void setup(){
  for (count=0;count<5;count++){
    pinMode(ledArray[count], OUTPUT);
  }
  attachInterrupt(0, ledOnOff, RISING);
  pinMode(stopLed, OUTPUT);
  pinMode(goLed, OUTPUT);
  randomSeed(analogRead(0));
}

void loop(){
  //start state
  if (state == 0) {
    digitalWrite(stopLed, HIGH);
    digitalWrite(goLed, LOW);
    for (count=0;count<5;count++){
      digitalWrite(ledArray[count], LOW);
    }
  }
  // start button pressed
  if (state == 1) {
    // random start
    startDelay = random(randMin,randMax);
    delay(startDelay);
    digitalWrite(stopLed, LOW);
    digitalWrite(goLed, HIGH);
    for (count=0;count<5;count++){
      digitalWrite(ledArray[count], HIGH);
      delay(timer);
      if (state == 2) {
        break;
      }
    }
  }
}

void ledOnOff() {
  static unsigned long lastMillis = 0;
  unsigned long newMillis = millis();
  if (newMillis - lastMillis < 50){
  }
  else {
    state = state++;
    if (state == 3) {
      state = 0;
    }
    lastMillis = newMillis;
  }
}
```

Function to generate ❸ random seed

In this sketch, you set the two pins 6 and 7, which are connected to your two new LEDs, as OUTPUTs. You also use one of the Arduino functions, random, which can take two arguments—in this case, randMin ❶ and randMax ❷. The function returns a long value between randMin, inclusive, and randMax, exclusive.

Figure 2.11 Completed connections with two additional LEDs for stop and start

Seeding the random number generator

To seed the random number generator, you call `randomSeed` during setup ❸:

```
randomSeed(analogRead(0));
```

The value given to `randomSeed` is obtained by reading in an analog value from the unconnected analog 0 pin. An analog pin that's unconnected will have varying values on it due to electrical noise.

The `state` variable is used to control the sketch logic and is tied to presses of the push button. The first press starts the sequence of events with the original five LEDs being turned off, the red `stopLed` on, and the green `goLed` off. After a random amount of time, the `stopLed` goes off and the green `goLed` goes on, starting the sequence of the original five LEDs lighting up one by one. Pressing the push button stops the LEDs from lighting up. Pressing the push button again restarts the whole sequence.

2.3.4 *Upload and test*

Connect the Arduino to the USB cable, verify that the sketch compiles correctly, and upload it to the Arduino. Press the push button, and play to see how quick your reaction times are. Play with other people to see whose reaction time is the quickest.

You can add some more code to your sketch to more accurately record reaction times using a timer. We'll cover that in the next section.

2.4 Reactometer: Who really has the fastest reaction time?

For the last sketch of this chapter, you're going to more accurately measure your reaction times using a timer. The circuit stays the same, but you're going to make some changes to the sketch.

2.4.1 Sketch to measure reaction speed

The following listing shows your new reactometer sketch; either edit the previous sketch or create a new one and type in the following listing.

Listing 2.5 Reaction timer

```
volatile int state = 0;
int ledArray[] = {8, 9, 10, 11, 12};
int count = 0;
int timer = 50;
int stopLed = 6;
int goLed = 7;
int randMin = 250;
int randMax = 750;
int startDelay;
volatile float time;
float start_time;

void setup(){
  for (count=0;count<5;count++){
    pinMode(ledArray[count], OUTPUT);
  }
  attachInterrupt(0, ledOnOff, RISING);
  pinMode(stopLed, OUTPUT);
  pinMode(goLed, OUTPUT);
  randomSeed(analogRead(0));
  Serial.begin(9600);             ◄── ❶ Sets up serial
}                                         communication.

void loop(){
  //start state
  if (state == 0) {
    digitalWrite(stopLed, HIGH);
    digitalWrite(goLed, LOW);
    for (count=0;count<5;count++){
      digitalWrite(ledArray[count], LOW);
    }
  }
  // start button pressed
  if (state == 1) {
    // random start
    startDelay = random(randMin,randMax);
    delay(startDelay);
    start_time = millis();
    digitalWrite(stopLed, LOW);
```

```
    digitalWrite(goLed, HIGH);
    for (count=0;count<5;count++){
      delay(timer);
      if (state == 2) {
        time = (time - start_time)/1000;
        Serial.print("Reaction time: ");
        Serial.print(time);
        Serial.println(" seconds");
        delay(1000);
        break;
      }
      digitalWrite(ledArray[count], HIGH);
    }
  }
}

void ledOnOff() {
  static unsigned long lastMillis = 0;
  unsigned long newMillis = millis();
  if (newMillis - lastMillis < 50){
  }
  else {
    state = state++;
    if (state == 2){
      time = millis();
    }
    if (state == 3) {
      state = 0;
    }
    lastMillis = newMillis;
  }
}
```

❷ **Serial.print prints the reaction time.**

❸ **Serial.println prints a carriage return at the end of the line.**

In this sketch you've added a timer so you can more accurately determine your reaction time. When it has been calculated, the time is sent out to the serial port. The serial port is enabled during the setup function in your sketch with this command ❶:

```
Serial.begin(9600);
```

The 9600 is the baud rate, or speed, at which the Arduino sends data. To understand the data, the host computer (in this case, the serial monitor) must have its baud rate set to the same speed.

When printing out the data, you use two functions: Serial.print ❷ and Serial.println ❸. The only difference between the two is that the Serial.println function appends a carriage return and newline character to the end of the string.

2.4.2   *Upload and test*

Verify that the sketch compiles correctly and then upload it to the Arduino. As before, the push button controls the start and stop of the reactometer. Figure 2.12 shows the working completed project.

Figure 2.12 Final circuit running the reactometer

To see the reaction times, you'll need to select the serial monitor in the Arduino IDE; make sure the baud rate is set at 9600. Figure 2.13 shows some recorded reaction times.

Displaying these reaction times will help settle arguments between you and your friends!

2.5 *Summary*

In this chapter, you've seen how a typical project can develop, starting from a simple sketch and gradually building in complexity. Building a project by making small changes with each development makes it easier to debug and find errors. If the sketch doesn't compile correctly or the correct result isn't displayed, you only need to look at the most recent changes and additions.

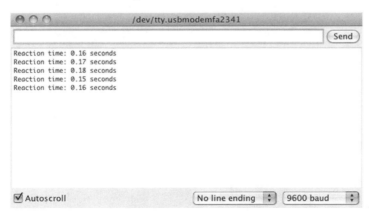

Figure 2.13 Serial monitor displaying reaction times

This project introduced you to the digital world with digital inputs and outputs: HIGH or LOW. You've explored some of the capabilities of Arduino, including the available functions, such as interrupts, which can be powerful. In later chapters, you'll look further at some of the digital pins and at the more specialized functionality those pins can have.

In the next chapter, you're going to leave the digital world for a while and look at some of the analog functionality that Arduino provides.

Simple projects: input and output

3

This chapter covers

- Looking at the analog world
- Reading an analog input
- Producing sound from a speaker
- Building a pentatonic keyboard

In the previous chapter, we looked at the digital side of the Arduino, building a series of incremental projects that showed off Arduino features like digital inputs and outputs and interrupts. In this chapter we're going to look at another aspect of the Arduino and how it interfaces with the world around us.

In basic terms, the world around us can be split into two parts—digital and analog—and in this chapter we're going to investigate interacting with the analog part. We'll once again start from a basic component, a potentiometer, which reads analog inputs into the Arduino. Then we'll experiment by adding a sensor—a piezo transducer that can be used as an analog input or output. We'll round up by adding four more piezo transducers and a small speaker to build a working five-key pentatonic keyboard.

These are the components required to complete this chapter:

- An Arduino board.
- A breadboard and a selection of jumper leads.

- A small potentiometer. (A trimpot is ideal, as it can easily plug into a breadboard.)
- Five zener diodes, 0.5 watt 5V1. (We used a BZX55C5V.)
- Five uncased piezoelectric transducers (knock sensors) with wire connectors.
- Five resistors, 1M ohm (1 mega ohm).
- One resistor, 1k ohm.
- A small speaker, 8 ohm.

Let's start by learning the basics of working in analog.

3.1   *Time to get analog*

In previous chapters, you experimented with buttons that could be either on or off, but what if you wanted to measure an analog input like a photo or force-sensing resistor? If the Arduino was purely a digital device, you wouldn't be able to measure these devices, which would limit the scope of your projects. Luckily, the Arduino has this covered and can interact with the analog world as well.

The Arduino can alter the brightness of an LED not by varying the voltage applied to it but by using a special technique called *pulse width modulation*, or PWM (more on this in a moment). In addition to providing an analog output using PWM, the Arduino can also take an analog input of between 0 and 5 volts.

The standard Arduino has six analog inputs labeled ANALOG IN A0, A1, A2, A3, A4, A5; in addition, there are six analog outputs.

In this chapter, we'll concentrate on the `analogRead` function; we'll leave `analogWrite` to a later chapter.

Let's start by taking a look at the difference between digital and analog devices.

3.1.1   *What's the difference between analog and digital?*

So what's the difference between the analog and digital worlds? In the digital world, everything has two states; a switch can only be on or off, an LED is either lit or it isn't, you're either awake or asleep. These states can be thought of in a variety of ways as ones or zeros, on or off, high or low. The Arduino digital pins work in the same way; when set as an output, they're either 0 or 5 volts, with a 0 voltage being a logical zero and 5 volts being logical one. In the analog world, things have a range of values. Music has notes that span a range of frequencies, a car accelerates through a range of speeds, a sine wave flows smoothly between maximum and minimum values, and temperature varies between a maximum and minimum.

We often want to explore the analog world, and the Arduino has six analog inputs that help us with this. But the Arduino is still a digital device, so you need a means of converting the input signal to a digital representation. This is done with an *analog-to-digital converter* (ADC). Table 3.1 shows the resolution, voltage range, and pins used for analog input and output for the Arduino and Arduino Mega.

In the next section, you're going to use a potentiometer to provide an analog input that you can manually vary, and you'll instantly see the effect of these changes by displaying the results using the serial monitor.

Table 3.1   The Arduino's analog resolution and analog input and output pins

	Analog input	Analog output
Resolution	10 bit (0 through 1023)	8 bit (0 through 254)
Voltage range	0 through 5 volts	0 through 5 volts
Arduino pins	A0 through A5	Digital pins 3, 5, 6, 9, 10, 11
Arduino Mega pins	A0 through A15	Digital pins 2 through 13

3.1.2   *Reading a potentiometer*

A potentiometer is one of the simplest ways to show how the Arduino's analog input works. Potentiometers come in all shapes and sizes, as shown in figure 3.1, and they're used in many different devices all around us. If you have a stereo with a rotary volume control, it's likely based on turning a potentiometer. Other examples include dimmer controls on lights and temperature controls on electric cookers or ovens. Despite the different shapes and sizes, they all have some means of varying resistance, either in a linear or logarithmic way.

The majority of potentiometers have three connections; the middle one is usually called the wiper and is used to vary the resistance by moving a contact along a fixed resistor. For this chapter, you want a potentiometer that varies resistance linearly and that's suitable for plugging into a breadboard; trimpots are often ideal.

Figure 3.2 shows the schematic symbols for a potentiometer. The central arrow, known as the wiper, is overlaid over the standard symbol for a resistor and indicates that the resistance is variable.

Let's now move on to connecting a potentiometer to the Arduino.

3.1.3   *Connecting the hardware*

Now that you know which potentiometer to use, let's get it set up. The circuit diagram shown in figure 3.3 has your potentiometer, labeled R1, connected between

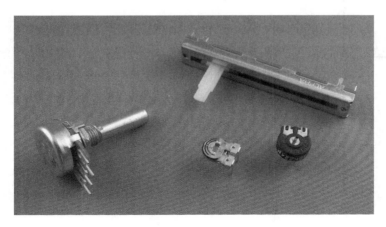

Figure 3.1   A selection of potentiometers

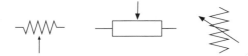

Figure 3.2   Schematic symbols for a potentiometer:
U.S. (left), International (center), Fritzing (right)

five volts and ground, with the wiper connected to analog input A0. As you turn the potentiometer clockwise or counterclockwise, you'll adjust the voltage between 0 and 5 volts on A0.

Plug the potentiometer into the breadboard. The central leg is normally the wiper, and this is the one you want to connect to your analog input, A0. The completed connections are shown in figure 3.4.

The potentiometer shown in figure 3.4 doesn't have a rotary knob, but it can be turned by inserting a *pot trimmer tool*. If you don't have a pot trimmer tool, you can use a small slot-head screwdriver instead.

With the potentiometer connected, you can move on to writing a sketch to read values from it.

3.1.4   *Sketch to read a potentiometer*

The following listing shows the sketch you're going to use to read an analog value between 0 and 5 volts into analog pin A0.

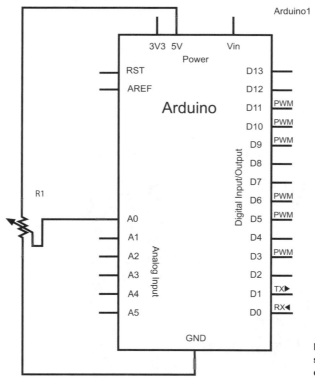

Figure 3.3   A circuit diagram showing the potentiometer connected to the Arduino

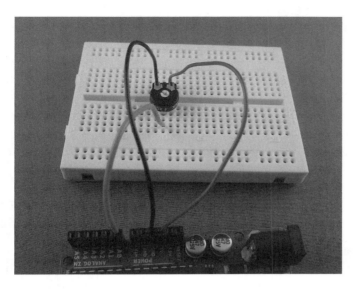

Figure 3.4   The potentiometer connected to the Arduino

Listing 3.1   Reading a potentiometer

```
int sensorPin = A0;
int sensorValue = 0;

void setup(){
  Serial.begin(9600);
}

void loop(){
  sensorValue = analogRead(sensorPin);
  Serial.print("Sensor = ");
  Serial.println(sensorValue, DEC);
  delay(10);
}
```

You don't need to set the `sensorPin` as an input during the setup routine because all analog input pins are set by default to be input. The `sensorValue` variable stores the value read by the `analogRead` function, which returns a number between 0 and 1023 inclusive, with 0 representing 0 volts and 1023 representing 5 volts.

The 10 millisecond delay between each reading gives the Arduino's ADC time to settle and capture an accurate reading. The `DEC` in the `Serial.println(sensorValue, DEC);` line instructs the `println` function to output data as base decimal. Other options include `HEX` (hexadecimal), `BIN` (binary), and `OCT` (octal).

3.1.5   *Upload and test*

After entering the sketch into the IDE, verify that it compiles, and then connect the Arduino to your computer and upload the sketch to it. Load the serial monitor in the IDE and rotate the potentiometer fully clockwise and counterclockwise. You should

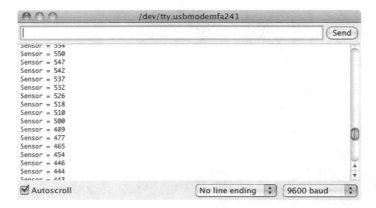

Figure 3.5   Output displayed as the potentiometer is rotated

see the number output to the serial monitor changing as the potentiometer is rotated. Example output is shown in figure 3.5.

You've now seen how to read a value into one of the analog input pins. In the next section, you're going to connect the Arduino to a *piezoelectric transducer*. For this you'll need some additional components, because a piezoelectric transducer can produce some very high voltages that could potentially damage the Arduino.

3.2   *A piezoelectric transducer*

If you've ever received a birthday card that plays a tinny version of "I'm So Excited" by the Pointer Sisters when opened, you've likely encountered a piezoelectric transducer being used as a speaker. Piezoelectric transducers are also found in a variety of other devices, including mobile phones, door buzzers, and underwater sonar.

Figure 3.6 shows a typical piezoelectric transducer that can be used to produce sounds similar to those used in some musical cards.

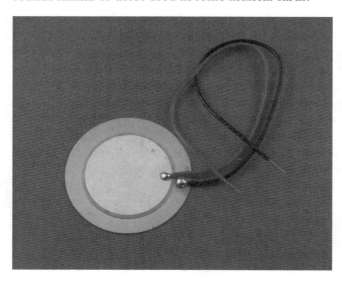

Figure 3.6   A typical piezoelectric transducer used in some musical cards and as sensors on drum kits

How do they work? The word *piezoelectricity* means "electricity resulting from pressure." When a piezoelectric device is squeezed, it produces an electric charge, as shown in figure 3.7. A typical application for this with an Arduino is to use the transducer as a knock sensor. When the transducer is hit or *knocked,* the Arduino detects this and performs the required action, such as switching on an LED or producing a tone from a speaker.

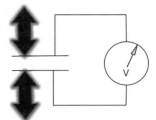

Conversely, when an electric charge is applied to a piezoelectric transducer, it distorts or changes shape as shown in figure 3.8. If you apply a varying voltage at a certain frequency, the movement of the transducer can cause it to produce a sound or note. It's in this mode that piezoelectric transducers are used in musical greeting cards or as buzzers.

Figure 3.7   When a piezoelectric transducer is distorted, it produces an electric charge; alternately squeezing and releasing the transducer will produce a varying voltage.

As you've seen, a single piezoelectric transducer can be used either as an input or an output device. Sonar devices, which have at their heart a piezoelectric transducer, send out a sound signal and listen for the echo. This is most familiar as the classic *ping* sound in submarine movies. The time it takes for the ping to return gives an indication of how far away a target is. We'll look at another example of this in chapter 6 when the Devantech SRF05 is used as a rangefinder.

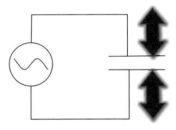

Figure 3.8   When varying voltage is applied to a piezoelectric transducer, the transducer's shape distorts.

Now that you've had a quick look at piezoelectric transducers and how they work, you're going to use a piezoelectric transducer as a knock sensor. When the Arduino detects that the knock sensor has been hit or knocked, it will light up an LED.

3.2.1 The circuit diagram

For this project, you'll need the following components:

- An Arduino.
- A breadboard and jump wires.
- A zener diode 0.5 watt 5V1. (We used a BZX55C5V.)
- An uncased piezoelectric transducer. (We used a 27 mm one from eBay.)
- A resistor, 1M ohm.

You'll use an uncased piezoelectric transducer because this will give better results than a cased one.

When hit, piezoelectric transducers can produce very high voltages, which are capable of causing damage to the Arduino. A zener diode is used to protect the

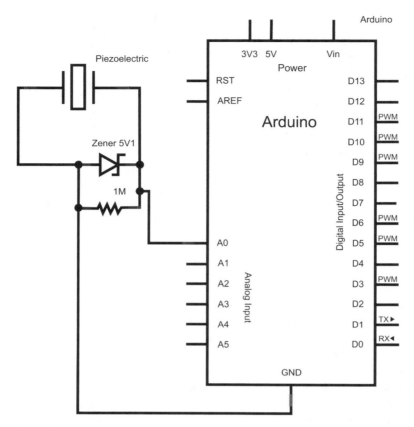

Figure 3.9 A piezoelectric transducer attached to analog input A0. The zener diode protects the Arduino from the high voltages produced by the transducer when it's struck.

Arduino from these high voltages, and the resistor is there to bleed off the voltage from the transducer.

Figure 3.9 shows the complete circuit diagram. Note the orientation of the zener diode and how both it and the resistor are parallel to the piezoelectric transducer.

Now that you've looked at the circuit diagram, you can move on to assembling the circuit on your breadboard.

3.2.2 *Connecting the hardware*

The circuit has three main parts in addition to the Arduino: a 5.1 V zener diode, a 1M ohm resistor, and a piezoelectric transducer. As already described, the zener diode and the resistor are connected in parallel to the piezoelectric transducer.

Start by placing the three components onto the breadboard, paying careful attention to the polarity of the piezoelectric transducer, which normally has a red and black wire presoldered onto it using a special low-melting-point solder. The

Diodes

Diodes are two-terminal devices that have low resistance to current flow in one direction, and high (ideally infinite) resistance in the other. Zener diodes are a special type of diode that is designed to allow current to flow in either direction once its *breakdown* or *knee* voltage is exceeded.

black wire connects to the GND part of the circuit, and the red connects to the Arduino's analog input A0.

The zener diode needs to be connected the correct way so that it protects the Arduino's analog input from any voltages exceeding 5 volts. Conventionally, the cathode or negative end of the diode, normally designated with a black band, would be connected to GND, but in your circuit you're going to reverse-bias the diode and connect it the other way so that the cathode is connected to the positive side of the circuit. The zener diode works by only conducting electricity when its breakdown voltage is exceeded, which in this case is 5.1 volts. Any voltages over 5.1 volts will cause the diode to connect and short circuit the voltage to GND, thus protecting the input of the Arduino.

When the three components have been connected to the breadboard, you can make the final connections to the Arduino's GND and analog input A0. Figure 3.10 shows a picture of the completed circuit, including the connections to the Arduino.

With your components connected together and to the Arduino, you can now move on to writing your sketch and interfacing the Arduino with your piezoelectric transducer.

3.2.3 *Sketch to measure output from a piezoelectric transducer*

To start with, you're going to use the sketch that was shown in listing 3.1. If you didn't save the sketch before, create a new sketch and type in the listing.

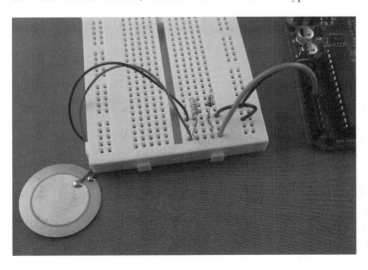

Figure 3.10   The completed circuit connected to the Arduino. Note the orientation of the zener diode and the polarity of the piezoelectric transducer.

Figure 3.11 The serial monitor showing the results of squeezing or tapping the piezoelectric transducer

Go ahead and plug in the Arduino to the USB port, upload your sketch, and start the serial monitor. Initially the serial monitor should just print 0 values. Now try lightly hitting or squeezing the transducer, and notice how the sensor values change. A typical output is shown in figure 3.11.

When the transducer is hit, the numbers should quickly rise to a maximum value and then fall back to 0. The differing values indicate how hard the transducer is squeezed or hit: the higher the value, the harder it has been hit or squeezed. If nothing happens, check your connections, paying careful attention to the orientation of the transducer and the zener diode.

You're now going to amend your sketch so that only values over a certain threshold are printed. You can either alter your existing potentiometer sketch or create a new one. The new sketch is shown in the following listing; save this sketch as `threshold`.

Listing 3.2 Threshold for a piezoelectric transducer

```
int sensorPin = A0;
int sensorValue = 0;
int threshold = 200;

void setup(){
  Serial.begin(9600);
}

void loop(){
  sensorValue = analogRead(sensorPin);
  if (sensorValue > threshold) {
    Serial.print("Sensor = ");
    Serial.println(sensorValue, DEC);
  }
  delay(10);
}
```

In listing 3.2, you set a threshold value of 200. In the loop part of the sketch, you're only going to print out sensor values that are greater than this threshold.

Now let's move on to testing it.

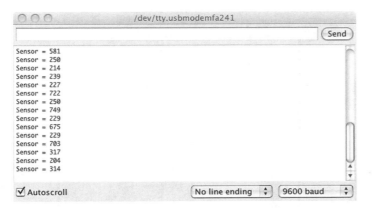

Figure 3.12 Output from hitting the piezoelectric transducer with varying degrees of force

3.2.4 Upload and test

After entering the sketch shown in listing 3.2, verify that it compiles and then upload it to the Arduino. Load the serial monitor and try hitting the transducer with varying degrees of force. Note that the harder you hit it, the higher the sensor value that's returned. Figure 3.12 shows some example output.

Now you have a sketch that checks the value at analog input A0 and prints the value if it exceeds a certain threshold. Next, you want to make it do something more useful than just report a value. If you added a speaker to your circuit, you could get the Arduino to play a note or tone when the piezoelectric transducer is hit, and that's what you're now going to do.

3.2.5 Circuit with added speaker

For this section, you need to add two components:

- A small speaker, 8 ohm
- One 1k ohm resistor

Figure 3.13 shows the circuit from figure 3.9 with the speaker and resistor added.

Now it's time to assemble the circuit onto a breadboard.

3.2.6 Connecting the hardware

Connect the hardware with the speaker connected to digital pin 8 through a 1k ohm resistor. The completed circuit is shown in figure 3.14.

We had to solder a couple of jumper wires to the speaker because the original speaker wire was too soft to plug directly into the breadboard. If you don't have soldering equipment, you can either use some insulating tape to tape the wires onto the wire jumpers or use alligator clips.

Once all the components have been connected, you can move on to writing your sketch.

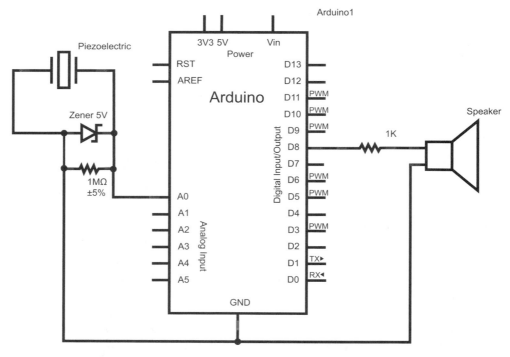

Figure 3.13   A speaker has been added to the circuit, with which you'll output a tone.

Figure 3.14   Connections with the addition of the speaker

3.2.7   *Sketch to generate a tone*

Listing 3.3 shows the code for your new sketch, in which you set three new variables:

- toneDuration denotes how long a tone is played in milliseconds.
- toneFrequency sets the frequency of the tone being played in Hertz (262 Hz is middle C).
- speakerPin defines the pin to which the speaker is connected.

Listing 3.3   Generating a tone in the speaker

```
int sensorPin = 0;
int sensorValue = 0;
int threshold = 200;
int toneDuration = 40;
int toneFrequency = 262;
int speakerPin = 8;

void setup(){

}
void loop(){
  sensorValue = analogRead(sensorPin);
  if (sensorValue > threshold) {
    tone(speakerPin,toneFrequency,toneDuration);
  }
}
```

In this sketch, you're using one of the Arduino's built-in libraries, tone, which can take three arguments:

```
tone (pin, frequency, duration)
```

pin is the pin to which the tone is output; frequency is the frequency of the output tone; and duration is the time in milliseconds to play the tone. If the duration parameter isn't provided, the tone will play until a noTone command is issued to it:

```
noTone(pin)
```

In this sketch, the tone is only played if the sensorValue is greater than the threshold. Now let's try it out.

3.2.8   *Upload and test*

After verifying that the sketch compiles with no errors, connect the Arduino to your computer and upload the sketch to it. Try hitting the piezoelectric transducer and check that a tone is produced in the speaker. If no sound is produced, try checking all your connections.

> **TIP** If your speaker is very quiet or you've checked all the connections and you still hear no sound, try increasing the toneDuration from 40 to 1000 or changing the value of toneFrequency.

Once everything is working, you can change the value of the `toneFrequency` variable to alter the note that the speaker plays. The higher the frequency, the higher the pitch; the lower the frequency, the lower the pitch. You can also try altering the value of the `threshold` variable. The lower the value, the softer you can hit the transducer to play a note from the speaker.

In the next section, you're going to add more piezoelectric transducers to your circuit so you can make a keyboard, with the transducers acting as keys.

3.3   Making a pentatonic or five-tone keyboard

The word *pentatonic* comes from *penta*, meaning five, and *tonic*, meaning tones. A pentatonic scale has five notes per octave, compared to the heptatonic scale, which has seven notes per octave. Pentatonic scales are popular the world over and are featured in a variety of musical types and styles including blues, Celtic, jazz, and ancient Greek music. The pentatonic scale is ideal for introducing children to music. Its simplicity and ease of use make it easy to quickly produce recognizable tunes, and many nursery rhymes are based on a pentatonic scale.

You're now going to build the final project in this chapter by adding another four piezoelectric transducers to your existing circuit, for a total of five piezoelectric transducers, which you'll use as keys. When each key is hit, it will produce a different note, or tone, from the speaker—hence, a pentatonic keyboard.

3.3.1   Circuit diagram

Each additional piezoelectric transducer requires a 1M ohm resistor and a zener diode in parallel, exactly the same as the first one you used. Figure 3.15 shows the complete circuit diagram. It looks complex with the additional components, but you're only repeating the circuit used in figure 3.9.

The circuit diagram shows the five piezoelectric transducers, each with a parallel resistor and diode. You use the analog inputs A0 through A4 as inputs to the Arduino.

Now it's time to connect the hardware together.

3.3.2   Connecting the hardware

Add the additional piezoelectric transducers, resistors, and diodes to the breadboard. Pay careful attention to the orientation of the piezoelectric transducers and the zener diodes. As you can see in figure 3.16, I've made a common ground using one of the horizontal strips on the breadboard.

Having completed the assembly of the keyboard, it's a good idea to check that each transducer is connected correctly. You can do this by uploading the sketch from listing 3.3 to the Arduino and testing that the transducer connected to analog input A0 produces a sound from the speaker when hit. If no sound is produced, check that all connections are properly made; it's easy to plug a component into the wrong hole on the breadboard, because the board is now getting crowded. Also check the orientation of the zener diode and the polarity of the piezoelectric transducer.

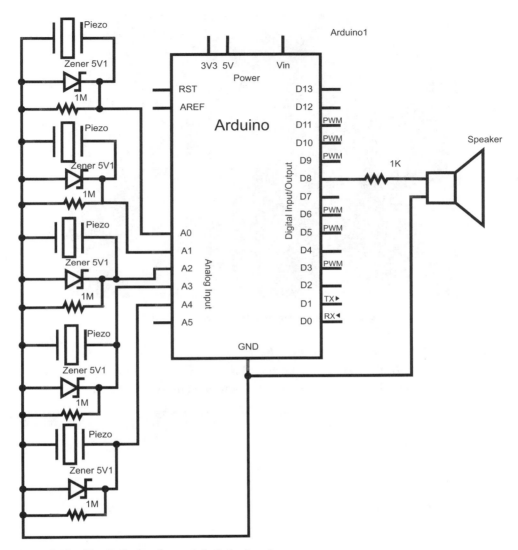

Figure 3.15   Circuit diagram for pentatonic keyboard

Once everything is working, you can test the other transducers one at a time by making a small change to the sketch. Change the value of the sensor pin in the topmost line from int sensorPin = 0 to int sensorPin = 1. Upload the revised sketch to the Arduino and test the transducer connected to analog input A1. When the transducer is hit, a sound should be produced from the loudspeaker.

Repeat this procedure for the other three transducers by changing the value of the sensorPin each time. Once all the piezoelectric transducers have been tested and are working, you can move on to the code for the pentatonic keyboard sketch.

Figure 3.16   The pentatonic keyboard fully assembled

3.3.3 *Sketch to create a pentatonic keyboard*

The code for the pentatonic keyboard is shown in the following listing. You can either adapt your existing sketch or create a new one and type in the listing.

Listing 3.4   Pentatonic keyboard sketch

```
int sensorValue = 0;
int threshold = 50;
int toneDuration = 10;
int speakerPin = 8;

int tones[]={262,294,330,392,440};

void setup(){

}

void loop(){
  for (int sensorPin = 0; sensorPin < 5; sensorPin++) {
    sensorValue = analogRead(sensorPin);
    if (sensorValue > threshold) {
      tone(speakerPin,tones[sensorPin],toneDuration);
    }
  }
}
```

This sketch loads the frequencies of the notes into the tones array; the tones used are based on the major pentatonic scale and middle C:

- C = 262 Hz
- D = 294 Hz
- E = 330 Hz
- G = 392 Hz
- A = 440 Hz

The loop routine tests the value of each analog input in turn. When a tap on a piezo-electric transducer is detected, and the value returned is above the threshold value, the corresponding tone is played through the speaker for 10 milliseconds.

> **NOTE** In this sketch, the threshold is set at 50. You previously used a value of 200, but we found during testing that one of the transducers needed to be hit much harder than the others, so we reduced the threshold to 50, thus making the keys more sensitive.

Once all the code has been typed into the sketch, save it with a memorable name. You can then move on to uploading and testing your pentatonic keyboard. You might even want to try playing a couple of tunes.

3.3.4 *Upload and test*

Verify that the sketch compiles. When it does, connect the Arduino to your computer and upload the sketch to it. Now you can test that everything is working by tapping the transducers and making sure each produces a tone. Try playing some simple tunes. It might sound a little tinny because you're only using a small speaker, but you've built your own working keyboard.

You can alter the notes by changing the frequencies loaded into the tones array. You might try the C minor pentatonic scale with the following values:

- C = 262 Hz
- E = 311 Hz
- F = 349 Hz
- G = 392 Hz
- B = 466 Hz

By loading different frequencies into the tones array, you can produce very different sounds and tunes.

The main thing is to have fun and show off your new creation. Using the major pentatonic scale, try the following note progressions. See if you can recognize the tunes, or better yet, see if someone else can recognize them.

1 GGAGCB GGAGDC—Hint: everybody has one of these each year.
2 CDECCDEC EFG EFG—French brother.
3 CCGGAAG FFEEDC—Heavenly.

Now try making some of your own note progressions. One of the beauties of using the pentatonic scale is that it's relatively easy to produce pleasant-sounding melodies.

3.4   *Summary*

In this chapter you looked at the analog-input side of the Arduino using `analogRead`. You experimented by reading values from two separate analog devices, a potentiometer and a piezoelectric transducer. You saw how the analog signal is converted to a digital format using an analog-to-digital converter (ADC) that can be interpreted by the Arduino. This approach allows you to confidently read data from many other analog devices.

Your final project in this chapter made extensive use of `analogRead,` and you built a pentatonic keyboard with five piezoelectric transducers that each produced a different note when hit. Hopefully you had some fun showing off your musical prowess to anyone who would listen, even if the sound was a little tinny.

In the next chapter, you'll look at the two main ways of extending the Arduino: the first using software libraries that enable the Arduino to communicate with other sensors, such as two-wire devices and SPI communication, and the second using hardware shields that plug directly into the headers of the Arduino. You'll also look at a couple of the most common shields.

Part 2

Putting Arduino to work

Part 2 of this book (chapters 4 to 13) looks at the Arduino in more depth, and this is where you'll really start to put the Arduino to work, learning a number of advanced techniques that you can use in your own projects. This part of the book includes chapters on using libraries, controlling various motors, using sensors and LCD displays, communicating with other devices, connecting to game controllers and iOS devices, creating wearables, building your own Arduino shields, and integrating with other software packages.

Extending Arduino

4

In previous chapters, you looked at the digital input and output and analog input functionality of the Arduino, and you constructed a few projects based on this functionality, including a reactometer and a pentatonic keyboard. But the Arduino is capable of much more, and you can also extend its functionality by using software libraries or hardware shields. In this chapter you're going to learn different ways of connecting the Arduino to other devices or equipment.

For example, if you were building an obstacle-avoidance robot that could detect objects in its path and maneuver around them, the Arduino would be an obvious choice. There are software libraries and hardware shields readily available that can enable the Arduino to drive motors, connect to infrared or ultrasonic sensors that detect objects, and communicate over Wi-Fi.

Let's get started by learning about software libraries.

4.1   *Extending the Arduino with libraries*

In the software world, a library is a piece of software that provides some sort of functionality, such as writing text to an LCD screen or calculating your position from a GPS navigation system. Software libraries work in the same way as conventional reference libraries: you request information and then use it within your project. Imagine you're working on a research project: you take a reference book out of a library and use the parts you need in your project. It's exactly the same with a software library.

In the Arduino world, a library is a piece of software that you include in your sketch and that provides some form of functionality. For example, there's a Liquid-Crystal library that, when included in your sketch, will give you the ability to communicate simply with some LCD displays. A library is often used many times across many projects.

Some libraries can be used on their own, whereas others need to be used with additional electronic components, often in the form of *shields*. We'll cover the use of shields later in this chapter.

There are three different types of Arduino libraries: core, standard, and contributed. We'll start with the built-in core library.

4.2   *Core library*

The core library is built into the main Arduino IDE and is central to what makes the Arduino such a great device for both beginners and more experienced users. The core library hides much of the complexity traditionally involved when working with a microcontroller. Members of the Arduino development team, who were involved with teaching students how to use microcontrollers in their projects, recognized that the downfall of many traditional microcontrollers was the difficulty of programming them. They looked at what actions many of their students wanted to perform with a microcontroller and, based on this, designed a core library that makes these actions easy to perform.

Most projects read data in (input) or write data out (output), and the core library makes these common tasks simple to execute. For example, to read the value of a digital pin, you just need to use the easily remembered `digitalRead`. Other common functions you've already used include `digitalWrite` and `analogRead`.

In your last project, the pentatonic keyboard, you used another core function, `Tone`, to output sound to a loudspeaker, and you used the `Serial` functions to send code output to the serial monitor:

- `Serial.begin(9600)`
- `Serial.print("Hello World")`

In later chapters, you'll come across other core functions, but for now we're going to look at the standard libraries that are included as part of the Arduino IDE.

4.3   *Standard libraries*

When you downloaded and installed the Arduino IDE, some standard libraries were included with the installation. The standard libraries are ones that the Arduino development team thinks will be needed by many people in their own projects. They aren't included by default in your projects like the core library, because the Arduino has limited resources; automatically including the libraries would be a waste of these resources, leaving little room for code in your own sketches.

To use the standard libraries, you have to explicitly include them in your sketches. To do so, you need to add an `include` statement at the top of your sketch. For example, if you wanted to include the LiquidCrystal library, which is used to display data on an LCD screen, you would place the following at the top of your sketch:

```
#include <LiquidCrystal.h>
```

> **NOTE** The name of the library is bounded by angle brackets: < and >. Also, the line doesn't end with a semicolon (;) as is usual.

The standard libraries are described in the following sections:

- ArduinoTestSuite library
- EEPROM library
- SD library
- Ethernet library
- Firmata library
- LiquidCrystal library
- Servo library
- Stepper library
- SPI library
- Wire library
- SoftwareSerial library

We'll also revisit some of these libraries in later chapters, where we'll go into much more detail about them.

4.3.1   *Test-driven development with ArduinoTestSuite*

The ways that code and sketches are written and developed are always evolving, and hopefully improving. One of the more recent innovations is a software process called *test-driven development* (TDD).

In TDD, a software project is split into small pieces, and before you write any of the pieces of code, you first write tests, with each test checking a particular function. When you write the code, it's run against the tests and must pass for that piece to work correctly; if it doesn't pass, you correct any errors and test the code again. When the piece of code passes its tests, you repeat the process for the next piece of code. This continues until the project is finished. If a change is made to a piece of code at a later date, you can run the tests to make sure everything still functions correctly and that the change has not caused other areas of the program to malfunction.

The ArduinoTestSuite library is the first step in bringing this methodology to Arduino development. It's a relatively new library, but it's seen as being essential to future development on Arduino. The ArduinoTestSuite library provides standard methods and functions that can be used to test your sketches before uploading them to the Arduino. This ensures that your code sketch works as intended before using it with expensive real-world devices that may be harmed if used incorrectly.

The library is still in active development, but it currently has tests for the processes listed in table 4.1.

Table 4.1   The tests available in the ArduinoTestSuite library

Test	Description
ATS_begin	Initiates the beginning of the test process
ATS_end	Completes the test process
ATS_Test_DigitalPin	Tests the given digital pin
ATS_Test_PWM	Tests PWM output
ATS_Test_AnalogInput	Tests analog input
ATS_Test_EEPROM	Tests the EEPROM
ATS_TestSerialLoopBack	Tests the RX and TX of serial ports
ATS_GetFreeMemory	Returns the amount of free memory available on the Arduino

The idea of incorporating software testing as part of Arduino development is new, but it will likely become more important as development of the IDE continues and functionality increases.

4.3.2   *Storing values using EEPROM*

Electrically Erasable Programmable Read-Only Memory (EEPROM) is a type of memory that retains its values even when a microcontroller is turned off. The amount of EEPROM on an Arduino board is dependent on the microcontroller at its core. Table 4.2 lists the amount of EEPROM memory available on the microcontrollers used on different Arduino boards.

Table 4.2   EEPROM memory on microcontrollers used on Arduino boards

Microcontroller	EEPROM memory (bytes)
ATMega8 and ATMega168	512
ATMega328	1,024
ATMega1280 and ATMega2560	4,096

NOTE The Arduino Uno is based on an ATMega328; it has 1,024 bytes of EEPROM memory.

The EEPROM library gives sketches access to the Arduino's EEPROM and provides two functions, read and write, as shown in table 4.3.

Table 4.3 The functions available in the EEPROM library

Function	Description
read	Reads the value of a byte stored at a location in EEPROM
write	Writes a value to a location in EEPROM

NOTE Any data written to the EEPROM remains there even when the Arduino is switched off.

A good use of the EEPROM library would be to store settings in between Arduino restarts—for example, constants that might be used by an LCD interface, data in a counting application, or the highest score in a game. If you want to store more data than this, it might be time to think about using SD cards.

4.3.3 Storing more data with SD

The Arduino doesn't have a convenient way of storing data, apart from the onboard EEPROM, which is only suitable for storing configuration settings and tiny amounts of data. To store the data logged from that GPS guided rocket project you've been working on, you're going to need to look elsewhere. Luckily, others have already paved the way, and there are a number of shields available that can use SD or SDHC memory cards, which are commonly used in digital cameras for storing pictures.

One of the advantages of using SD or SDHC cards is that they're readily available in a variety of memory sizes, and they're relatively cheap, with prices starting at just a few dollars. Table 4.4 shows the typical differences between SD and the higher-capacity SDHC cards.

Table 4.4 Key differences between SD and SDHC memory cards

	SD	SDHC
Capacity	0–2 GB	4 GB–32 GB
File storage system	FAT16 or FAT32	FAT32

William Greiman wrote an Arduino library called SdFat that supports the FAT16 and FAT32 filesystems on SD cards. The SdFat library provides a comprehensive range of functions: creating and deleting files and directories, and performing basic formatting.

The Arduino team realized that many users would find it difficult to use the SdFat library, so they built a wrapper around it, making it friendlier to use by exposing only a subset of its functions.

NOTE   The SdFat library uses a lot of program memory, which limits the size of your sketches, so it's recommended that you use it with an Arduino that has at least an ATMega328P processor.

When included in your sketch, the SD library provides a range of basic functions, as listed in table 4.5, enabling the Arduino to interact with SD cards.

Table 4.5   The functions provided by the SD library

Class	Function	Description
SD	begin	Initializes the SD library and card
	exists	Tests existence of file or directory on the card
	mkdir	Creates directory on the card
	rmdir	Deletes directory on the card
	remove	Deletes file from the card
	open	Opens file on the card
File	available	Checks if any bytes are available to read from a file
	close	Closes file and makes sure data written to it is saved on the card.
	seek	Seeks a position in the file
	position	Returns current position within the file
	size	Returns size of the file
	print	Prints data to already open file
	println	Prints data to file and appends newline
	write	Writes data to the file
	read	Reads a byte from the file

NOTE   The SD library can only use the 8.3 filesystem—an eight-character filename and a three-character extension, separated by a period. You can't use long descriptive filenames or names with spaces in them.

Arduino uses a serial peripheral interface bus (SPI; more about this in section 4.3.9) to communicate with the SD card, which uses digital pins 11, 12, and 13 on a standard Arduino and 50, 51, and 52 on a Mega. In addition, pin 10 is commonly used to select the card device on a standard Arduino and pin 53 on the Mega; an alternative pin can be used by specifying it in the call to SD.begin.

NOTE Before an SD card can be used by the Arduino, it must first be properly formatted as either FAT16 or FAT32 using your computer and a card reader.

A microSD shield is available from SparkFun Electronics, as shown in figure 4.1.

A range of shields is also available with onboard microSD card connectors, including the latest official Ethernet shield and data logging shields available from SparkFun Electronics and Adafruit Industries.

Figure 4.1   The microSD shield from SparkFun Electronics

4.3.4   *Get connected with Ethernet*

An increasing number of people want their projects to be remotely accessible so that they can share their data or results over a home network, or so that the project can be controlled over an internet connection. Sending status messages via Twitter is a favorite goal in many projects, which requires the Arduino to tweet the results of some form of input. An early example came from a baker whose oven was connected to an Arduino: it tweeted a message to his customers whenever a fresh batch of bread was ready for sale.

The Ethernet library simplifies the TCP/IP stack, making it easier to get an Arduino to communicate over the internet or home network. The library is designed to work with WIZnet W5100-based boards. The latest official Arduino Ethernet board also has an onboard microSD card connector that's great for data-logging applications. You could use the Arduino to take readings in a remote location and display the readings on a basic web page as well as log them to a microSD card that could be retrieved and further analyzed at a later date.

The Ethernet library is very extensive and allows the Arduino to be set up as either a server, which receives connections from clients, or as a client, which connects to servers. Table 4.6 shows some of these functions.

Table 4.6   Some of the functions provided by the Ethernet library

Class	Function	Description
Ethernet	begin	Initializes library and network settings
	localIP	Returns local IP address
	dnsServerIP	Returns DNS server address
Server	Server	Creates server
	begin	Starts to listen for connections
	available	Retrieves a client that has data available to read

Table 4.6 Some of the functions provided by the Ethernet library *(continued)*

Class	Function	Description
Client	write	Writes data to clients; data is `byte` or `char`
	print	Writes data to clients; data can be `byte`, `char`, `int`, `long`, or `string`
	println	Writes data to clients, followed by a newline
	Client	Creates client
	connected	Returns `true` if client is connected to server
	Connect	Connects to IP address and port specified
	write	Writes data to a connected server
	print	Writes data to server; data can be `byte`, `char`, `int`, `long`, or `string`
	println	Writes data to server, followed by a newline
	available	Returns number of bytes to be read from server
	read	Reads next byte from server
	flush	Discards bytes waiting to be read by client
	stop	Disconnects from the server

As you can see in table 4.6, the Ethernet library is rich in functionality and is under active development as we head to a more connected world.

4.3.5 *Serial communication with Firmata*

Firmata is a communication protocol that allows a host computer to use software to control a microcontroller. The Firmata library provides the serial communication protocols for communicating with the software on a host computer.

Using Firmata, a host computer can control devices attached to the Arduino, such as servos, motors, and LEDs. You can have your own glorious Technicolor light-and-sound show controlled by a host PC that sends commands to one or more Arduinos.

Table 4.7 shows some typical Firmata functions.

Table 4.7 Typical Firmata functions

	Method	Description
Common	begin	Initializes Firmata library
	printVersion	Sends protocol version to host computer
	setFirmwareVersion	Sets firmware version

Table 4.7 Typical Firmata functions *(continued)*

	Method	Description
Sending messages	sendAnalog	Sends an analog message
	sendDigitalPortPair	Sends digital pin value
	sendsysex	Sends a command with an array of bytes
	sendString	Sends a string to the host PC
Receiving messages	available	Checks buffer for incoming messages
	processInput	Processes incoming messages
	attach	Attaches a function to an incoming message type
	detach	Detaches a function from an incoming message type

The Firmata protocol is evolving all the time; visit http://firmata.org/wiki/ to get the latest updates and information. We'll take a more detailed look at Firmata in chapter 13.

4.3.6 *Displaying data using the LiquidCrystal library*

You've seen in previous chapters how the Arduino can display information on the Arduino IDE's built-in serial monitor, but what about when the Arduino isn't connected to a host computer? It can be handy to use a small 16-character-by-2-row (16 x 2) LCD to display information to your project users. Most of these small LCDs are based on a Hitachi HD44780 or compatible chip.

This requirement is so common that we've devoted a whole chapter—chapter 7—to just dealing with LCD displays. You'll learn how to show your project users GPS data, status messages, and other cool and useful stuff.

Central to all this is the LiquidCrystal library that's used to drive the display. Table 4.8 lists some of the functions available in the library.

You'll learn more about LCD displays in chapter 7.

Table 4.8 Some LiquidCrystal library functions

Function	Description
begin	Sets the dimensions of the LCD screen in rows and columns
LiquidCrystal	Initializes the library and sets up the pins used to communicate with the LCD
print	Prints data to the LCD
clear	Clears the LCD screen
setCursor	Positions the cursor on the LCD screen

4.3.7   *Controlling a servo motor*

Servo motors are commonly used in the radio-control world to accurately control movement in models, such as the flaps on a model airplane or the rudder on a model boat. They're ideal for projects needing accurate movement, such as obstacle-avoidance robots that scan an ultrasonic sensor from side to side looking for objects to avoid.

You'll be looking at servo motors in much greater detail in the next chapter; for now let's look at some of the main features of the Servo library. The Servo library allows the Arduino to control up to 12 servo motors on a standard Arduino, and a whopping 48 on the Mega. Table 4.9 shows the main functions provided by the Servo library.

Table 4.9   The main functions provided by the Servo library

Function	Description
attach	Attaches servo to a pin.
attached	Checks servo attached to pin.
detach	Detaches servo from pin.
read	Reads angle of servo.
write	Writes shaft angle to servo—between 0 and 180 on a normal servo. On a continuous rotation servo, sets the speed of rotation.
writeMicroseconds	Writes value to the servo in microseconds, to set the angle of the shaft.

NOTE   Using the Servo library disables analogWrite on the PWM pins 9 and 10 for a standard Arduino. On the Mega, using more than 12 servos will disable analogWrite on pins 11 and 12.

Another type of motor is a stepper motor, and there's another library for driving them.

4.3.8   *Turning a stepper motor*

A stepper motor rotates its motor shaft in steps; the specification of a stepper motor is often given in steps, so a motor with a specification of 200 steps would take 200 steps to rotate one revolution.

Sometimes the specification is given in degrees; this can easily be converted to steps by dividing one revolution, which is 360 degrees, by the number of degrees given in the specification. For a stepper motor with a specification of 1.5 degrees, you would calculate the number of steps per revolution as follows:

```
360 degrees / 1.5 degrees per step = 240 steps
```

Stepper motors are therefore a great way of controlling devices precisely.

The Stepper library gives the Arduino control over both unipolar and bipolar types of stepper motors. Using the library, you can set the speed of rotation of the motor, the number of steps to take, and the motor direction. Table 4.10 lists the main functions provided by the Stepper library.

Table 4.10 Main functions provided by the Stepper library

Function	Description
Stepper	Initializes Stepper library and sets the number of steps per revolution
setSpeed	Sets speed at which motor should turn, in rotations per minute (RPM)
step	Steps the motor the number of steps specified; positive numbers rotate one way, negative numbers the other

We'll cover the Stepper library in much greater detail in chapter 5, where we'll also look at the different types of stepper motors available.

4.3.9 *Communicating with SPI peripherals*

Serial peripheral interface bus (SPI), sometimes called *four-wire bus*, is a synchronous serial communications protocol used for communicating over short distances with external peripherals. SPI can be used to communicate with a variety of peripherals or sensors, including temperature sensors, pressure sensors, analog-to-digital converters, touch screens, videogame controllers, and onscreen displays. You've already seen that the Arduino uses SPI to communicate with SD cards.

The protocol has a single master, the Arduino, and one or more slave devices. Because of the lack of a formal standard, there's some variation in how individual manufacturers apply SPI to their own devices, so you'll probably need to resort to a data sheet if you want to connect to a particular peripheral.

The protocol uses four wires, three of which are common to each device, and one that's a slave select. Their designations are shown in table 4.11.

Table 4.11 Four wire designations for SPI on the Arduino

Designation	Description	Arduino pin	Mega pin
MISO	Master In Slave Out, sending data to master	12	50
MOSI	Master Out Slave In, sending data to slave	11	51
SCK	Serial clock	13	52
SS	Slave select	Normally 10	53

Each slave has a *slave select* wire but shares the other three wires. Digital pin 10 (53 on the Mega) is normally used as the *slave select* line, but others can be set during setup. The Arduino Ethernet shield uses pin 4 to connect to the onboard SD connector and pin 10 to connect to the Ethernet controller.

The SPI library provides functions to interact with SPI peripherals, as shown in table 4.12.

Table 4.12   SPI functions

Function	Description
begin	Initializes the SPI bus and sets the MOSI and SCK pins low and the SS pin high
end	Disables SPI bus
setBitOrder	Sets the order in which bits are loaded into the bus
setClockDivider	Sets the SPI clock divider as a division of the system clock
setDataMode	Sets SPI data mode
transfer	Transfers one byte over the bus

Let's have a closer look at a couple of those functions:

- setBitOrder—This sets the order in which data is sent to the bus. The choices are either Most Significant Bit (MSB) or Least Significant Bit (LSB). The peripheral data sheet should give you this information.
- setClockDivider—This governs the speed that the SPI bus runs at, as a divisor of the system clock. The default divider setting is 4, which reduces the speed of the SPI bus to a quarter of the system clock; other divisors are 2, 8, 16, 32, 64, and 128.
- setDataMode—This controls the mode of transmission of data between the slave peripheral and the master. There are three main transmission modes, and these depend on whether data is shifted in or out on the rising or falling edge of the clock pulse, which is called *clock phase*. The other consideration is whether the clock is idle when set high or low; this is the *clock polarity*.

Table 4.13 summarizes the setDataMode modes.

Table 4.13   The setDataMode modes dependent on clock phase and clock polarity.

Mode	Clock polarity (CPOL)	Clock phase (CPHA)
0	0	0
1	0	1
2	1	0
3	1	1

Although this looks complicated, by making good use of the data sheet and carefully following each step for setting up the SPI bus, you should be able to communicate with SPI peripherals with confidence.

4.3.10 *Communicating with the two-wire interface*

I2C, commonly known as *two-wire interface* (TWI), is used to communicate with a wide range of low-speed devices and components, including real-time clocks. It's perfect for logging applications, LCD displays, ultrasonic rangers for distance measurements, and digital potentiometers whose resistance can be read or set remotely. Interestingly, I2C is also used in Nintendo game controllers, the Wii Motion Plus, and Wii Nunchuks. We'll look at interfacing with those in chapter 9.

Only two pins are needed for the I2C bus interface. Table 4.14 identifies these for the standard Arduino and Mega.

Table 4.14 Pin designations on the standard Arduino and the Mega for I2C

	Standard Arduino	Mega
SDA data line	Analog input pin 4	Digital pin 20
SCL clock line	Analog input pin 5	Digital pin 21

With the Wire library, the Arduino can act as either a master or slave device. In most cases, the Arduino will be the master device and will interact with one or more slave devices on the I2C bus; each slave device has a unique address to distinguish it on the bus network. It's possible to string devices together, up to a maximum of 112.

The Arduino can also be set up as a slave device, and when in this mode, it interacts with a master device.

Table 4.15 lists the main functions of the Wire library.

We'll take a more detailed look at using the Wire library in chapter 9.

Table 4.15 List of main Wire library functions

Function	Description
begin	Initializes the Wire library and joins I2C bus either as master or slave.
requestFrom	Requests data from slave to master.
beginTransmission	Prepares to start transmission of data.
send	Sends data from slave to master or queues bytes for transmission from master to slave.
endTransmission	Ends transmission (begun by beginTransmission) of data to a slave, and sends the bytes queued by send.
available	Returns number of bytes available for retrieval with receive. Should be called on the master device after a call to requestFrom or on a slave inside the onReceive handler.
receive	Retrieves byte transmitted by slave device after a call to requestFrom or from a master to a slave.
onReceive	Registers function to call when the slave receives a transmission from the master.
onRequest	Registers function to be called when the master requests data from the slave device.

4.3.11   *Get more serial ports with SoftwareSerial*

Many projects require at least one serial port. GPS devices send position and status messages serially, and some LCDs can be interfaced to a serial controller. A serial port is made up of just two connections: one RX for receiving messages, and one TX for transmitting or sending messages.

The beauty of a serial port is its simplicity. At one time every computer had a serial port; in fact, the original Arduino used a serial port for connecting to the computer, and even through the connection is now made by USB, it still emulates a serial port and appears to the host computer as a serial port.

The Arduino Uno and Duemilanove have one hardware serial port connected to digital pins 0 and 1, but if your project needs to connect to more serial devices than this—for example, to both a GPS and a serial LCD controller—you have a choice. You can either purchase the more powerful Arduino Mega, which has four dedicated hardware serial ports, or use the SoftwareSerial library that's distributed with the Arduino IDE.

The original SoftwareSerial library could only provide one software serial port in addition to the hardware port, and it was limited to a speed of 9600 baud. These limitations were addressed by Mikal Hart with his NewSoftSerial library. Realizing the advantages this library had, the Arduino development team renamed it and incorporated it as a replacement for the existing SoftwareSerial library in mid-2011. Table 4.16 shows the functions provided by the new library.

Table 4.16   The functions of the SoftwareSerial library

Function	Description
begin	Activates port and sets baud rate
available	Switches to that port
isListening	Returns current active port
listen	Listens to port and makes active
end	Terminates port
read	Reads data from port
write	Writes data to port

The updated library can create multiple instances of software serial ports, which can communicate at up to speeds of 115,000 baud. But all this additional functionality comes at a price, because the Arduino can only listen or receive data on one software serial port at a time, although it can transmit data on any port. When using the library with more than one software port, you'll need to think carefully about your sketch structure and the order in which data will be received.

Let's consider an example: You want to connect to both a GPS and a serially connected thermometer using software serial ports. GPS devices tend to send their data in bursts at intervals of a second, so your sketch could start by listening to the software serial port connected to the GPS, and after it has received the burst of data, switch to listening to the other port and process its data before switching back to the port connected to the GPS. Here's a sketch demonstrating how this would work in practice.

Listing 4.1 Using the SoftwareSerial library with two ports

```
#include <SoftwareSerial.h>                      Includes
SoftwareSerial gpsPort(2, 3);                    SoftwareSerial
SoftwareSerial thermPort(4, 5);                  library

void setup()
{
  gpsPort.begin(9600);                           Sets up
  thermPort.begin(9600);                         two ports
}

void loop()
{
  gpsPort.listen();                              Listens to the
  while (gpsPort.available() > 0) {              two devices
    char inByte = gpsPort.read();
  }
  thermPort.listen();
  while (thermPort.available() > 0) {
    char inByte = thermPort.read();
  }
}
```

As you can see, the SoftwareSerial library is a great addition to your toolbox, but you must be careful when using it with more than one software serial port.

This concludes our roundup of the standard libraries. But what if you want to work with other devices or peripherals that aren't covered by the standard libraries? There's a good chance that someone has written a library that you can use in your project. In the next section, we're going to look at how to use these user-contributed libraries.

4.4 *Contributed libraries*

Contributed libraries are libraries that are contributed by users of the Arduino but that aren't distributed as standard with the Arduino IDE. You'll find many of these libraries listed on the main Arduino website.

Some of these libraries are extensions to the standard libraries, offering a few more functions, and over time, if these additions are deemed suitable, the development team may add them to the standard libraries or even to the core library. Other contributed libraries are designed to work with particular devices, such as game controllers—you'll see one of these used in chapter 9.

So how do you add a contributed library to your project? Because these libraries aren't distributed with the IDE, you need to perform a couple of additional steps before you can use one of them.

4.4.1   *Installing a new library*

Adding a contributed library to the Arduino IDE requires a few simple steps:

1   Download the library, usually a zip file.
2   Install it into the Arduino IDE by copying the unzipped files to your default sketch directory libraries folder. If the libraries folder doesn't exist, you'll need to create it.
3   If the IDE is already started, you'll need to restart it. The library should now be available to your code.
4   Add the library to your sketch by selecting Sketch > Import Library from the menu, as shown in figure 4.2, where a couple of contributed libraries are displayed.

NOTE   Once a library is added to the IDE, it will be available for use with future projects, just like the standard libraries are.

Once a library has been imported to a sketch, all its functions are available to the sketch.

This concludes our look at Arduino software libraries for now. In the chapters ahead, we'll come back to some of them, and we'll also introduce more contributed libraries to help you get even more functionality out of the Arduino. In this section, you've seen how the use of software libraries can extend the functionality of the Arduino, allowing it to interface with many devices and peripherals, thus allowing you to quickly produce complex projects. In the next section we're going to look at another common way to extend the Arduino: using hardware shields.

Figure 4.2   **The contributed libraries available to a sketch after installation**

4.5   *Expanding the Arduino with shields*

Shields are another great way to add functionality to the Arduino. Want to control that robot by Wi-Fi? Get a Wi-Fi shield! Want to use your television as a display? Get the TellyMate shield! Want to program games like *pong*? Buy a game shield! These and a host of other shields are available and let you connect the Arduino to a wide range of hardware and peripherals.

Arduino shields are pluggable hardware boards that connect to the headers on an Arduino. Many of the shields have their own headers, so they can be stacked on top of each other. To get the most out of a shield, you'll often need additional libraries, and these are usually downloadable from the manufacturer of the shield, ensuring that you have the latest version.

Shields are a great way of expanding the Arduino, and they can come fully assembled or as a kit. If you're unsure of your soldering skills, it might be a good time to learn. Check to see if there's a local electronics hobby group or hacker space where someone can teach you. Alternatively, you can often purchase shields fully assembled and tested, although this will be more expensive.

You can even make your own shields from scratch. Many shield manufacturers have fully embraced the open hardware movement and provide the necessary files and drawings to make your own *printed circuit boards* (PCBs).

In later chapters, you'll make extensive use of shields in your projects because they're such a quick and neat way of extending the Arduino. But first, let's learn about some of the common shields that are available.

4.5.1 *Common shields*

These are some common shields that are generally available:

- Motor shields
- Ethernet shields
- Wi-Fi shields
- Prototyping shields

Let's start with motor shields.

MOTOR SHIELDS

Motor shields are usually suitable for controlling small DC motors. They're sufficiently powerful to power small robots or vehicles, and they can also be used with stepper and servo motors.

There are a variety of versions available. Adafruit Industries produces a motor shield, shown in figure 4.3, capable of driving two servo motors, two stepper motors, and up to four DC motors. We'll be making extensive use of this shield in chapter 5, where Arduino goes mobile.

ETHERNET

Looking to get your project connected to the internet, tweeting status messages, or responding to remote commands? We've already looked at the standard Ethernet library, and this is the hardware to go with it.

The official Arduino Ethernet shield, shown in figure 4.4, is based on the WIZnet W500 with its full TCP/IP stack. If you plan to purchase the official Arduino version new, make sure you purchase the latest version, which has an onboard microSD socket. Adafruit Industries produces an alternative version that's also compatible with the library. A cheaper option is to purchase a shield based on the ENC28J60 SPI Ethernet controller version, but this isn't directly supported by the Arduino team and has less functionality, though it may be enough for your project.

Figure 4.3   A motor shield from adafruit.com

Wi-Fi

Everything seems to be going wireless nowadays, and the Arduino is no exception. Wi-Fi gives you wireless control, which is ideal for remote-operated robots, as well as connecting to the internet.

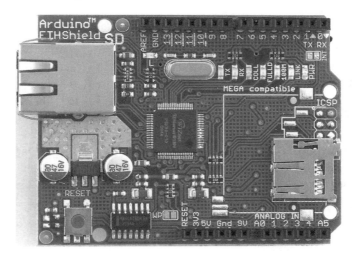

Figure 4.4   The official Arduino Ethernet shield

Figure 4.5 The WiFly shield from SparkFun

There are a couple of different shields available that provide Wi-Fi functionality. The WiFly shield from SparkFun is shown in figure 4.5.

PROTOTYPING SHIELDS

Bare or prototyping shields are excellent for use with your own projects. There are a few different versions available; some have an onboard breadboard, and others have a prototyping area you can solder components to. Figure 4.6 shows an example of a prototyping shield available from adafruit.com.

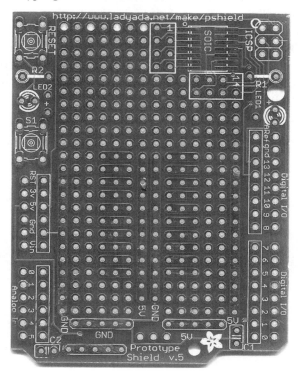

Figure 4.6 A prototyping shield from adafruit.com

NOTE Shields that are available as kits aren't always provided with headers, so you may need to purchase these separately.

4.5.2   *Gotchas: will it work with my Arduino?*

When using shields on a project—particularly if using more than one—care must be taken as to which pins are used by an individual shield. There's a great website, www.shieldlist.org, that has a comprehensive list of shields and which pins they use. It's worth checking the site for compatibility between shields that you want to use in your project.

A further consideration is the components on a shield. Some components are very tall and may interfere with any shields stacked on them.

You must also determine whether a shield is compatible with your Arduino. Some don't work with the Arduino Mega or require modifications to work with it. Others require a minimum of a 328 processor and won't work with the older 168 processor found in Diecimila and an early version of the Duemilanove Arduino.

4.6   *Summary*

In this chapter, we've looked at ways of expanding the functionality of the basic Arduino by using software libraries and hardware shields to interface the Arduino with a wide range of hardware and peripherals.

We started off by looking at software libraries, including the core library and those provided as standard with the Arduino IDE. We then looked at the vast range of contributed libraries and how they can be used in your projects.

In the second part of the chapter we looked at hardware shields, which are another excellent way of expanding the Arduino. We looked at some of the common shields and discussed some considerations you need to be aware of, mainly when using more than one shield or using the Arduino Mega.

In the next chapter, we'll use both libraries and shields to add motor functionality to your Arduino projects.

Arduino in motion

This chapter covers

- Connecting to small DC motors
- Reverse and speed control of DC motors
- Stepper motors
- Servomotors
- Brushless motors
- Using a purpose-designed motor shield

Earlier chapters provided you with a strong foundation for using the Arduino to communicate in the digital and analog worlds. You've built and developed a small number of projects from start to finish that have demonstrated these principles. You've also explored how to use libraries and shields to extend the basic functionality of the Arduino and enable it to work with an increasingly wide range of devices.

It's now time to consider the ways that the Arduino can be used in your own projects, whether it's a tweeting bread oven, an internet remote-controlled robot, or an automatic cat door. This and successive chapters will give you the tools and techniques to achieve these goals.

Starting with this chapter, you're going to look at ways of adding mobility to a project. You'll examine different ways of controlling a variety of off-the-shelf motors or motors you may already have. Perhaps you have an old junk printer that can be stripped for its stepper motors, or old toys powered by small DC motors; these are all motors you can use!

If you want to use the Arduino to control small DC motors to power a robot, to adjust the control on an unmanned aerial vehicle with a servomotor, to step a stepper motor on a 3D printer, or to control a quadrocopter powered by brushless motors, this chapter will show you how.

Let's get started with a look at DC motors, which are typically used to power small robots or vehicles.

5.1 *Getting up to speed with DC motors*

Small direct current (DC) electric motors can be found in a wide range of devices, including radio-controlled cars and boats, electric car windows, DVD players, and hand-held electric fans. Many of these can be repurposed for use with an Arduino. Alternatively, new motors can be purchased from Arduino suppliers, model shops, or eBay.

Voltages for small DC motors normally range from 1.5 to 30 volts, delivered through two wires; each motor manufacturer provides a recommended voltage. Exceeding the recommended voltage by too much will cause the motor to burn out; delivering too little voltage will result in the motor not turning at all.

To make a motor reverse, you normally just need to reverse the two wires connected to it. If you're using a motor to power a small robot, it's often connected to a gearbox. Why a gearbox? A small DC motor normally produces high speed and low torque. A gearbox converts this to low speed, high torque, making it more suitable for powering a small robot.

A gearbox can normally be purchased with the motor. Figure 5.1 shows a typical motor with a gearbox.

The Arduino can only provide a small amount of current—not enough to power a motor—so you'll need to use an external power supply. You'll use the Arduino to switch the motor on and off, as well as to provide speed control. Initially, we'll look at switching a motor on and off, and then we'll move on to controlling its speed.

For this section you'll need the following items:

- A small DC motor
- An external power supply suitable for the motor
- An external power supply for the Arduino (9 volts recommended)
- A miniature relay DPDT 5 volt coil rated 2 amps or more
- A 2N2222 NPN transistor
- A 1N4003 diode
- A small breadboard

Figure 5.1   A DC motor complete with gearbox from solarbotics.com

5.1.1   *Stopping and starting*

You start a DC motor by applying an appropriate voltage to it, and you stop it by removing that voltage. One of the simplest ways to do this is by using a switch that when switched one way starts the motor and when switched the other stops it.

You're going to use an Arduino to turn the motor on and off, and one way to do that is to use a relay as an electrical switch. Relays are available in a number of types and packages. To switch the motor on and off, you need a type of relay called *single pole double throw* (SPDT), rated for a current of 2 amps or more and with a 5 volt coil.

Figure 5.2 shows the layout of an SPDT relay. A relay has a coil that, when energized by applying a voltage to it, moves the contact one way (contact 1 in figure 5.2), and when de-energized moves it the other way (contact 2 in the figure).

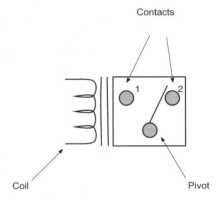

Figure 5.2   The elements of an SPDT relay

NOTE A double pole double throw (DPDT) relay is basically two SPDT's together on the same device. It's easier to connect a DPDT relay on a breadboard, so that's what you're going to use in the following circuit.

You can't use the Arduino to supply the 5 volts to the coil of the relay because it can't provide enough current, so you'll need to use a transistor to power the coil and switch the relay. The transistor you're going to use is a general-purpose type 2N2222 NPN transistor. The transistor will be configured as a switch to turn the relay's coil on and off.

The 2N2222 transistor is available in either a plastic or metal package and has three wires: collector, base, and emitter. Figure 5.3 shows a

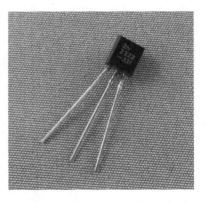

Figure 5.3   A NPN 2N2222 transistor in a TO-92 plastic package

2N2222 transistor in a plastic package. The transistor works as a switch by applying a small voltage to the base wire, which causes current to freely flow between the collector and the emitter.

We'll discuss the circuit in more detail when we come to connecting the hardware. Next we're going to look at the sketch.

5.1.2 Sketch to turn a small DC motor on and off

In your sketch, you're going to repeatedly switch a motor on for five seconds and then off for five seconds. The next listing shows the sketch you'll use to stop and start your motor. Enter it into the Arduino IDE.

Listing 5.1   Sketch to turn a small DC motor on or off

```
int transistorBasePin = 13;

void setup()
{
  pinMode(transistorBasePin, OUTPUT);
}

void loop()
{
  digitalWrite(transistorBasePin, LOW);
  delay(5000);
  digitalWrite(transistorBasePin, HIGH);
  delay(5000);
}
```

The sketch works by switching on a transistor whose base is connected to digital pin 13 on the Arduino. In the next section, you'll learn more about the hardware and how the circuit works, starting with the electronic switch.

5.1.3 Connecting the hardware

You're going to use a transistor to operate a relay to switch a motor on and off. The transistor is a bipolar NPN 2N2222, which is a general-purpose transistor. The transistor has three legs: a base, a collector, and an emitter. Figure 5.4 shows the typical connections for a 2N2222 NPN transistor in plastic and metal packages.

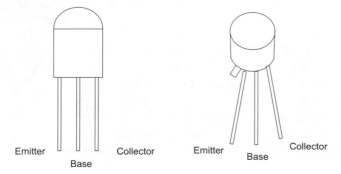

Emitter   Collector   Emitter   Collector
        Base   Base

Figure 5.4   A 2N2222 NPN transistor with legs connected to a TO-92 plastic package on the left and a TO-18 metal package on the right

NOTE There's no guarantee that the leg arrangement will be exactly as shown in figure 5.4. If in doubt, consult the manufacturer's data sheet.

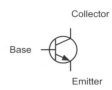

You're using the transistor so that it acts as a switch; figure 5.5 shows the schematic symbol for an NPN transistor.

**Figure 5.5
Schematic symbol
for an NPN
transistor showing
the base, collector,
and emitter**

NOTE There are two types of standard transistors: NPN and PNP. The letters in the acronyms refer to the layers of semiconductor materials used to make them. The majority of transistors used today are NPN, because they're the easiest type to make.

When no voltage is applied to the base of the transistor, the switch is off. When a voltage greater than 0.6 volts above the emitter is applied to the base, the transistor switches on and current flows from the collector to the emitter. Turn off the voltage to the base, and the transistor switches off again.

NOTE The transistor is never fully switched off because a small amount of leakage current is passed.

Figure 5.6 shows the complete circuit diagram for your circuit.

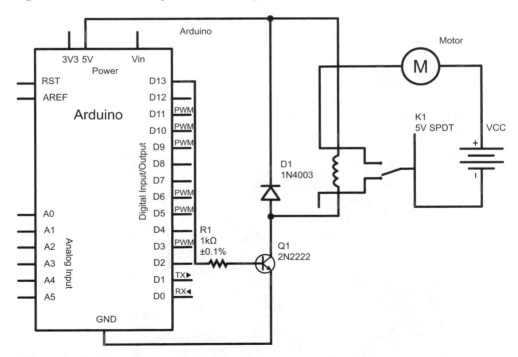

Figure 5.6   Schematic diagram for switching a motor on and off with a transistor and a relay

The relay you're going to use is a DPDT; you could use an SPDT relay, but its pinouts are difficult to fit onto a breadboard. Figure 5.7 shows the pinouts for a typical DPDT relay.

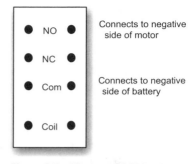

You'll need to check the datasheet for the relay you use to identify its pinouts, but as a general rule, the coil is at one end and is spaced differently from the other pins. The *common* (COM) pins are closest to the coil, with the *normally closed* (NC) pins next and the *normally open* (NO) connection at the far end. Figure 5.7 shows the pinouts of the relay we used.

Figure 5.7   Pinouts of DPDT relay

In the circuit diagram in figure 5.6, the D1 diode is a protection diode. When a relay coil is switched off, it can generate high voltage spikes that could potentially damage transistors and integrated circuits. The diode deals with these spikes safely, protecting the other components in the circuit.

When the Arduino sends a HIGH signal to the base of the transistor, it switches the transistor on; this in turn energizes the relay coil, which moves the contacts and completes the circuit to the motor, causing it to turn. When the Arduino sends a low signal to the transistor base, it turns it off, causing the relay coil to de-energize and move the contacts to the NC position, which breaks the motor circuit and turns it off.

Using the circuit diagram in figure 5.6 as a guide, assemble the circuit on a breadboard. Figure 5.8 shows the completed circuit.

Having completed the circuit, you can now move on to testing it.

5.1.4   Upload and test

Once you've made your connections, upload your sketch to the Arduino. You should notice the motor switching on for five seconds and then switching off for five seconds in a continuous loop.

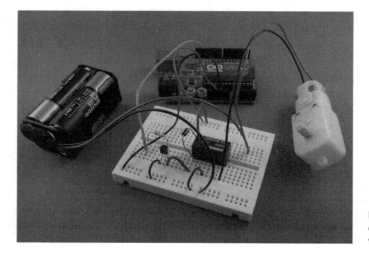

Figure 5.8   Completed circuit controlling a motor with a relay

Using a transistor and relay like this is a great way to switch a motor on and off, but there are times you'll want to be able to control the motor's speed and direction. That's what you're going to do next.

5.2 *Speed control and reverse*

Reversing a DC motor just involves swapping the wires from the power supply to the motor. But if your motor is installed in a remote place or on a mobile robot zipping across a room, switching wires becomes more difficult.

Controlling the speed of a motor is even trickier. The speed of a motor can be varied by altering the voltage applied to it. The less voltage, the slower the motor will turn, and the more voltage, the faster the motor will turn.

NOTE   Running a motor at too high a voltage is likely to cause it to overheat, resulting in permanent damage.

One way to vary the voltage is to use a potentiometer to produce variable resistance. This is shown in figure 5.9.

This is a very simple way to control a motor, but it's very inefficient because the potentiometer can quickly become very hot. A much more efficient way is to use a method called *pulse width modulation* (PWM), which we'll discuss next.

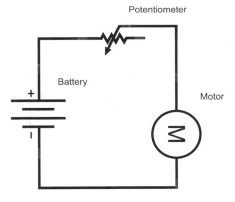

Figure 5.9   Using a potentiometer to control the speed of a motor

5.2.1 *PWM to the rescue*

A motor is at its most efficient when its design voltage is supplied to it. PWM is the most efficient way to power a motor, and it works by applying a series of voltage pulses to the motor.

We like to use the analogy of a playground carousel: if you start a carousel spinning, it will continue to spin and gradually slow down. To keep it turning, you need to give it another spin. To make the carousel turn faster at a constant speed, you need to give it lots of small spins; fewer spins will lower the speed. In the same way, you can control a motor's speed by switching the voltage on and off quickly.

You previously met the `analogRead` function, which measures an analog voltage and converts it to a digital number using the Arduino analog-to-digital converter (ADC). You would be forgiven for thinking that the Arduino `analogWrite` function does the opposite and outputs a voltage relative to a digital value given to it, but, in fact, the `analogWrite` function produces a PWM output. Figure 5.10 shows a graphical representation of the output from an Arduino using the `analogWrite` function.

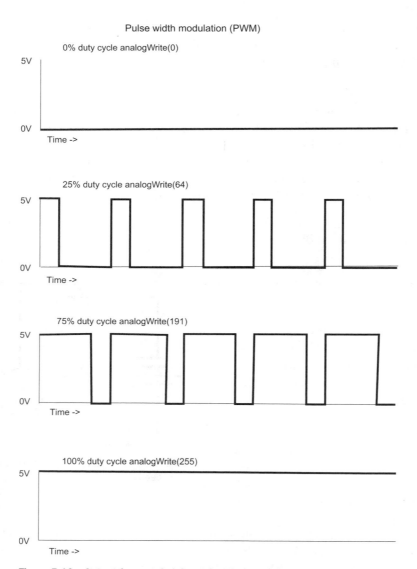

Figure 5.10   Output from an Arduino using the analogWrite function

The Arduino produces the output as a series of pulses, which, when coupled with the correct components, make it ideal for controlling motor speed.

NOTE   The Arduino's software automatically configures all of an Arduino CPU's available timers for hardware PWM duty at the beginning of every sketch. The Arduino's programming language makes PWM easy to use: call analogWrite(pin, duty cycle), where duty cycle is a value from 0 to 255, and pin is one of the PWM pins (3, 5, 6, 9, 10, or 11 on a standard board, or pins 2 through 13 on an Arduino Mega).

As we've said before, the Arduino can't itself provide enough current to drive a motor, but you can use the Arduino to control the speed and direction of rotation. In the next section, you're going to learn about a special circuit called an *H-bridge*. The H-bridge allows you to power a small DC motor and will give you more control over it than the transistor relay combination used previously.

5.2.2 *The H-bridge for motor control*

An H-bridge is a common way of controlling the speed and direction of a DC motor. Initially we'll use an H-bridge to turn a motor on and off and control its direction of rotation, and then we'll return to what we learned in the last section and use PWM to control its speed.

Figure 5.11 shows a typical circuit diagram of an H-bridge made up of four switches.

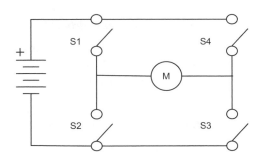

Figure 5.11   An H-bridge made up of four switches to control the direction of a motor

A good way to visualize how the circuit in figure 5.11 works is to use a table. Table 5.1 shows the motor's action based on the position of the four switches.

Table 5.1   Motor action based on position of switches in the H-bridge shown in figure 5.11

S1	S2	S3	S4	Motor action
Closed	Open	Closed	Open	Turns clockwise
Open	Closed	Open	Closed	Turns counterclockwise
Open	Open	Open	Open	Free runs
Closed	Open	Open	Closed	Brakes
Open	Closed	Closed	Open	Brakes

In two of the rows, the motor brakes, which is caused by the motor terminals being short-circuited. If the motor is turning, it will free-run (coast to a stop) if all the switches are open.

We could duplicate the H-bridge in figure 5.11 using transistors to replace the switches, but for ease of use and speed of assembly, you're going to use an excellent, readily available, purpose-designed integrated circuit that has two H-bridges on it. The L293D dual H driver provides a ready means of controlling both the direction and speed of a small DC motor. It's suitable for use in small robots or vehicles.

NOTE Make sure you get the L293D, not just an L293; the L293D comes equipped with built-in protection diodes.

You'll need the following items:

- A small DC motor
- An external power supply
- A breadboard
- An L293D dual H driver

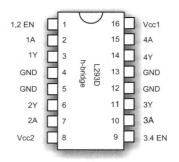

Figure 5.12   Pinouts of the L293D dual H driver

5.2.3   *The L293D dual H driver*

The L293D comes in a 16-pin package with pinouts as shown in figure 5.12.

Table 5.2 provides descriptions of each of the L293D pinouts.

Table 5.2   Pinouts of L293D dual H driver

Pin	Label	Description
1	1,2 EN	Enables half-H driver 1 and 2
2	1A	Half-H driver 1 input
3	1Y	Half-H driver 1 output
4, 5, 12, 13	GND	Ground
6	2Y	Half-H driver 2 output
7	2A	Half-H driver 2 input
8	Vcc2	Motor supply 4.5–36V
9	3,4 EN	Enables half-H driver 3 and 4
10	3A	Half-H driver 3 input
11	3Y	Half-H driver 3 output
14	4Y	Half-H driver 4 output
15	4A	Half-H driver 4 input
16	Vcc1	5V logic voltage

The L293D has the following characteristics:

- Peak output current of 1.2 amps
- Continuous output current of 600 milliamps
- Voltage range of 4.5–36 volts
- Drivers enabled in pairs
- Can drive two DC motors or one stepper motor

You're now going to look at how you can use the L293D to drive your small DC motor.

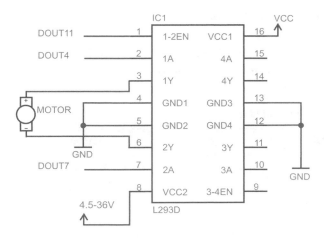

Figure 5.13   Circuit diagram showing connections between the motor, the L293D, and the Arduino

5.2.4   *Connecting the hardware*

Although the L293D is capable of driving two DC motors, we're only going to show how to drive one. The same techniques are used to drive two motors, so you can easily expand this if your own project requires you to use two.

Figure 5.13 shows the circuit diagram for the connections between the motor, the H-bridge and the Arduino; figure 5.14 shows the assembled project on its breadboard.

NOTE   Make sure you connect the grounds of the two power supplies together.

Once you've completed assembling the circuit, you can move on to constructing your sketch.

Figure 5.14   DC motor control using an L293D integrated circuit

5.2.5 *Sketch to control a motor with an L293D*

Looking at the circuit diagram shown in figure 5.13, you can see that the motor is connected to pins 3 and 6 with pins 1, 2, and 7 connected respectively to pins D11, D4, and D7 on the Arduino. You can draw up a truth table (table 5.3) based on these connections, and use this information to write your sketch.

Table 5.3   Truth table for L293D connected to a DC motor

1,2 EN	1A	2A	Motor
HIGH	LOW	HIGH	Turns clockwise
HIGH	HIGH	LOW	Turns counterclockwise
HIGH	LOW	LOW	Brakes
HIGH	HIGH	HIGH	Brakes
LOW	(doesn't matter)	(doesn't matter)	Brakes

Looking at the table, you can see that for the motor to operate, the enable pin (1,2 EN) must be HIGH with the 1A and 2A pins controlling the direction. Armed with this information, you can now write your sketch, as shown in the next listing.

Listing 5.2   Using an L293D to control a small DC motor

```
int enablePin = 11;
int in1A = 4;
int in2A = 7;

void setup()
{
  pinMode(enablePin, OUTPUT);
  pinMode(in1A, OUTPUT);
  pinMode(in2A, OUTPUT);
  digitalWrite(enablePin, LOW);
}

void loop()
{
  digitalWrite(in1A, HIGH);          Drives motor
  digitalWrite(in2A, LOW);           counterclockwise
  digitalWrite(enablePin, HIGH);
  delay(5000);
  digitalWrite(enablePin, LOW);      Brakes
  delay(2000);
  digitalWrite(in1A, LOW);
  digitalWrite(in2A, HIGH);
  digitalWrite(enablePin, HIGH);     Drives motor
  delay(5000);                       clockwise
  digitalWrite(enablePin, LOW);
  delay(2000);
}
```

Listing 5.2 shows a sketch that you can use to switch your motor on and off with the L293D H-bridge. You first set the enable pin to LOW, thereby disabling the H-bridge. During the loop, you enable the H-bridge by setting the enable pin to HIGH. The in1A and in2A pins, which are connected to pins 2 (1A) and 7 (2A) on the L293D, are changed in the loop so that the motor turns in one direction for five seconds and then the other direction for five seconds with a two-second gap in between. Let's move on and test your sketch.

5.2.6 Upload and test

Check your connections, and then upload the sketch to the Arduino. If everything is working correctly you should observe the motor rotating one way and then the other way with a pause in between. The sequence then repeats.

We've just shown you how to use a circuit to control one motor; controlling another is just a matter of duplicating the circuit. By changing your code and using the same circuit, you can also alter the speed of the motor, which you'll do next.

5.2.7 Changing motor speed

We previously talked about how PWM can be used to control the speed of a motor, and you can do the same with this circuit. You'll use PWM on the enablePin to enable and disable the H-bridge. Here's the new sketch.

Listing 5.3   Controlling motor speed with an L293D

```
int enablePin = 11;
int in1 = 4;
int in2 = 7;

void setup()
{
  pinMode(enablePin, OUTPUT);
  pinMode(in1, OUTPUT);
  pinMode(in2, OUTPUT);
  digitalWrite(enablePin, LOW);

}

void loop()
{
  digitalWrite(in1, HIGH);          ◁——— Counterclockwise
  digitalWrite(in2, LOW);
  digitalWrite(enablePin, HIGH);
  for(int i = 0 ; i <= 255; i++) {
    analogWrite(enablePin, i);
    delay(50);
  }

  digitalWrite(in1, LOW);           ◁——— Clockwise
  digitalWrite(in2, HIGH);
  for(int i = 0 ; i <= 255; i++) {
```

```
    analogWrite(enablePin, i);
    delay(50);
  }

}
```

This sketch is similar to the previous one; you're using a `for` loop that varies the PWM output on the `enablePin` from 0 to 255, first rotating the motor in one direction and then the other. After either changing your existing sketch or creating a new one, you can move on to testing it.

5.2.8   *Upload and test*

Check over your connections, and then upload the sketch to the Arduino. If everything is working correctly, you should see the motor rotating in one direction and then the other, with the motor gradually increasing in speed from stationary to full. The sequence then repeats.

> **NOTE**   You may notice a delay between each start of the motor because it may need a minimum PWM value to start turning. This depends on an individual motor's characteristics, but is perfectly normal.

We've shown you how to use this circuit to control one motor, but as before, controlling another is just a matter of duplicating the circuit.

The circuit you've built in this example is only suitable for driving small motors. Large DC motors can be similarly controlled with PWM, but they require suitably rated components; unfortunately, these components tend to be more specialized and expensive.

This concludes our look at controlling small DC motors. Next, we'll look at stepper motors, which can be precisely controlled

5.3   *Stepper motors: one step at a time*

A stepper motor is a special type of motor that can move in a series of discrete steps. Stepper motors are a good choice for projects requiring controlled and accurate movement. Typical projects include 3D printers, telescope positioning systems, and computer numerical control (CNC) lathes and mills.

Good sources for obtaining stepper motors are old inkjet or laser printers, where they're used to move the print heads and to control paper feed. You can also purchase new ones from electronics suppliers or from eBay.

Figure 5.15 shows a typical stepper motor purchased from eBay.

Stepper motors are classified according to their frame size, which corresponds to the diameter of the body: a size 11 has a body diameter of 1.1 inches, and a size 23 has a body diameter of 2.3 inches. Stepper motors are also often rated in terms of the torque they can provide, with the torque being proportional to body length: the longer the body, the greater the torque. The step angle is also normally provided; a stepper motor with an angle of 9 degrees will require 40 steps to complete a full revolution.

Figure 5.15   A stepper motor purchased from eBay

NOTE   Torque is a measure of the rotational force a motor can provide, often given in ounce-inches.

There are two main types of stepper motors—bipolar and unipolar—each with its own advantages and disadvantages. Let's take a look at the differences between them.

5.3.1   Unipolar or bipolar

Bipolar and unipolar describe the internal method of construction of a stepper motor. The two types are also controlled in slightly different ways. Table 5.4 shows the main differences.

Table 5.4   Main differences between unipolar and bipolar stepper motors

Unipolar	Bipolar
Simpler to control	More efficient
Generally lower cost	Greater torque per unit of power
Five or six wire connections (can be more)	Four wire connections
	Greater speed of rotation
	Simpler construction

NOTE   A unipolar stepper motor can be electronically controlled in the same manner as a bipolar motor if it's connected in a particular way.

Choosing a stepper motor can be quite involved, depending on your intended usage. For projects requiring extremely accurate high torque, choose the bipolar variant; for simpler projects, the cheaper unipolar type is a good choice, although bipolar motors are now becoming more readily available because of the reduction in cost of the integrated circuits needed to control them.

Figure 5.16   Label on the back of a stepper motor

If you're scavenging a motor from existing equipment or purchasing a motor from eBay, you'll need to identify the type of stepper motor and which wires connect to which coil.

Let's take a look at the steps required to identify the motor type and connections of a stepper motor we purchased from eBay.

A visual inspection revealed a label on the back, as shown in figure 5.16. This indicated that the motor has a step angle of 1.8 degrees and that it draws 0.5 amps of current. The description provided by the seller also indicated the motor was rated at 6.5 volts.

The stepper motor has a step angle of 1.8 degrees, so we calculated the number of steps to complete one revolution by dividing 360 degrees by the step angle:

```
360 / 1.8 = 200
```

Based on our calculation, the stepper motor takes 200 steps to complete one revolution.

The motor has six wires connected to it, and based on what we already know, this identifies it as a unipolar motor. We can work out the motor connections by using a multimeter to measure the resistance between individual wires and recording the results in a table. Figure 5.17 demonstrates taking a measurement between two wires using a multimeter.

Draw a truth table and record the resistance between each wire, with *X* denoting no connection. Our truth table for our motor is shown in table 5.5.

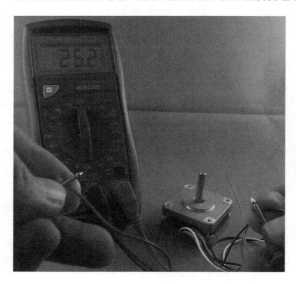

Figure 5.17   Measuring the resistance between two stepper motor wires

Table 5.5 Record of resistance between stepper motor wires

	Red	Blue	Green	Yellow	Black	White
Red	X	26	X	X	X	13
Blue	26	X	X	X	X	13
Green	X	X	X	13	26	X
Yellow	X	X	13	X	13	X
Black	X	X	26	13	X	X
White	13	13	X	X	X	X

What we're measuring is the resistance in the coils of the stepper motor. The unipolar stepper motor has two coils, each with a wire connected halfway along the coil. Notice how some measured values are half the values of others—13 ohms instead of 26 ohms. Figure 5.18 shows this more clearly.

Using the preceding method, we identified the coil wires of our unipolar stepper motor.

We should also take a quick look at bipolar stepper motors, because these are readily available in surplus equipment such as old printers. Figure 5.19 shows a bipolar stepper motor from an old surplus Epson printer.

The only identification is a label on the back of the stepper motor, as shown in figure 5.20.

The label identifies the stepper motor as an Astrosyn P/N EM-257. A search on the internet turns up some information for its specification, which is summarized in table 5.6.

Like the unipolar motor, the bipolar motor has two coils. We can identify the coils using a multimeter to measure their resistance. Because there are only four wires and no center taps, we just need to find out which two wires connect together.

One of the wires has a red stripe on it. We call this wire *number one*, and then number the other wires sequentially. Using the multimeter we discovered that wire number one was connected to wire three, and that wire two was connected to wire four.

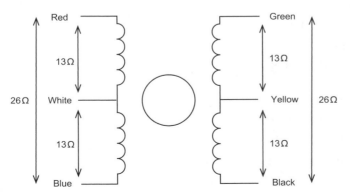

Figure 5.18 Resistance measured from coils of a unipolar stepper motor

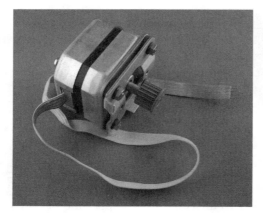

Figure 5.19   A surplus bipolar stepper motor
pulled from an old printer

Figure 5.20   Label on reverse of
bipolar stepper motor

Table 5.6   Specification of surplus bipolar stepper motor

Specification	Value
Voltage	7 volts
Current	0.7 amps
Wires	4
Steps/revolution	200
Step angle	1.8 degrees
Frame size	17 (1.7 inches)

You've now seen how to identify the wires for both unipolar and bipolar stepper motors.

You now need to work out how to connect a stepper motor to the Arduino, and for this you're going to use the L293D chip that you previously used to power your DC motor.

5.3.2   Connecting the hardware

You'll need the following items:

- A stepper motor
- An external power supply
- A breadboard
- An L293D dual H driver
- A selection of jumper wires
- Two 2-pin screw connectors

The L293D can drive either a bipolar or a unipolar stepper motor. Figure 5.21 shows the schematic for your circuit to drive a bipolar stepper motor.

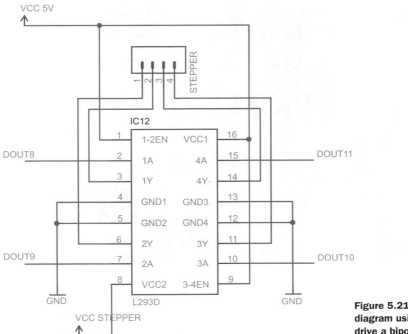

Figure 5.21 A schematic diagram using an L293D to drive a bipolar stepper motor

You use the Arduino digital pins 8 through 11 to provide the control inputs for the L293D chip. Pins 1 and 9 of the L293D are tied to the 5 volt supply so that the H-bridges are always enabled (when you controlled the DC motor, you used these pins to provide the PWM control by switching them to either HIGH or LOW).

Pin 8 on the L293D provides the power for the motor; make sure you tie the grounds for the 5 volt supply and the stepper motor supply together. One coil connects to pins 3 and 6, and the other to pins 11 and 14 of the L293D chip.

> **NOTE** The circuit diagram shown in figure 5.21 is for a bipolar stepper motor; when using a unipolar stepper motor with an L293D, connect the center tap of the coils to ground.

Now that you've studied the schematic, you can move on to assembling the circuit on a breadboard. Figure 5.22 shows the completed circuit.

5.3.3 *Stepper motor library functions*

The Arduino IDE has excellent support for stepper motors and provides a library appropriately called Stepper that can be used with either bipolar or unipolar stepper motors. We took a brief look at the Stepper library in chapter 4 and saw that the library has three main functions that together control the speed and direction of rotation of the stepper motor. Let's look at each of these in turn, starting with the Stepper function.

Figure 5.22   Circuit connections between the L293D and the unipolar stepper motor

STEPPER

The Stepper function has two forms depending on the circuitry used to drive your stepper motor, because it's possible to control a stepper motor using only two pins of the Arduino by adding additional components. These are the functions:

```
Stepper(number_steps, pin1, pin2)
Stepper(number_steps, pin1, pin2, pin3, pin4)
```

The number_steps variable is the number of steps your stepper motor takes to complete one revolution, which, if you'll recall, you can calculate by dividing 360 by the step angle. For example, if you have a motor with a step angle of 1.5 degrees, the calculation is as follows:

```
360 / 1.5 = 240 steps
```

The remaining variables—pin1, pin2, and the optional pin3 and pin4—are the Arduino digital pins that are used to control the stepper motor.

NOTE   In our example, we used all four pins.

SETSPEED

This optional function sets the motor's speed of rotation in revolutions per minute (RPM). This function doesn't actually cause the stepper motor to turn, but it sets the speed at which it will turn when it's commanded to by the steps function.

```
setSpeed(rpm)
```

STEPS

This function moves the motor the number of steps specified: a negative number causes the stepper motor to turn one way, and a positive number causes it to turn the other way.

```
steps(num_steps)
```

The rate at which the stepper motor moves between steps is set by the `setSpeed` function; if this function isn't called in your sketch, the stepper motor will move as quickly as it's able to between steps.

Now that you've seen the functions available to you, let's look at the sketch you're going to use to step your motor.

5.3.4 Sketch to control a stepper motor

This sketch is shipped with the Arduino IDE, and it's a great way to ensure that you have your stepper motor wired correctly. Because it moves the motor one step at a time, the sketch is called *stepper_oneStepAtATime*, and it can be found in the Files > Examples > Stepper menu. We've provided a copy of it in the following listing.

Listing 5.4 Sketch to drive a stepper motor

```
#include <Stepper.h>                                   ①  Loads Stepper library
const int stepsPerRevolution = 200;
Stepper myStepper(stepsPerRevolution, 8,9,10,11);
                                                          Sets motor steps
int stepCount = 0;                                     ②  and pin numbers
void setup() {
    Serial.begin(9600);
}
void loop() {
  myStepper.step(1);
  Serial.print("steps:" );
  Serial.println(stepCount);
  stepCount++;
  delay(500);
}
```

The first line of the sketch loads the Stepper library; you need to do this because even though the library is provided as part of the Arduino IDE, it isn't part of the core libraries ①. You next set the number of steps for your stepper motor; this listing is set for a 200-step motor, but yours may be different ②. You next make a call to set up your `Stepper` object and set the pin numbers to use.

During the setup function, you set up the serial port so that you can see the number of steps taken.

In the loop function, the stepper motor is moved one step at a time, and the number of steps is sent as output to the serial port. The `stepCount` is incremented by 1, and then a delay of 500 milliseconds occurs before you go through the loop and step the motor again.

Take some time to make sure you understand the code in the sketch before moving on to test it.

5.3.5 Upload and test

Check over your connections and upload the sketch to the Arduino. Make sure everything is powered correctly, and hopefully the stepper motor turns one step at a time.

If it doesn't turn, you may need to switch the wires going to the coils—these must be configured correctly for the sketch to work. Remove the power to the Arduino, swap the wires, and try again. You might need to make a couple of wire swaps to get everything connected correctly and get the stepper motor turning one step at a time.

In this section on stepper motors, we've covered both unipolar and bipolar stepper motors and how to connect them correctly to your L293D chip. You now have a working stepper motor that you can use in any future projects. Next, we're going to take a look at another type of motor, called a *servomotor*.

5.4   *Try not to get in a flap with servomotors*

Servomotors are very common in the model-control world and are excellent for moving flaps on model airplanes or rudders on model boats, and for steering model cars or robots. They're also widely available from a number of suppliers.

A servomotor is a geared motor that can be set to turn to an angle, usually between 0 and 180 degrees, and is normally powered by a voltage of approximately 4.8 volts. Because of their low cost and their simplicity of control, they're ideal for use in a wide variety of projects that require accurate movement. We've previously used a servomotor to scan an ultrasonic module from side to side to locate objects in a small robot's path.

A typical servomotor is shown in figure 5.23.

Let's take a look at how a servomotor is controlled.

5.4.1   *Controlling a servomotor*

A servomotor has three connections to it: ground, power, and a control or signal connection. The majority of modern servo connectors have the center connector as the power line.

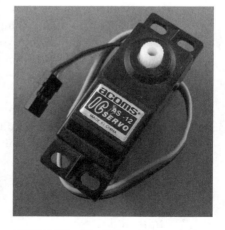

The control or signal connection controls the angle the servomotor turns to by sending a pulse. The *pulse width* tells the motor to turn to an angle somewhere between 0 and 180 degrees. The pulse has to be repeated every 20 milliseconds or the motor will return to an arbitrary position. Figure 5.24 shows the relationship between pulse width and servo angle.

As you can see in figure 5.24, the neutral position for a servo is 90 degrees, which is obtained with a pulse width of 1.5 milliseconds. The pulse width ranges roughly between 1.0 milliseconds and 2.0 milliseconds, with the servomotor angle being 0 degrees for the former and 180 degrees for the latter.

Figure 5.23   A typical small servomotor

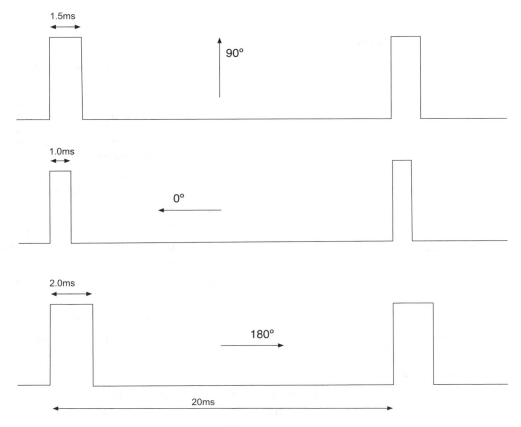

Figure 5.24   Relationship between pulse width and servo angle

Now that you've seen what is required to power and set the angle for a servomotor, let's look at what the Arduino IDE provides.

5.4.2 Servomotor functions and methods

Just as it does for the stepper motor, the Arduino IDE ships with a Servo library to help you control a servomotor. In fact, the library gives you the ability to control up to 12 servomotors on a standard Arduino and a whopping 48 on the Arduino Mega.

The functions and methods provided by the Servo library are listed in table 5.7.

NOTE   Using the Servo library disables `analogWrite` on pins 9 and 10 for a standard Arduino. On the Mega, using more than 12 servos will disable `analogWrite` on pins 11 and 12.

Let's look at a sketch you can use with a servomotor.

Table 5.7   Servo library functions

Function name	Usage	Description
`Servo`	`Servo myServo`	Creates a servo object to control a servomotor.
`attach()`	`attach(pin)` `attach(pin, min, max)`	`pin` is the Arduino pin that the servomotor is attached to; `min` and `max` are values in microseconds for the maximum and minimum values of the pulse width. The defaults are minimum `544` and maximum `2400`.
`write()`	`write(angle)`	Sets the angle of rotation for the servomotor to turn to in degrees.
`writeMicroseconds()`	`writeMicroseconds (pulse_width)`	Sets the servomotor's pulse width in microseconds.
`read()`	`read()`	Returns the last written pulse width angle as degrees, from 0 to 180.
`readMicroseconds()`	`readMicroseconds()`	Returns the last written pulse width angle in microseconds.
`attached()`	`attached()`	Returns `true` if servo is attached.
`detach()`	`detach()`	Stops attached servomotor from pulsing pin.

5.4.3   *Sketch to control a servomotor*

The sketch you're going to use is one that's shipped with the Arduino IDE and shows the range of motion of a servomotor. The sketch is called *sweep*, and it can be located in the IDE under Files > Examples > Servo.

Listing 5.5   Sketch to rotate a servomotor between 0 and 180 degrees

```
#include <Servo.h>

Servo myservo;
int pos = 0;

void setup()
{
  myservo.attach(9);
}

void loop()
{
  for(pos = 0; pos < 180; pos += 1)
  {
    myservo.write(pos); delay(15); }
  for(pos = 180; pos>=1; pos-=1)
  {
    myservo.write(pos); delay(15); }
}
```

You first need to include the Servo library because although the library ships with the Arduino IDE, it isn't included in the core functions. You next create a `servo` object.

In setup you attach the servo to digital pin 9 on the Arduino.

In the main loop, the code sweeps the servomotor from 0 to 180 degrees with a 15-millisecond delay between each new position to give the servomotor time to move to the new angle. The servomotor is then swept the other way from 180 to 0 degrees, again with a 15-millisecond delay between each move. The loop then repeats the process.

Let's now move on and connect the Arduino to a servomotor so you can see the sketch in action.

5.4.4 Connecting the hardware

You'll need the following items:

- A servomotor
- An external power supply
- A breadboard
- A selection of jumper wires
- A section of 0.1-inch header

A servomotor usually has three connections, with the center connector typically being the power connector. The other two connections are the ground and signal connections. The ground is normally black or brown, although this can vary among manufacturers.

Because you're just using one servomotor, you can use the 5 volt supply on the Arduino to provide power, although we recommend powering the Arduino with an external power supply and not just using the USB connection.

Figure 5.25 shows the section of single-row header 0.1-inch pitch we used on the breadboard to make it easier to connect to a servomotor. Figure 5.26 shows the connected circuit.

Having connected the servomotor to the Arduino, it's time to try out your sketch.

Figure 5.25 Section of single-row header 0.1-inch pitch to connect servomotor to breadboard

5.4.5 Upload and test

Check your connections and upload the sketch from listing 5.5 to the Arduino. You should observe the servomotor turning smoothly from 0 to 180 degrees and from 180 back to 0 degrees. If the motor doesn't turn, check the ground and signal connections and try again.

We're now going to look at another type of DC motor called a *brushless motor*.

Figure 5.26   Connections
between servomotor and
Arduino

5.5   *Mighty power comes in small packages with brushless DC motors*

The humble DC motor has been around for more than a century, and the brushless motor is the new kid on the block. Mass production has rapidly brought the price down on these highly efficient motors, but what advantages and disadvantages do they have over their older cousins?

5.5.1   *Why go brushless*

Brushless motors provide more torque per weight, are more efficient, offer increased reliability, and have reduced electrical noise compared to standard DC motors. A disadvantage is that they require a more specialized controller than a standard motor does, although you'll soon see how, with the correct electronics package, they're easy to control and even allow you to use some existing code.

Brushless motors are often labeled with a value of Kv, which is the theoretical RPM per volt that a motor can rotate at. Consider a motor labeled 2400 Kv as an example. If you're supplying 6 volts, the maximum speed the motor could turn at would be 6 x 2400 = 14,400 RPM.

Brushless motors come in two types: *inrunner* and *outrunner*. With an inrunner motor, only the inner shaft rotates; with an outrunner motor, the outer shell, or can, rotates as well. Inrunners tend to have a higher Kv and less torque, whereas outrunners tend to be lower Kv and higher torque. Figure 5.27 shows examples of both types.

Inrunner motors tend to be used in model cars and boats, so they're probably a good choice for any land-based vehicles or projects. Outrunner motors are normally found in model airplanes and helicopters. They're a good choice if you want to build

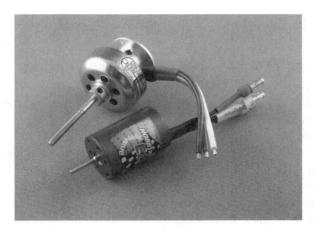

Figure 5.27   An outrunner (top) and an inrunner (bottom) brushless motor

a quadrocopter. We've used outrunner motors previously in an underwater robot because of their better torque.

This completes our overview of these small and powerful motors. Let's take a look at how you control them.

5.5.2   Gaining control

Brushless motors require specialized controllers because they're really three-phase motors. Luckily, electronic speed controllers (ESCs) are readily available in the model radio-control world at reasonable prices and have a range of functions that you can take advantage of.

When choosing a brushless ESC, make sure that it will work with your chosen motor, because current load and voltage requirements can vary significantly from one motor to another. ESCs designed for use in model aircraft and some boats are normally only able to control the speed of rotation of a motor but can't reverse a motor's direction of rotation.

> **CAUTION**   It's possible to reverse the direction of a brushless motor by switching any two of the three connecting wires with each other. Don't reverse the connections from the battery to the controller, because you'll destroy the ESC and may also cause damage to the motor or battery pack.

ESCs designed for use in model cars and some boats are usually able to control both a motor's speed and its direction of rotation, but make sure you check this before purchasing.

To power a brushless motor, you need to use batteries designed to take the high current required by these motors. These can be NiCd, NiMH, or the newer lithium polymore (LiPo) battery packs.

> **NOTE**   Specialized chargers are needed to charge these batteries; using incorrect equipment, particularly with LiPos, can cause them to explode.

One of the great things about ESCs is that they can be controlled in exactly the same way as servomotors; this means you can use the Servo library and the things you learned in the last section to control them. Just like servomotors, they expect a pulse every 20 milliseconds with a width of between 1.0 and 2.0 milliseconds, with 1.0 millisecond being the slowest speed and 2.0 milliseconds being the highest. With ESCs that can reverse direction, the pulse range will be different: a width of 1.5 milliseconds will cause the motor to stop, a 2.0-millisecond pulse width will be the fastest forward speed, and a 1.0 millisecond pulse width will be the fastest reverse speed.

When a motor and its controller are first powered on, the motor won't instantly start—this is a safety feature—but it will wait a period of time and may expect a particular pulse width before starting. You'll need to consult the ESC's manual to see if this is the case. The first brushless motor we used expected a 1.0-millisecond pulse width for a period of one second before it would function correctly.

NOTE   You'll often hear a series of tones when an ESC and its motor are first powered up; this is all part of the normal startup process and can even sound quite musical.

Now that you have a basic understanding of how to control a brushless motor, let's move on and look at some code in a sketch.

5.5.3 *Sketch to control a brushless motor*

Take a look at the next listing. You should recognize the code because it's almost the same as the code in listing 5.5, with the addition of a start pulse during setup to allow the ESC and motor to stabilize.

Listing 5.6 Sketch to control a brushless motor in one direction

```
#include <Servo.h>

Servo myservo;
int pos = 0;

void setup()
{
  myservo.attach(9);
  myservo.write(pos);
  delay(1000);
}

void loop()
{
  for(pos = 0; pos < 180; pos += 1)
  {
    myservo.write(pos);
    delay(15);
  }
  for(pos = 180; pos>=1; pos-=1)
  {
    myservo.write(pos); delay(15); }
}
```

The code shown in listing 5.6 is for use with an ESC that only controls speed, not direction. The next listing shows a sketch you can use with an ESC that can control a motor's speed as well as its direction of rotation.

Listing 5.7 Sketch to use with ESC that can control speed and direction

```
#include <Servo.h>

Servo myservo;
int pos = 90;

void setup()
{
  myservo.attach(9);
  myservo.write(pos);
  delay(1000);

}

void loop()
{
  for(pos = 90; pos < 180; pos += 1)
  {
    myservo.write(pos);
    delay(15);
}
  for(pos = 180; pos>=90; pos-=1)
  {
    myservo.write(pos);
    delay(15); }
}
```

Once you've typed in the sketch that's applicable to your type of ESC and motor, you can build your circuit.

5.5.4 Connecting the hardware

You'll need the following items:

- A brushless motor
- A brushless ESC
- An external power supply for the motor
- A selection of jumper wires

For this example, we used an inrunner brushless motor with an ESC that can control both speed and direction. We also used a NiCd battery pack to supply power to the ESC.

TIP You'll need to connect the motor to something quite solid because these motors are very powerful when rotating.

There's a servo-type connector connected to the ESC, and this can be connected to your breadboard in the same manner as in the previous section on servomotors. Figure 5.28 shows the completed setup.

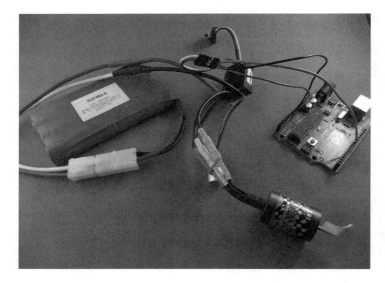

Figure 5.28   Brushless motor controlled by an Arduino

When you've completed your connections, you can move on and test your circuit.

5.5.5   *Upload and test*

Upload your sketch to the Arduino before connecting the power pack to the ESC. Once the sketch has uploaded, connect the power pack to the ESC and reset the Arduino. After a short delay, you should observe the motor speeding up and then slowing down.

Once you've completed this part, it's time to control the direction of rotation as well as speed.

5.5.6   *Reverse*

To control the direction as well as the speed of a brushless motor requires an ESC that's normally found in radio-control model cars and some boats. Controlling them still involves treating the control as a type of servo, but instead of the 1.5-millisecond pulse width being the midrange speed, it's the motor's off position. The 2.0-millisecond pulse width is now the full forward direction, and the 1.0-millisecond pulse width is the full reverse position. You need to change your sketch to reflect this.

5.5.7   *Sketch to reverse a brushless motor*

The new sketch is shown in the following listing. It's similar to listing 5.7, with a few additions.

Listing 5.8   Sketch to control a brushless motor in both forward and reverse

```
#include <Servo.h>

Servo myservo;
int pos = 90;
```

```
void setup()
{
  myservo.attach(9);
  myservo.write(pos);
  delay(1000);

}

void loop()
{
  for(pos = 90; pos < 180; pos += 1)
  {
    myservo.write(pos);
    delay(15);
  }
  for(pos = 180; pos>=90; pos-=1)
  {
    myservo.write(pos);
    delay(15);
  }
 for(pos = 90; pos > 0; pos -= 1)
  {
    myservo.write(pos);
    delay(15);
  }
  for(pos = 0; pos<=90; pos+=1)
  {
    myservo.write(pos);
    delay(15);
  }

}
```

Reverse motor

Code added to listing 5.7

The sketch has a delay in `setup` to allow the ESC to stabilize.

During the loop, you use a `for` loop to increment the servo position up to a maximum of 180 and then another `for` loop to decrement it to 90. Another `for` loop decrements the servo position from 90 to 0 before a final `for` loop increments the servo position from 0 to 90. The delays allow the motor to stabilize between commands.

Let's move on now and construct the circuit.

5.5.8 Connecting the hardware

We're going to use the inrunner motor and controller from before, so you quickly test your new sketch.

5.5.9 Upload and test

Upload your sketch to the Arduino before connecting the power pack to the ESC. Once the sketch has uploaded, connect the power pack to the ESC and reset the Arduino. After a short delay, you should observe the motor speeding up and then slowing down, then doing the same in the reverse direction.

We'll finish this chapter off by discussing a motor control shield that can be used when you want to control more than one motor.

Figure 5.29   Components supplied in the Adafruit Industries motor control shield kit

5.6   *The motor control shield for more motors*

There are a few different motor control shields available; we're going to look at one from Adafruit Industries. The shield is reasonably priced and is supplied as a kit that you assemble yourself. Figure 5.29 shows the components supplied in the kit.

The shield is ideal if you want to control more than one stepper motor or a couple of DC motors. The shield is based on the L293D integrated circuit that you've been using in this chapter, but instead of one, it uses two of them. The shield can drive up to four DC motors or two stepper motors or servomotors, making it very versatile.

The assembled shield is shown in figure 5.30.

This kit is available from a number of suppliers, and it's a great addition to your toolbox if you want to control more than a couple of motors at a time. It would be ideal for obstacle-avoidance robots where DC motors provide the motion and a servomotor controls an ultrasonic module that looks out for obstacles.

Figure 5.30   The fully-assembled motor controller shield

5.7 Summary

In this chapter you've looked at a variety of different motors and have seen which types of projects they would be suitable for and how you can control them using an Arduino and a handful of components.

You started with a small DC motor that can be used to power a wide range of robotic vehicles, and you learned how to control both its speed and direction using an L293D integrated circuit.

You then investigated stepper motors that can be accurately and precisely controlled and are used in CNC mills, lathes, and 3D printers. You learned how to identify the different types of commonly available stepper motors and then learned how to control them using the Stepper library shipped with the Arduino IDE.

Next, you learned about servomotors, which are commonly used in radio-controlled models. These small, powerful, geared motors are great in projects requiring accurate movement, like moving an ultrasonic transducer on an obstacle-avoidance robot. You used the Servo library that lets you control up to 12 servomotors on a standard Arduino, and for those more ambitious projects, up to 48 on an Arduino Mega.

You then applied what you learned about servomotors to control brushless motors. These highly efficient powerhouses are suitable for a wide range of projects, including quadrocopters and remote-piloted drones.

We ended the chapter with a brief look at a motor controller shield kit from Adafruit that's capable of controlling up to four DC motors or two stepper motors or servomotors.

In chapter 6, you're going to look at using ultrasonic and infrared sensors with an Arduino and see how they can be used for object detection.

Object detection

6

This chapter covers

- Detecting objects with ultrasound
- Range finding with active infrared
- Detecting motion with passive infrared

In this chapter we're going to begin exploring how to get meaningful data from the objects and environments around your Arduino controller and use it in your Arduino programs. Of course, *meaningful data* could mean any number of things: temperature, sound, light, color, and so on. To start, we'll focus on detecting objects.

There are a number of fields where this is important, including robotics, monitoring, interactive applications, security, and home automation, to name a few. There are three simple technologies that this chapter will explore: *ultrasonic* sensors, *active infrared* sensors, and *passive infrared* sensors. All are relatively low-power and easy to configure and control, but each has distinct advantages and disadvantages that you'll want to understand before creating sensing applications.

We'll start with ultrasound.

6.1 Object detection with ultrasound

Ultrasound is an excellent way of figuring out what's in the immediate vicinity of your Arduino. The basics of using ultrasound are like this: you shoot out a sound, wait to hear it echo back, and if you have your timing right, you'll know if anything is out there and how far away it is. This is called *echolocation* and it's how bats and dolphins find objects in the dark and underwater, though they use lower frequencies than you can use with your Arduino.

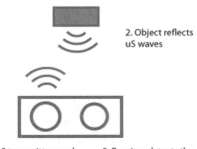

2. Object reflects uS waves

1. uS transmitter sends a uS signal

3. Receiver detects the reflected uS waves.

Figure 6.1   How ultrasonic waves are transmitted and received by a distance sensor

An ultrasonic sensor consists of two separate components: one that sends out the sound, and one that listens for it to bounce back. The sensor will also contain additional components, including a small microcontroller, that are responsible for determining the time between sending and receiving a sound. The time value is encoded in a voltage; the longer the delay, the higher the voltage. Because ultrasonic sensors communicate at 5V, the value is between a maximum 5V and a minimum 0V.

The trick of echolocation is in knowing what to do with the length of time between sending the signal and receiving it back. The meaning of that time will always be dependent on the particular component that you're using, be it a Parallax Ping (also known as the *PING)))*), the Devantech SRF05, or another ultrasonic range sensor. This information can always be found in the product's data sheet in one format or another. For instance, the datasheet for the Parallax Ping contains the following: "The PING))) returns a pulse width of 29.033 uS per centimeter."

That's helpful and points you in the right direction, but there's one catch: you get the time for every centimeter travelled, when what you really want is the centimeters travelled *to* the object, not *to* and *back*. So you divide by two and you're good to go.

Let's examine two specific sensors.

6.1.1 Choosing an ultrasonic sensor

We're going to focus on two different ultrasonic sensors: the Devantech SRF05, shown in figure 6.2, and the Parallax Ping, shown in figure 6.3.

Both of these sensors work the same way: you signal the sensor that you want it to send out a signal, and then you read the response. The response comes back using what the Arduino calls a *pulse*, or simply a HIGH signal with microsecond fidelity, which means that

Figure 6.2   The Devantech SRF05, an ultrasonic sensor

the difference between an object that's 30 cm away and 2 m away is approximately 40 millionths of a second.

You need a special method to read values that quickly, and the Arduino provides one:

```
pulseIn(pin, value)
```

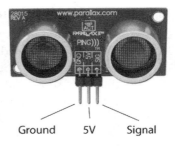

Ground   5V   Signal

Figure 6.3   The Parallax Ping, an ultrasonic sensor

The first value is an integer that indicates which pin you're going to read the pulse on, and the second specifies whether you're expecting a pulse that's LOW or HIGH. Some components communicate by pulling the pin LOW to 0V, and others communicate by setting the pin HIGH to 5V (or 3.3V if you're using a 3.3V powered Arduino), so it's important to know which one you should be expecting.

The differences are slight but significant. The Parallax Ping operates in a single mode, which is to say there's only one way to do it. It can read ranges from 3 cm to 3 m. The Devantech SRF05 has two modes, a three-wire mode and a four-wire mode, and it can read ranges from 3 cm to 4 m.

Because there's only one way to operate the Ping, we'll return to it later; the Devantech's three-wire versus four-wire modes are worth exploration.

6.1.2   *Three wires or four*

The fourth and fifth extra pins on the Devantech SRF05 might seem strange at first, because the Ping needs only three, but there's a good reason for it. The SRF05 had a predecessor called the SRF04, and when Devantech updated their ultrasonic range finder, they made the SRF05 compatible with wiring for the SRF04. This meant that older designs that couldn't be changed could still easily update to a newer controller.

The slight disadvantage is that the SRF05 is a little more complex than the Ping: it has two modes. It can either use one pin to send the signal and another to listen to the result, or it can use a single wire to both send the signal and get the resulting data. Connecting the mode pin to ground means that you're going to use the SRF05 in three-wire mode, just like the Ping. Connecting the mode pin to 5V indicates that the SRF05 will be used in four-wire mode.

6.1.3   *Sketches for ultrasonic object finding*

First we'll cover working with the Parallax Ping and then the Devantech SRF05.

SKETCH FOR THE PARALLAX PING

To begin, you need to configure the Arduino pin to whichever signal pin of the Ping will be connected as an input. To trigger the sensor, you set the connection pin LOW briefly and then HIGH for 5 microseconds. After that you can read the distance to any object as a length of time using pulseIn(). Note the *microseconds*, which are millionths of a second and can be set using delayMicroseconds(); they're not *milliseconds*, which are thousandths of a second and can be set using delay().

Something else important to note is that you don't want to send a pulse more frequently than every 30–50 milliseconds or so, because, depending on the distance of objects from the sensor, you might end up with ultrasound waves interfering with one another travelling to and from an object. After you send a pulse, calling `delay(50)` will ensure that your readings are free from interference.

To build this example, you'll need the following components:

- 1 Arduino Uno (or similar)
- 1 Parallax Ping

This sketch will let you read ranges from the Ping.

Listing 6.1 Reading ranges with the Parallax Ping

```
const int signalPin = 9;                    ◁──┐  Any PWM-enabled
                                                 pin can be used.
void setup()
{
  Serial.begin(9600);
}

unsigned long ping()
{
  pinMode(signalPin, OUTPUT);
  digitalWrite(signalPin, LOW);
  delayMicroseconds(2);

  digitalWrite(signalPin, HIGH);
  delayMicroseconds(5);
  digitalWrite(signalPin, LOW);

  pinMode(signalPin, INPUT);
  digitalWrite(signalPin, HIGH);

  return pulseIn(signalPin, HIGH);
}
void loop()
{
  int range = ping() * 29;
  delay(50);
}
```

SKETCH FOR THE DEVANTECH SRF05

Now we'll look at the SRF05 configured in *classic* or four-wire mode. The three-wire mode code for the SRF05 (using 5V, ground, and input/output pin) is very similar to the Ping, so for the sake of brevity we'll omit that listing.

The four-wire mode requires that you set the output pin HIGH for 10 milliseconds to signal to the sensor that you'd like it to fire an ultrasonic signal, and then you can read it back in. Because the input pin is a separate pin, you pass that pin number to the `pulseIn()` method to read the echo distance from the SRF05.

For the example in the next listing you'll need the following:

- 1 Arduino Uno (or similar)
- 1 Devantech SRF05

Listing 6.2   Reading distances with the SRF05

```
const int inputPin = 9;
const int outputPin = 8;

void setup()
{
  pinMode(inputPin,INPUT);
  pinMode(outputPin, OUTPUT);
}
unsigned long ping()
{
  digitalWrite(outputPin, HIGH);        ❶ Set 10-microsecond
  delayMicroseconds(10);                  pause
  digitalWrite(outputPin, LOW);

  return pulseIn(inputPin, HIGH);
}

void loop()
{
  int range = ping() / 74 / 2;          Convert
  delay(50);                            range to cm
}
```

The 10-microsecond pause is necessary to signal to the SRF05 that you want it to send a signal ❶. If the pause is any shorter, it won't send out an ultrasonic wave. If it's any longer, you might miss the wave coming back.

Now that you've seen the code, we can look at connecting the two controllers.

6.1.4   Connecting the hardware

To use the Ping, connect the signal pin to a digital pin on the Arduino, the 5V pin to either the power out on the Arduino or on a breadboard rail, and the ground to either the ground or a ground rail. This is shown in figure 6.4.

To use the SRF05, you'll connect differently depending on the mode that you decide to use. Figure 6.5 shows how to use the four-wire mode because that setup is different from the Ping.

Connecting the pin marked MODE to 5V tells the SRF05 that you'll be using it in four-pin mode, whereas connecting the MODE pin to ground indicates that you'll be using three-pin mode.

6.1.5   Upload and test

When you upload your code, you should see the LED stay lit for a period of time proportional to the distance that the ultrasonic sensor is detecting. If you want to continue exploring, you might consider building one of the classic tropes of physical computing: the electronic theremin, which we'll explore in the next section with a different technique: infrared (IR).

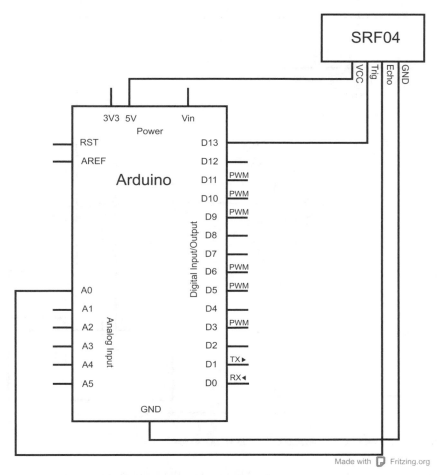

Figure 6.4   Connecting the Parallax Ping to the Arduino

6.2   *Infrared for range finding*

You might choose to use infrared because it has a few advantages over ultrasound. It works much more quickly than ultrasonic sensors because, as your intuition might tell you, light travels more quickly than sound. That means the danger of interference is much lower. It also uses a much narrower beam, meaning that you can pinpoint the location you want to monitor more easily. This also avoids the problem of *ghost echoes*, where the width of a beam hitting a corner and echoing back creates a ghost reading for an object that isn't there.

Infrared has disadvantages as well, though. It relies on light, so in bright direct sunlight, infrared sensors often won't work well, if at all—sunlight will saturate the sensor, creating a false reading. Furthermore, infrared is often not able to read at the same distances as ultrasonic. For instance, the SRF05 ultrasonic sensor can clearly detect

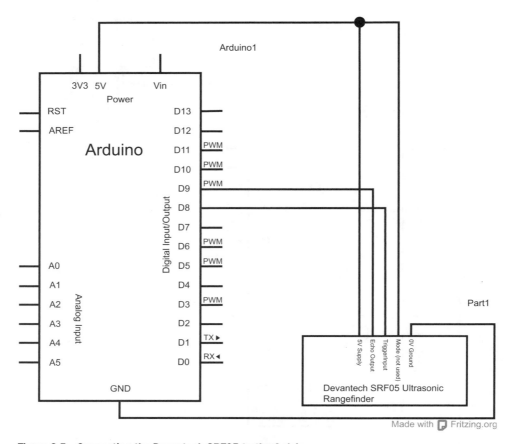

Figure 6.5   Connecting the Devantech SRF05 to the Arduino

objects up to 4 m away, whereas the Sharp GP2D12 infrared sensor that we'll use in this chapter has a maximum range of 80 cm.

6.2.1   *Infrared and ultrasound together*

Certain objects don't respond well to infrared beams, and other objects don't respond well to ultrasound. For instance, an ultrasound sensor doesn't do particularly well with window curtains or very soft fabrics. An infrared sensor, as you might imagine, doesn't do well with fog, smoke, particulate matter, or focused sunlight. Because the two types of sensors use very different ways of detecting objects, you can easily pair them—set them side by side or on top of one another—without risking interference.

There are many infrared distance sensors. In this chapter we're going to focus on one in particular: the Sharp GP2D12.

6.2.2 *The Sharp GP2D12 range finder*

The GP2D12 has been around for a long time and consists of two components: an infrared LED that projects a focused beam, and an infrared receiver that detects the variance in the angle of the returned beam. The sensor is durable and reads from 10 cm to 80 cm without the delay that the ultrasonic sensor requires to avoid signal interference. The Sharp GP2D12 is shown in figure 6.6.

Figure 6.6 The Sharp GP2D12 IR Ranger

6.2.3 *Nonlinear algorithm for calculating distance*

One of the interesting aspects of working with infrared distance sensors is that the results are nonlinear, which means that getting the results from the distance sensor involves a bit more math than simply dividing or multiplying. To understand why, take a look at figure 6.7.

As you can see, the voltage returned from the GP2D12 isn't a straight line; it's a curve, so to interpret that correctly you need a way of dealing with the tail of that curve. Luckily, there's a way. The following bit of code will correctly convert the voltage to centimeters:

```
float ratio = 5.0/1024;
float volts = analogRead(PIN);
float distance = 65*pow( (volts*ratio), -1.10);
```

This accounts for the nonlinear slope that you can see in the diagram.

Now that you know how to convert the data, let's look at some more full-featured code that will show you how to set up and use the GP2D12.

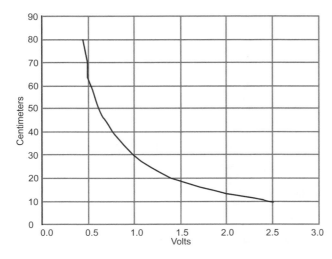

Figure 6.7 Distance to voltage output from the GP2D12

6.2.4 *Sketch for range finding*

It's time to do something interesting with the values that the infrared ranger is return-ing. As we mentioned earlier, you're going to build one of the classic tropes in physi-cal computing: the theremin.

For this example you'll need:

- One Arduino
- One speaker
- One Sharp GP2D12

Positioning the GP2D12 facing upwards allows you to hold your hand out over the beam, and by moving your hand up and down, you can change the notes that are played. The Arduino is never going to make particularly great sounds, but it can accurately reproduce notes by using the delayMicroseconds() method to modulate the note.

The sketch in listing 6.3 maps the distance from the infrared sensor to the 12 notes. You can create a specific tone by powering a speaker for very short periods of time. You'll see in the following sketch that different notes are defined as lengths of time—microseconds—between powering and then stopping power to the speaker. This will create an approximation of the note.

Listing 6.3 Creating a theremin with the GP2D12

```
#include <math.h>
const int FREQOUT_PIN = 4;

const int RANGER_PIN = 9;

const float A      = 14080;
const float AS     = 14917.2;
const float B      = 15804.3;
const float C      = 16744;
const float CS     = 17739.7;
const float D      = 18794.5;
const float DS     = 19912.1;
const float E      = 21096.2;
const float F      = 22350.6;
const float FS     = 23679.6;
const float G      = 25087.7;
const float GS     = 26579.5;

float lastDistance;
float notes[12] = { A, AS, B, C, CS, D, DS, E, F, G, GS };

float read_gp2d12_range(byte pin)
{
  int distance = analogRead(pin);
  if (distance < 3)
    return -1; // invalid value

  return (6787.0 /((float) distance - 3.0)) - 4.0;
}
```

```
void freqout(int frequency, int time)                          ◁──┐ Specify hertz
{                                                                   │ and length in
  int hperiod;                                                      │ milliseconds
  long cycles, i;
  pinMode(FREQOUT_PIN, OUTPUT);
  hperiod = (500000 / frequency) - 7;
  cycles = ((long) frequency * (long) time) / 1000;

  for (i=0; i<= cycles; i++)
  {
    digitalWrite(FREQOUT_PIN, HIGH);
    delayMicroseconds(hperiod);
    digitalWrite(FREQOUT_PIN, LOW);
    delayMicroseconds(hperiod - 1);
  }
  pinMode(FREQOUT_PIN, INPUT);                                  ◁──┐ Shut off pin to
}                                                                   │ avoid getting noise

void setup()
{
  pinMode(RANGER_PIN, INPUT);
  Serial.begin(57600);
  lastDistance = 0;
}

void loop()
{
  float distance = read_gp2d12_range(RANGER_PIN);
  Serial.print(distance);

  freqout( notes[map(distance, 10, 80, 0, 11)],
           lastDistance - distance * 50 );

  lastDistance = distance;
}
```

The freqout() method in listing 6.3 uses the distance to create a note that's appropriate for the distance that the infrared ranger is returning and reacts to the amount of change the ranger detects: the larger the movement, the shorter the note. This has the effect of making the notes feel as if they're being more precisely controlled by the user. You might want to play around with different techniques for creating this sensation of control by parameterizing the sounds even further.

6.2.5 Connecting the hardware

Connecting the GP2D12 is simple, as shown in figure 6.8. Select the pin that you would like to receive the signal on, and then connect the other two pins of the GP2D12 to 5V power and ground. The speaker should be connected to digital pin 4, with the resistor between the PWM pin that will power the speaker and the speaker itself.

6.2.6 Upload and test

When you run the code, you should hear the frequency of the note that's played changing as you move your hand closer and further from the infrared sensor. You can

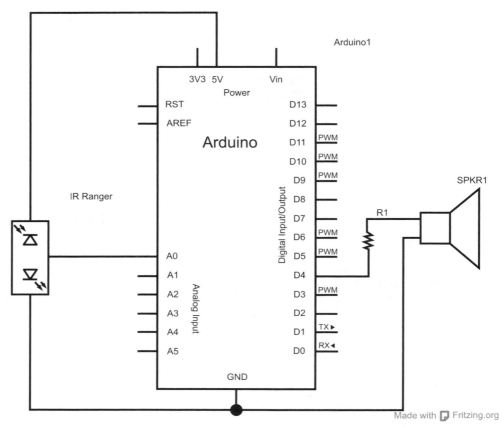

Figure 6.8   Connecting the GP2D12 to the Arduino

position the sensor so that it points upwards or outwards, depending on which motion you think makes the most sense.

6.3   *Passive infrared to detect movement*

While an infrared ranger shoots a beam of light out and waits for it to come back, there are times when you might want to monitor a larger area and you don't need such specific data. You simply want to know if something moved. You're in luck, because that's exactly the purpose of passive infrared (PIR) sensors. It's quite likely that at some point you've turned a light on or off by triggering a PIR sensor either in a large room or in a yard.

A PIR sensor is essentially an infrared camera that measures infrared light radiating from objects in its field of view. Typically it calibrates for a short period of time to create a map of the infrared energy in front of it, and once the calibration is done, it triggers a signal when the amount of infrared changes suddenly. Everything emits some low-level radiation, and the hotter something is, the more radiation it emits.

The sensor in a motion detector is split in two halves because we're trying to detect motion (change), not average infrared levels. The two halves are wired up so that they cancel each other out. If someone walks through an area that's monitored by a PIR sensor, the hot spot on the surface of the chip will move as the person does. If one half sees more or less infrared radiation than the other, the output will swing HIGH or LOW.

As mentioned at the beginning of this section, PIR sensors are simply triggers. They typically only report movement, not information on the amount of movement, the location of that movement, or any other information beyond the amount of time that the movement lasted. But there are plenty of times when that's all you need.

6.3.1 Using the Parallax PIR sensor

One of the more venerable and commonly used PIR sensors is the one made by Parallax. The PIR sensor has a range of approximately 20 feet, though this can vary with environmental conditions.

The sensor requires a warm-up time in order to function properly—the settling time required to learn its environment—which can be anywhere from 10 to 60 seconds. During this time, there should be as little motion as possible in the sensor's field of view. The sensor is designed to adjust to the slowly changing conditions that would happen normally as the day progresses and as environmental conditions change. But when sudden changes occur, like someone passing in front of the sensor or something quickly changing the infrared field in front of the sensor, it will detect the motion.

The sensor's output pin goes to HIGH if motion is present and to LOW when the infrared detected is the same as the background. But even if motion is present, it goes to LOW from time to time, which might give the impression that no motion is present. The program in listing 6.4 deals with this issue by ignoring LOW phases shorter than a given time, assuming continuous motion is present during these phases.

The sensor itself is small, light, and easy to connect. It's shown in figure 6.9.

Notice the three connector pins, which are power, ground, and the signal pin.

6.3.2 Sketch for infrared motion detection

The first thing you may notice about the following PIR sensor code is how the calibration time is used to essentially stall the loop() from reading the PIR sensor until 30 seconds have passed. This is because the PIR sensor needs time to create an accurate map of the environment to compare against.

The next thing to note is how the loop() method contains a conditional statement to detect whether the sensor is returning HIGH or LOW and how long it's

Figure 6.9 The Parallax PIR sensor

been pulled HIGH, if it has been. The Parallax PIR sensor returns HIGH until the motion ceases, so by keeping track of the amount of time since the sensor was pulled HIGH, you can determine how long the object or entity moved in the field of vision of the PIR sensor (see the following listing).

Listing 6.4 Detecting motion with the Parallax PIR sensor

```
const int calibrationTime = 30;                    Ensures adequate
const unsigned long pause = 5000;                  time to calibrate

unsigned long lowIn;
boolean waitForLow = true;
int pirPin = 3;

void setup()
{
  Serial.begin(57600);
  pinMode(pirPin, INPUT);
  digitalWrite(pirPin, LOW);
}

void loop()
{
  if(calibrationTime > 1) {
    calibrationTime--;
    delay(1000);
    return;
  }

  if(digitalRead(pirPin) == HIGH) {
    if(!waitForLow && millis() - lowIn > pause) {
      waitForLow = true;
      delay(50);
    }
  }

  if(digitalRead(pirPin) == LOW) {
    if(waitForLow) {
      lowIn = millis();
      waitForLow = false;
    }
    if(!waitForLow && millis() - lowIn > pause) {    Checks for end
      waitForLow = true;                             of movement
      Serial.print("length of motion ");
      Serial.print((millis() - pause)/1000);
    }
  }
}
```

When the motion ends, the program writes the duration of the motion in front of the PIR sensor to the serial monitor.

6.3.3 *Connecting the hardware*

For this example you'll need the following components:

- A Parallax PIR sensor
- An Arduino
- A 10k resistor

To connect the PIR sensor, you simply connect the power pin to 5V, ground to GND, and the data pin to D3, as shown in figure 6.10. A pull-up resistor is used to ensure that

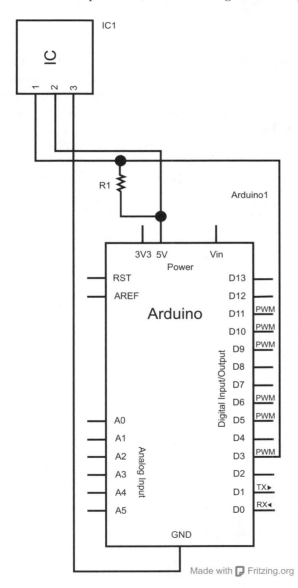

Figure 6.10 Connecting the Parallax PIR sensor to the Arduino

the pin stays HIGH until it's actually pulled low by the PIR sensor. Without this, the readings from the sensor might float after the initial HIGH reading.

6.3.4 Upload and test

An easy way to test that the sensor is detecting motion is to point it at the ceiling, count to 30, and then wave your hand a meter or so above the sensor. You should see the length of time that your hand moves in front of the sensor returned in the Arduino IDE serial monitor. This will also give you a sense of the width of the field of vision of the sensor.

6.4 Summary

In this chapter, you've learned a few different techniques to make the Arduino contextually aware, enabling it to perform simple object detection, range finding, and motion detection. This sort of capability goes a long way toward making interactive systems that can react to their users and respond to the location of their users or objects in their environments. These are the first steps toward creating autonomous vehicles, detection systems, security systems, simple presence-activated systems, and of course, fun musical instruments.

In the next chapter, you'll learn about using LCD screens with your Arduino.

LCD displays 7

This chapter covers

- Communicating with the common Hitachi HD44780 parallel LCD
- Building a serial LCD weather station
- Displaying text and images on the KS0108 graphic LCD

By now you've begun to master the art of interacting with your Arduino in both the analog and digital domains. You've made LEDs blink, you've transformed piezos into pentatonic musical keyboards, and in chapter 6 you graduated from interfacing with everyday components such as potentiometers to working with ultrasonic and infrared distance sensors.

Aside from blinking your first LEDs in chapter 1, most of your interaction with the Arduino thus far has been concerned with obtaining real-world input and output from your Arduino. Most of the work you do with the Arduino will be concerned with doing exactly that. But you'll also encounter scenarios where your project will need to receive information *back* from the Arduino, so in this chapter we'll revisit the realm of visual feedback by exploring various liquid crystal displays, more commonly called LCDs.

LCDs are embeddable screens found in all sorts of consumer electronics. There are many different types of LCDs, however, so in section 7.1 you'll learn about the common LCDs you'll use in your future Arduino endeavors.

7.1 Introduction to LCDs

Liquid crystal displays (LCDs) have become ubiquitous: from the moment you wake up to the moment you go to bed, your day is guided by many interactions with LCD screens.

You wake up in the morning and, upon seeing the LCD on your alarm clock, you realize you're running an hour late. You use the LCD on your mp3 player to navigate to the song you absolutely must listen to next. You look at the number on your phone's LCD and decide to answer or ignore the call. And before bed, you look at the alarm clock again to make sure it's set for tomorrow.

Viewing LCD displays is one of the primary ways we experience electronic data, and in this chapter we'll look at the common types of LCDs you can add to your future Arduino projects.

The first two types of LCD displays are parallel and serial LCDs, and they're normally character displays. Character displays are ideal for displaying some sort of text to the user, and even small shapes or icons (usually 5 x 7 pixels). The other type of LCD we'll cover in this chapter is basic graphic LCDs, which as you may have guessed are great for drawing graphics and images.

But before we explore character displays, let's take a look at String variables, which are how we deal with text in Arduino.

7.1.1 String variables: String type vs. char type

Pairing an Arduino with an LCD is a great way to display text feedback and add menu-browsing capabilities to your project. So how exactly does one send text to an LCD?

In the Arduino and other computer programming languages, text is thought of as a sequence of characters. For example, if you were to put together the four characters T, e, x, t, you would make the word Text. In this way, all text is represented in code as an array of characters.

There are two main ways to create your text in code (or, more generally, to create any sequence of characters). One way is to use the String data type, and the other is to use a null-terminated array of type char. If that makes complete sense to you, great! If not, don't worry; it's much simpler than it sounds. Let's take a look and see what the fuss is all about.

As previously mentioned, all text in your code will actually be an array of characters. For more control, a container class called the String class was created, which enables you to manipulate this array of characters in many complex ways. You can compare two Strings against each other to see if they're the same, search a String of text for a substring, and append characters to the end of a String or even concatenate multiple Strings. Table 7.1 provides an overview of the various functions that can be performed on a String variable. As you can see, the String class is extremely powerful and can be useful for preparing text on your character display.

Table 7.1   The functions of the Arduino String class

Function	Description
charAt()	Accesses a particular character of a String
compareTo(String two)	Tests if two Strings are equal, or if one comes before or after the other
concat(String two)	Combines two Strings into one new String
endsWith(String two)	Tests whether a String ends with the chars of another
equals(String two)	Performs case-sensitive comparison of two Strings' equality
equalsIgnoreCase(String two)	Performs non-case-sensitive comparison of two Strings' equality
getBytes(char [ ], int length)	Copies a String's characters to the supplied buffer
indexOf(val) indexOf(val, int index)	Locates a character or String within another String, starting from the front (val can be a char or String)
lastIndexOf(val) lastIndexOf(val, int index)	Locates a character of String within another String, starting from the end (val can be a char or String)
length()	Returns the length of the String in characters
replace(String one, String two)	Replaces all instances of a character or substring with another
setCharAt(int index, char c)	Sets or changes a particular character of a String
startsWith(String s)	Returns a Boolean (true/false) indicating whether a String starts with the characters of another String
substring(int start) substring(int start, int end)	Returns a substring of a String
toCharArray(char [ ], int length)	Copies a String's characters to the supplied array
toLowerCase()	Returns a copy of the original String with all characters lowercase
toUpperCase()	Returns a copy of the original String with all characters uppercase
Trim()	Returns a copy of the original String with all whitespace before and after the String removed

Declaring a String is easy. Here are a couple of examples:

```
String s = "Arduino in Action Rocks!";
String s = String(13);
```

Both of these lines will create a String called s, the first from a constant string of characters, and the second from an integer number (defaults to base 10).

The String functions outlined in table 7.1 provide many utilities. For example, to combine these two lines,

```
String first = "Hello";
String second = " World";
```

into a new String third, simply call this function:

```
String third = first.concat(second);
```

String third would now be "Hello World". But as is often the case, this added functionality of the String class comes at the price of memory, and because memory can be precious on the Arduino, you may want to bypass the String type and use the more lightweight array of type char directly.

> **NOTE**   You may have noticed that up until now we've been referring to Strings with a capital S; for char strings, we'll use a lowercase s.

There are many ways to represent a string as a char array, as you can see in table 7.2. Character strings normally end with a null character (ASCII code 0), which ensures that Arduino functions such as Serial.print() know exactly where the end of the string is. This is why the arrays two[5] and three[5] in table 7.2 are five characters long, even though text is technically only four characters long; the Arduino compiler automatically inserts the extra null character at the end. One last important reminder: constant strings are always declared inside double-quotes, whereas single chars are declared in single-quotes. See table 7.2 for examples.

Table 7.2   Possible char type string array initializations

Declaration	Description
char one[10];	Declares a non-initialized char array
char two[5] = { 't', 'e', 'x', 't' };	Declares an array with an extra char so the compiler can automatically add the null char
char three[5] = { 't', 'e', 'x', 't', '\0' };	Same as the previous example with the null char added explicitly
char four[] = "text";	Compiler automatically sizes to the string constant plus the null character
char five[5] = "text";	Initializes to explicit size and string constant
char six[10] = "text";	Initializes the array with extra space for a larger string

At this point, we've hopefully demystified the differences between the `String` type and the array of `char` type `strings` that you'll encounter when working with the Arduino and LCDs. Next we'll look at wiring up your first LCD, so without further ado, please welcome the Hitachi HD44780.

7.2   Parallel character LCDs: the Hitachi HD44780

The Hitachi HD44780 is one of the most common LCD controller chips designed for embedded systems and microcontrollers. The chip supports many shapes and sizes of displays, and in this example, we'll use one to drive a 16 x 2 LCD (2 rows, 16 characters long).

The pervasiveness of the Hitachi HD44780 controller (and other similar LCD chips) is great news for you, because they can usually be purchased cheaply or salvaged from your old machines. Some are even pretty fancy, offering single and multicolor (RGB) backlighting.

Backlit LCDs have lights (LEDs) embedded in the screen, which can be turned on to make the screen glow. This isn't only great for low-lit situations, but also for visual feedback. For example, an LCD such as the Hitachi HD44780 that has an RGB backlight can light the screen with different colors, reporting the status of your Arduino. You might turn the screen red to let the user know something is wrong, or green to signal that things are OK.

7.2.1   4-bit or 8-bit?

Hitachi HD44780-based LCDs come in many different configurations, but there are two ways in which you can interface with the Hitachi HD44780 LCD: 4-bit and 8-bit. The main tradeoff between the 4-bit and 8-bit configurations is the number of pins needed on the Arduino versus speed of execution.

Because it's a parallel LCD, the simplest means of communication would be to send the full byte (8-bits) of data all at once (in a 1-byte message). To do this would require at least 10 I/O pins on the Arduino. In contrast, the 4-bit mode requires just 6 I/O pins and splits the byte into two 4-bit nibbles. This saves pins but takes a little more time (two messages versus one message). The 4-bit mode is still "parallel" in the sense that you receive 4 bits at a time, but it's split into two messages that are sent one after another.

7.2.2   Library and functions

Luckily for us, working with LCDs based on the Hitachi HD44780 chipset (or other similar chipsets) is a breeze. As was mentioned in chapter 4, one of the standard libraries preinstalled in the Arduino IDE is the LiquidCrystal LCD library. It's compatible with both 4-bit and 8-bit configurations and provides you with many useful functions for controlling your LCD.

Table 7.3 details the functions available in the LiquidCrystal library.

Table 7.3   The functions available in the LiquidCrystal LCD library

Function	Description
begin(int column, int row)	Sets the dimensions of the screen
clear()	Resets and clears everything on the display
home()	Sets the cursor to the upper left of the LCD
setCursor(int column, int row)	Sets the cursor to the position passed in
write(byte value)	Writes a character to the current cursor position
print(data)	Prints text to the string; can be a char, byte, int, long, or string/String
cursor()	Displays an underscore at the current position
noCursor()	Hides the cursor character
blink()	Blinks the cursor character
noBlink()	Disables the cursor character from blinking
display()	Turns the display on and restores text if turned off by noDisplay()
noDisplay()	Turns off the display, saving current text
scrollDisplayLeft()	Scrolls text one space to the left
scrollDisplayRight()	Scrolls text one space to the right
autoscroll()	Automatically scrolls text, pushing previous character one position to the left or right
noAutoscroll()	Disables autoscrolling
leftToRight()	Sets the direction of text being displayed
rightToLeft()	Sets the direction of text being displayed
createChar(int num, byte[] charData)	Defines a custom 5 x 8 character

7.2.3   *Circuit diagram*

Now that we have a good understanding of how the Hitachi HD44780 communicates on both the hardware and software level, we're ready to start connecting everything. For this, you're going to need the following components:

- An Arduino (such as Arduino Uno or Mega).
- A Hitachi HD44780-based LCD screen.
- A 10k ohm potentiometer or trimpot (R1).
- A resistor. (R2. This is only needed if your LCD has a backlight, and the value of the resistor will depend on the backlight of your LCD; see additional notes that follow.)

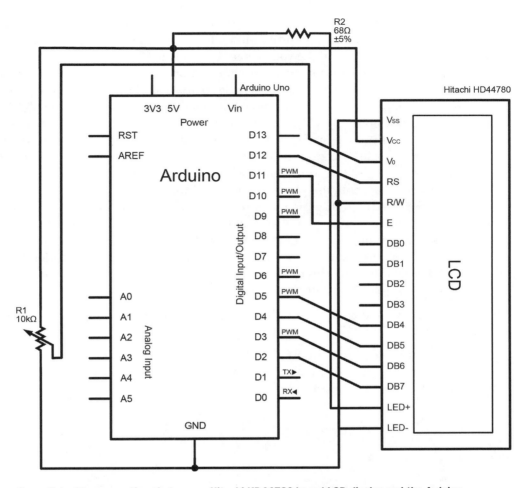

Figure 7.1   The connections between a Hitachi HD44780-based LCD display and the Arduino

Figure 7.1 shows the connections required to hook up your LCD to your Arduino.

NOTE   In figure 7.1, the backlight LED+ (if present) is connected to 5V on the Arduino via a 68-ohm current-limiting resistor. This value may differ and should be calculated based on the specification of your screen backlight. There are many tutorials and online calculators to help you determine the optimal value for your screen; a good place to start is the "LED Current Limiting Resistors" tutorial on the SparkFun Electronics site: http://www.sparkfun .com/tutorials/219.

7.2.4   Connecting everything up in 4-bit mode

To save your precious I/O pins for other sensors and devices, you can connect everything in 4-bit mode. The LiquidCrystal library automatically takes care of the logic required to communicate in 4-bit mode, so there's no difference in terms of coding. Your completed wiring will look similar to figure 7.2.

If possible, the first thing you should do is look up the data sheet for your particular LCD. This is useful for identifying the pin layout of your LCD if the layout isn't already silk-screened onto the LCD circuit board itself. If there isn't a printed label on your board, or a sticker with the model number, and you purchased the LCD from an online hobby store, check the retailer's website because they often provide links to the data sheets. If you salvaged your LCD from an old printer or other machine, and you can't find any information about the pin layout, be careful. Most 16-pin Hitachi 77480-compatible LCDs will follow a similar pin layout, but incorrectly wiring up the LCD can damage both the LCD and your Arduino.

As per the circuit diagram in figure 7.1, first connect the Vss pin to GND. The next pin, Vcc, supplies power to the LCD and should be connected to +5V on the Arduino (or 3.3V depending on your LCD). Next, you'll want to connect the V0 pin on the LCD to the wiper (middle leg) of a 10k linear potentiometer. Connect the left leg to +5V and the right to GND. This is used to set the contrast of your LCD, and you may prefer to use a trimpot if the contrast is something you want to set and forget.

NOTE   Ground and power rails have been created using the vertical columns labeled "+" and "-".

Now that power and contrast are all set, you can move on to your communication lines. Connect the Register Select (RS) pin on the LCD to Arduino digital pin 12. This RS pin is used to control where in the LCD's internal memory the Arduino will

Figure 7.2   Power and contrast wiring for the Hitachi HD44780 parallel LCD

write the current character. Next, wire the Enable (E) pin to Arduino digital pin 11. Enable is what actually allows writing to those registers. Read/Write (RW) can be connected directly to GND or to Arduino digital pin 10 (optional). Tying RW to digital pin 10 instead of ground gives you the added functionality of being able to send information back from the LCD if you so choose. If you don't wish to read from the LCD (which you won't in most cases), save yourself the digital pin and connect RW directly to ground.

Since you're running in 4-bit mode, the next four pins on the LCD (DB0–DB3) don't need to be connected. That brings you to LCD bits DB4–DB7: DB4 should be connected to Arduino digital pin 5, DB5 to digital pin 4, DB6 to digital pin 3, and DB7 to digital pin 2. If your LCD has a backlight, now would be the time to connect the backlight LED+ to +5V on the Arduino through a series resistor (see the earlier note in section 7.2.3), and the LED- to GND on your Arduino.

Voilà! You're now ready to test your first sketch and communicate with your LCD. If you want to triple-check your connections, please refer to table 7.4.

Table 7.4   The required circuit connections between the Hitachi HD44780 LCD and the Arduino

Arduino pin	LCD pin
GND	Vss
+5V	Vcc
Pin 2 (wiper) of 10k linear potentiometer	V0
D12	Register Select (RS)
D11	Enable (E)
GND or D10 (optional)	Read/Write (RW)
D5	DB4 (bit 4)
D4	DB5 (bit 5)
D3	DB6 (bit 6)
D2	DB6 (bit 7)
+5V through a series resistor (for example, 68 ohm)	LED+
GND	LED-

7.2.5   *Sketch for writing to the Hitachi HD44780*

Now that everything is wired up, let's print something to the screen. Open up the Arduino IDE and carefully copy the code from the following listing into your empty sketch (or simply run the provided sketch).

Listing 7.1   Writing text onto your LCD

```
#include <LiquidCrystal.h>                          ➊ Creates LCD class instance

LiquidCrystal lcd(12, 11, 5, 4, 3, 2);     ⊲──────┘
                                             ➋ Configures size
void setup() {                                  of the screen
  lcd.begin(16, 2);                    ⊲─────────┘
  lcd.print("Arduino in");                ⊲───── ➌ Prints text
  lcd.setCursor(0,1);                 ⊲──────┐
  lcd.print("Action Rocks!");  ⊲──────┐      Moves to
}                                      │   ➍ second line
void loop() {                ➎ Prints text
}
```

First, you must include the LiquidCrystal library header file to tell Arduino that you wish to use the LiquidCrystal library. Next, you create an instance of the Liquid-Crystal class, lcd, and pass in the Arduino pins to which your LCD is connected ➊. The number of arguments you pass in to the constructor automatically configures the lcd object to run in 4-bit or 8-bit mode.

In your setup routine, configure the size of your screen ➋, and then print some text to the LCD ➌. Because the text you want to print is longer than one row, you print the first half, then go to the second line using the setCursor ➍ method and then print the second half of the text ➎.

7.2.6   *Upload and test*

Connect the USB cable to your Arduino and verify that the sketch compiles. Make sure your board and serial port are selected in the Tools menu, and click the Upload icon. Shortly after the sketch completes, your LCD should display the words "Arduino in Action Rocks!" (It should look similar to the image in figure 7.3.) Exciting! If you

Figure 7.3   Completing the wiring for the Hitachi HD44780 parallel LCD

don't see anything displayed on the screen, or if the text is too dim, turn the potentiometer wired to V0 to adjust the contrast of the screen.

Seeing text on your LCD for the first time is always very exciting, especially when the display is giving you useful information. Now that you've tackled displaying static text in your first LCD project, let's build a weather station to monitor temperature in real time. And while we're at it, let's also learn about another type of character display, the serial LCD.

7.3 *Serial LCD weather station*

Want to save even more pins on your Arduino, or perhaps you'd just prefer fewer dangling wires? Serial LCDs are another affordable option, and they require only three pins to operate. They work a little differently than parallel LCDs, interpreting serial commands (TTL or transistor-transistor logic, to be exact) over your Arduino's TX pin into special commands or output to the LCD (more on this later). The catch is that they're a little more expensive than their parallel brethren, although prices have come down significantly in recent years. Additionally, you can purchase a serial LCD backpack, turning your Hitachi HD44780 parallel LCD into a serial LCD.

In this section, we're going to look at connecting and communicating with a serial LCD and build a real-time weather station to monitor the temperature of your home.

7.3.1 *Serial vs. parallel LCDs*

The way in which serial LCDs communicate with the Arduino is fundamentally different than the parallel LCDs we saw in section 7.2, although operationally they're very similar.

If you remember our study of parallel LCDs, we sent either 4- or 8-bit messages from the Arduino to the LCD, instructing it to move the cursor or print a character to the screen. The main difference is that serial LCDs send messages one bit at a time (serially), requiring only one communication line. Once wired up, communicating with the serial LCD is as easy as sending the appropriate single-byte command flag using `Serial.print(command)` to perform various tasks (move the cursor, turn the display off, and so on) or you can send plain old characters to print text to the screen: `Serial.print("text")`.

There are a number of commands you can send to the screen, so it would be helpful to create helper functions that automatically set the appropriate command before passing the message you want. Luckily, the Arduino community has already done this for various serial LCD models, and it has created Serial LCD libraries based on the official LiquidCrystal library, but with a few added features.

7.3.2 *SerLCD library and functions*

The library you'll be using to communicate with your serial LCD in this section is called SerLCD. The library is written to be used with the 16 x 2 SparkFun (or compatible) serial LCDs and backpacks, but with a simple modification the library can be used with most serial LCDs on the market.

Unlike the LiquidCrystal library that comes installed within the Arduino IDE, Ser-LCD is a contributed library, which means it has been written by a member of the Arduino community and isn't currently rolled into the official release. There are a few things you need to do in order to get SerLCD up and running, so please read the following instructions carefully.

First, you'll need to download the SerLCD library source from http://arduino.cc/playground/Code/SerLCD. Download and extract the folder called serLCD and put that folder in your sketchbook/libraries folder, as described in chapter 4 (section 4.4 on contributed libraries).

The SerLCD library uses the built-in SoftwareSerial library (discussed in section 4.3.11), allowing the LCD to work over the serial communication lines while leaving the hardware serial port open on the Arduino. This is great news, because it will allow the simultaneous use of multiple serial peripherals alongside the LCD, albeit with a few important considerations. Please refer back to section 4.3.11 for more information on using multiple serial devices simultaneously with the Software-Serial library.

The SerLCD library has implemented most of the functions available in the Liquid-Crystal library (table 7.3), so sharing your code between the parallel and serial LCDs will only require a few minor changes. Table 7.5 details the functions available in the SerLCD library, which even include the ability to adjust the contrast of the screen using pulse-width modulation (on SparkFun SerLCD and compatible displays).

Table 7.5 The functions available in the SerLCD library

Function	Description
serLCD(int pin)	Constructor that specifies the TX pin to the LCD
clear()	Resets and clears everything on the display
clearLine(int num)	Resets and clears a specific line
selectLine(int num)	Moves the cursor to the beginning of a specific line
setBrightness(int num)	Sets the contrast of the LCD (only on some LCDs)
home()	Sets the cursor to the upper left of the LCD
print(data)	Prints text to the LCD
setSplash()	Saves the first two lines displayed as the startup "splash" screen
toggleSplash()	Enables or disables a startup "splash" screen
leftToRight()	Sets the direction of text being displayed
rightToLeft()	Sets the direction of text being displayed

Table 7.5 The functions available in the SerLCD library *(continued)*

Function	Description
blink()	Blinks the cursor character
noBlink()	Disables the cursor character from blinking
cursor()	Displays an underscore character at the current position
noCursor()	Hides the cursor character
display()	Turns the display on and restores text if turned off by noDisplay()
noDisplay()	Turns off the display, saving current text
setCursor(int row, int column)	Sets the cursor to the position passed in
createChar(int num, byte[] charData)	Defines a custom 5 x 8 character
printCustomChar(int num)	Prints a custom character

NOTE If you're using a serial LCD that isn't compatible with the SparkFun serial LCD, there are a few changes you must make to the SerLCD library. If you open up SerLCD.h, you'll find a list of commands and flags set in hexadecimal notation. Refer to your LCD's datasheet and update these accordingly, and you should be all set.

With the SerLCD library installed, you're ready to start wiring up your LCD, but first let's take a look at the temperature sensor that you'll be using.

7.3.3 *The Maxim IC DS18B20 temperature sensor*

The DS18B20 temperature sensor by Maxim uses the Maxim one-wire protocol and is becoming one of the most popular temperature sensors on the market. The one-wire protocol allows one or more one-wire slave devices to communicate with a master device over a single data line, which means that you can easily connect many of these sensors to your Arduino without taking up many inputs on the Arduino. They're inexpensive, reliable, calibrated, and robust enough to communicate over long wires for remote applications.

Easy to wire up, the contributed OneWire and DallasTemperature libraries also make communicating with the sensor simple.

7.3.4 *OneWire and DallasTemperature libraries*

In order to communicate with your DS18B20 temperature sensor, you need the OneWire Arduino library; using the DallasTemperature library is optional. The OneWire library will allow you to begin communicating with your temperature sensor; the DallasTemperature library has some useful features such as Celsius to Fahrenheit conversion, and the ability to easily code and read more than one temperature sensor on the same bus. As such, we're going to be using the DallasTemperature library in this example, and recommend you do too.

> **NOTE** If you don't use the DallasTemperature library, you'll need to execute the less readable OneWire library commands, which can be referenced online at http://www.pjrc.com/teensy/td_libs_OneWire.html.

Download the latest version of the OneWire library from www.arduino.cc/playground/ Learning/OneWire and the DallasTemperature library from http://milesburton.com/ Dallas_Temperature_Control_Library (you'll want version 3.7.2 or greater). Place the two library folders into your Arduino sketchbook libraries directory.

You're now ready to wire everything up and upload the code.

7.3.5   *Circuit diagram*

Figure 7.4 is an overview of the circuit you'll wire up for the serial LCD–powered weather station.

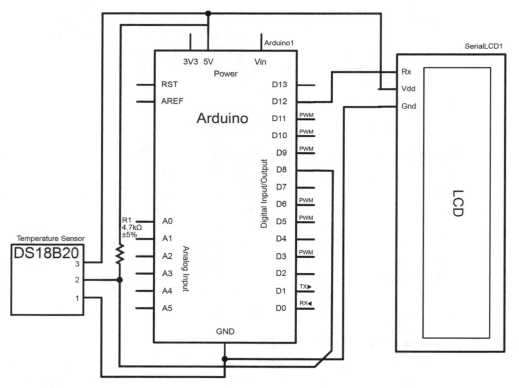

Figure 7.4   Circuit diagram for a weather station using the SparkFun (or compatible) serial LCD, and the DS18B20 one-wire digital temperature sensor

7.3.6 *Connecting everything up*

Before connecting everything up, you should prepare all the parts needed for the project:

- An Arduino
- A serial LCD (SparkFun-compatible 16 x 2 serial LCD or backup recommended)
- A DS18B20 temperature sensor
- A 4.7k ohm resistor (R1)

Once you have the required parts, making your weather station couldn't be any simpler. As described in table 7.6, simply connect the Vdd pin on the LCD to 5V on your Arduino to get power going to the LCD. Next, wire the GND pin on the LCD to your Arduino's GND pin. Finally, the RX (receive) pin on your LCD should connect to any of the digital pins on your Arduino—table 7.6 and the schematic in figure 7.4 show it connected to pin 12.

Table 7.6   Required circuit connections between the serial LCD and the Arduino

Arduino pin	LCD pin
GND	GND
5V	Vdd
D12 (or any digital pin)	RX

If you aren't using the serLCD library (which uses the SoftwareSerial library for communication), you can also directly connect the LCD's RX pin to the TX (D1) pin on the Arduino, although you'll lose the benefits of using a software serial port, as discussed earlier.

Wiring up the DS18B20 one-wire temperature sensor is also a breeze. As described in table 7.7, connect pin 1 on the sensor to GND, connect pin 2 to a digital input (such as digital pin D8 on the Arduino), and pin 3 on the sensor to 5V on the Arduino. Lastly, you need to wire a 4.7k ohm pull-up resistor between pin 2 on the DS18B20 and 5V—one simple way is to put the resistor directly between pins 2 and 3 on the sensor itself. For the DS18B20's pin layout, see figure 7.5. Your completed wiring should look similar to that in figure 7.6.

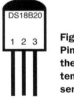

Figure 7.5 Pin layout for the DS18B20 temperature sensor

Table 7.7   Required circuit connections between the DS18B20 one-wire temperature sensor and the Arduino

Arduino pin	DS18B20 one-wire temperature sensor
GND	Pin 1
5V	Pin 3 and pin 2 through a 4.7k ohm resistor
Pin 8 (or any digital pin)	Pin 2

Figure 7.6   Completed wiring for a DS18B20-based LCD weather station

7.3.7   *Sketch for an LCD weather station*

Now that everything is wired up, you can get information from the temperature sensor and display it on the screen. Open up the Arduino IDE and carefully copy the following code into your empty sketch (or simply run the provided sketch).

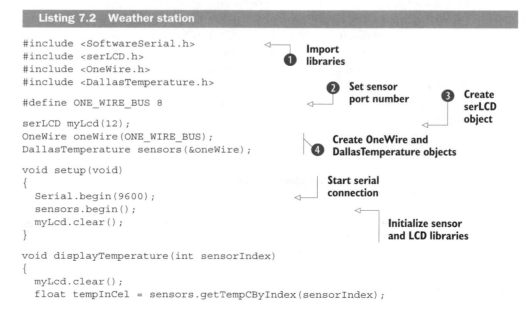

Listing 7.2   Weather station

```
#include <SoftwareSerial.h>                    Import
#include <serLCD.h>                            libraries
#include <OneWire.h>
#include <DallasTemperature.h>
                                               Set sensor        Create
#define ONE_WIRE_BUS 8                         port number       serLCD
                                                                 object
serLCD myLcd(12);
OneWire oneWire(ONE_WIRE_BUS);                 Create OneWire and
DallasTemperature sensors(&oneWire);           DallasTemperature objects

void setup(void)
{                                              Start serial
  Serial.begin(9600);                          connection
  sensors.begin();
  myLcd.clear();                               Initialize sensor
}                                              and LCD libraries

void displayTemperature(int sensorIndex)
{
  myLcd.clear();
  float tempInCel = sensors.getTempCByIndex(sensorIndex);
```

```
    myLcd.setCursor(0,0);
    myLcd.print("C: ");
    myLcd.print(tempInCel, 1);
    myLcd.setCursor(0,1);
    myLcd.print(" F: ");
    float tempInFar = DallasTemperature::toFahrenheit(tempInCel);
    myLcd.print(tempInFar, 1);
}
void loop(void)
{
    sensors.requestTemperatures();
    displayTemperature(0);
    delay(2000);
}
```

Update temperature readings

Update display with new temperatures

First you must import the three libraries we want to use ❶. Next, set up the temperature sensors by defining the port the temperature sensor is connected to ❷.

You can then create a new `OneWire` object and `DallasTemperature` object ❹. You configure the LCD by creating a new `serLCD` object with the `SoftwareSerial` port number (digital pin) the LCD is using ❸.

NOTE When printing the temperature value, you can change the decimal precision (how many decimal places are printed) by modifying the print function arguments. For example, `myLcd.print(tempInCel, 4);` prints temperatures with four decimal places.

Once you've copied the code into the Arduino IDE, you're ready to see the code in action.

7.3.8 Upload and test

If you haven't done so already, make sure you've properly installed the three required libraries (SerLCD, OneWire, and DallasTemperature). You're now ready to connect the USB cable to your Arduino and verify that the sketch compiles. Make sure your board and serial port are selected in the Tools menu, and click the Upload icon. Shortly after the sketch completes uploading, your LCD should display the temperature in both Celsius and Fahrenheit, updating its reading every two seconds.

Congratulations! Your Arduino will now monitor the temperature of your room. Want to take this one step further? You can purchase a tri-color (RGB) backlight parallel display and use the color of the screen to indicate from a distance whether you should turn on the heat or air conditioning. Perhaps when the temperature crosses a certain threshold, the screen turns red, letting you know you should cool the place off, or vice versa.

This leads us to a good question: how can LCDs be used to display things other than text? Well, pairing an LCD with LEDs is one way, but for many more possibilities, you can turn to graphic LCDs.

7.4   *Graphic LCDs: the Samsung KS0108 GLCD*

If you need feedback other than text displayed on a screen, look no further. Graphic LCDs (GLCDs) are one of the most common peripherals you'll come into contact with on a daily basis, from the cellphone in your pocket to the laptop on your desk.

Whereas parallel and serial character displays allocate a very small number of pixels for each character (typically 5 x 8 pixels), graphic LCDs use the entire screen as your canvas. That means you have complete control to draw whatever you like, pixel by pixel. Imagine the possibilities: you could use a graphic LCD to build a fully functional Arduino-powered video game, or perhaps to draw custom knobs and sliders to visualize your sensors' data stream. Graphic LCDs are extremely useful displays, unleashing the power of the pixel to create anything from homemade calculators to audio-responsive level meters.

So how many pixels do you get? Graphic displays come in many different sizes, but we're going to use the common KS0108-based GLCD, which typically comes in a monochrome 128 x 64 pixel configuration. Like the character displays discussed earlier in this chapter, the KS0108 GLCD has an extensive library that allows you to easily draw to your screen.

7.4.1   *Library and functions*

To communicate with the KS0108 GLCD, you'll be using the KS0108 Graphics LCD Library available at www.arduino.cc/playground/Code/GLCDks0108. Download the official release, or for the latest optimizations, download the bleeding-edge release candidate hosted at http://code.google.com/p/glcd-arduino/downloads/list.

Table 7.8 lists the various functions in the library that you'll use to move around on and draw to your display.

Table 7.8   The functions available in the GLCDks0108 library

Function	Description
Init(bool inverted)	Initializes the library
ClearScreen()	Resets and clears everything on the display
DrawBitmap(bitmap, int x, int y, color)	Draws the provided bitmap image at the x,y location
SelectFont(font)	Switches to the fixed-width font provided
PutChar(char c)	Prints a char at the current position
GotoXY(int x, int y)	Moves position to x,y (top left is 0,0)
CursorTo(int x, int y)	Locates cursor for printing text
PrintNumber(long n)	Prints a number to the screen at the current position

Table 7.8   The functions available in the GLCDks0108 library *(continued)*

Function	Description
`Puts(string t)`	Prints a text string at the current cursor position
`DrawLine(int x1, int y1, int x2, int y2, color)`	Draws a line
`DrawVertLine(int x, int y, int length, color)`	Draws a vertical line
`DrawHoriLine(int x, int y, int length, color)`	Draws a horizontal line
`DrawRect(int x, int y, int width, int height)`	Draws a rectangle
`InvertRect(int x, int y, int width, int height)`	Inverts pixels within given rectangle
`DrawRoundedRect(int x, int y, int width, int height, int radius, int color)`	Draws a rectangle with rounded corners
`FillRect(int x, int y, int width, int height, int color)`	Draws a filled rectangle
`DrawCircle(int x, int y, int radius, color)`	Draws a circle with the center at x,y
`SetDot(int x, int y, color)`	Fills a pixel at the specified location

NOTE   For the functions in table 7.8 with a `color` parameter, `WHITE` clears a pixel and `BLACK` fills a pixel.

While communicating with the KS0108 GLCD is intuitive using the GLCDks0108 library, wiring up the GLCD is a little more involved than the character displays we discussed earlier. Let's take a look at how exactly you can wire up your screen and what you should watch out for.

7.4.2   Circuit diagram

To connect up your KS0108 graphic LCD, you'll need the following:

- An Arduino Mega
- A KS0108 GLCD
- A 10k ohm potentiometer (R1)
- A 220 ohm resistor (R2)

Figure 7.7 is a circuit diagram showing how to wire a KS0108 (model with pinout A) to the Arduino Mega. There are four common versions of the KS0108 display, and the circuit diagram in this section only applies to the common LCD pinout A when connected to the Mega. If you're using a KS0108 with any of the other pinouts or Arduino

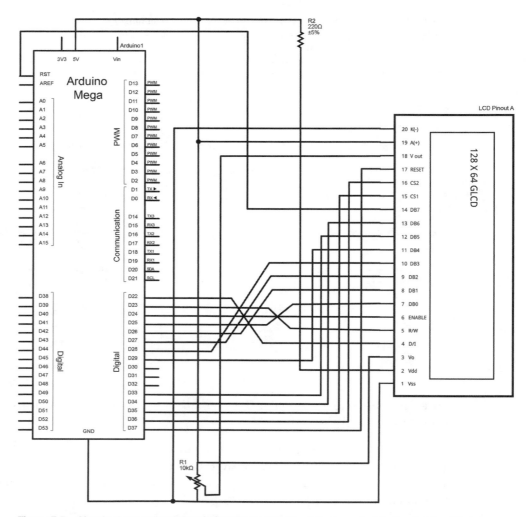

Figure 7.7   Circuit diagram for the KS0108 GLCD with pinout A connected to the Arduino Mega

models, please skip this diagram and go straight to section 7.4.3. There you'll find a table with all the appropriate connections you need to make. More information on determining which pinout your LCD has can also be found in section 7.4.3.

7.4.3   *Connecting everything up*

Wiring up the KS0108 isn't particularly difficult, although there are a lot of connections to make—20 to be exact.

The first thing you'll need to figure out is the pinout of the KS0108 version you have. Verify the labeling on your KS0108 screen (if labeled) or refer to the screen's data sheet. Additionally, a list of models and their pinout versions has been compiled for most of the common screens you'll come across at www.arduino.cc/playground/ Code/GLCDks0108. In this example, we used the standard SparkFun GLCD 128 x 64, which uses pinout A.

Table 7.9 provides an extensive overview of the pin assignments for each type of KS0108. Additionally, you'll notice in table 7.9 that depending on the Arduino you're using, the pin assignments between the GLCD and the Arduino change. This is very important and must be correct in order for the library to properly communicate with the screen.

Table 7.9   KS0108 GLCD pinouts and connections to the Arduino

Uno/168/328	Mega	Function	Pinout A	Pinout B	Pinout C	Pinout D	Description
5V	5V	5V	1	2	2	4	
Gnd	Gnd	Gnd	2	1	1	3	
n/a	n/a	V0	3	3	3	5	Wiper of 10k contrast pot
8	22	D0	4	7	7	9	
9	23	D1	5	8	8	10	
10	24	D2	6	9	9	11	
11	25	D3	7	10	10	12	
4	26	D4	8	11	11	13	
5	27	D5	9	12	12	14	
6	28	D6	10	13	13	15	
7	29	D7	11	14	14	16	
14 (analog 0)	33	CSEL1	12	15	16	1	Chip 1 select
15 (analog 1)	34	CSEL2	13	16	15	2	Chip 2 select
Reset	Rest	Reset	14	17	17		Connect to reset pin
16 (analog 2)	35	R_W	15	5	5	7	R/W
17 (analog 3)	36	D_I	16	4	4	6	RS
18 (analog 4)	37	EN	17	6	6	6	Enable
External	External	Vee (Contrast out)	18	18	18		Connect to one leg of 10k pot
External	External	Backlight +5V	19	19	119		100–330 ohm resistor to +5V
Gnd	Gnd	Backlight Gnd	20	20	20		Connect to other leg of 10k pot

7.4.4   *Sketch for drawing to a GLCD*

Now that it's wired up, let's get some graphics drawing. Carefully copy the following code into the Arduino IDE (or run the provided sketch), and you should be able to upload and see your screen animated.

Listing 7.3   Drawing to the KS0108 GLCD

```
#include <ks0108.h>                               ⊲──┤ Import KS0I08
                                                       library
int xc, yc = 0;
int d=1000;                                       ⊲──── Delay between drawing
                                                        examples (milliseconds)
void setup()
{
  GLCD.Init(NON_INVERTED);                           │ Initialize and
  GLCD.ClearScreen();                                │ reset screen
}

void loop()
{
  for (int a=1; a<20; a++)                        ⊲──── Draw circles
  {
    GLCD.DrawCircle(63,31,a,BLACK);
    delay(200);
    GLCD.DrawCircle(63,31,a,WHITE);
  }

  delay(d);                                          │ Delay and
  GLCD.ClearScreen();                                │ reset screen

  for (int a=0; a<128; a++)                       ⊲──┤ Draw vertical
  {                                                    lines
    GLCD.DrawVertLine(a, 0, 63, BLACK);
    delay(d-950);
  }

  delay(d-800);                                      │ Delay and white-
                                                     │ out each line
  for (int a=0; a<128; a++)
  {
    GLCD.DrawVertLine(a, 0, 63, WHITE);
    delay(d-950);
  }

  GLCD.ClearScreen();                                │ Reset screen and
                                                     │ draw horizontal lines
  for (int a=0; a<64; a++)
  {
    GLCD.DrawHoriLine(0, a, 127, BLACK);
    delay(d-950);
  }

  for (int a=0; a<64; a++)                        ⊲──┤ White-out
  {                                                    each line
    GLCD.DrawHoriLine(0, a, 127, WHITE);
    delay(d-950);
  }
```

```
GLCD.ClearScreen();
GLCD.DrawRoundRect(30, 30, 20, 20, 5,BLACK);
GLCD.DrawRoundRect(60, 30, 20, 20, 5,BLACK);
delay(d);
GLCD.ClearScreen();
delay(d);
GLCD.FillRect(30, 30, 30, 10, BLACK);
delay(d);
GLCD.ClearScreen();

for (int a=0; a<1000; a++)
{
  xc=random(0,127);
  yc=random(0, 63);
  GLCD.SetDot(xc, yc, BLACK);
  delay(2);
}

GLCD.ClearScreen();
}
```

Reset screen and draw rounded rectangles

Draw filled rectangle

Fill random pixels

Reset screen

7.4.5 Upload and test

If you haven't already installed the GLCDks0108 library, please follow the instructions to do so in section 7.4.1. Once the library has been installed, you're ready to connect the USB cable to your Arduino and verify that the sketch compiles. Make sure your board and serial port are selected in the Tools menu and click the Upload icon.

Immediately after the sketch has been uploaded, you'll begin to see your LCD come to life! You now have all the tools necessary to draw complex images and text to your KS0108 GLCD. You can create rich visual feedback in future applications.

7.5 Summary

In this chapter you learned how to connect three different kinds of LCD screens to your Arduino. These included parallel and serial LCDs—embeddable character displays that prove themselves useful time and time again when it's important to provide feedback about the state of your Arduino, data from sensors, or other information. You also learned about the nifty one-wire protocol while making a homebrewed LCD-powered weather station to monitor the temperature of your home. Lastly, you learned about GLCDs—powerful displays that give you the freedom to draw and visualize images and text on screen with great precision and control.

By themselves, LCDs don't do very much, but as you can imagine, the way you code your LCD to interact with your Arduino can enable many possibilities. Whether they're visualizing the state of your sensors, enabling you to change and interact with different modes on your Arduino-powered project, creating the world of your video game, or displaying information from the internet (discussed further in chapter 8), LCDs will afford you great control and provide feedback in many of your projects. In a general sense, LCDs can be thought of as one of the great communicators between you and your Arduino.

But LCDs aren't the only way for your Arduino to communicate to the outside world. It's now time to turn to chapter 8, on communications.

Communications

8

This chapter covers

- Creating an Ethernet web server to query data from your Arduino
- Tweeting messages from your Arduino to Twitter
- Wi-Fi network and Bluetooth communication with the Arduino
- Data logging onto an SD card and to the internet using the Cosm service
- Communicating with other devices over the Serial Peripheral Interface (SPI) protocol

In the previous chapter, we investigated how you can receive visual feedback from the Arduino by communicating with LCD screens. Imagine if you could display information from the Arduino on an external screen, and also send it out over the internet for the world to see! What if you could control your Arduino remotely?

Getting your Arduino on the internet and remotely talking to your computer are two of the many communication channels possible with the Arduino. We'll look at communicating with your Arduino via Ethernet, Wi-Fi, Bluetooth, and SPI.

As many of your projects will involve communicating over the internet, let's dive right in and look at how to communicate with the Arduino over a computer network.

8.1 *Ethernet*

One of the most powerful communication channels available on the Arduino is Ethernet. Ethernet is a standardized networking facility that allows all kinds of devices to communicate with each other by sending and receiving streams of data (called *packets* or *frames*).

Ethernet is extremely fast and robust, transmitting the data back and forth across the network without error. Each device on the network gets a unique identifier called an IP address, which allows the devices to communicate via different internet protocols.

The Arduino makes setting up internet communication easy using the Ethernet Shield and the Ethernet library, but before we discuss the library and shield, let's take a look at a few key networking concepts. If you're already familiar with networking concepts, it still may be worth reviewing the terminology and technologies in table 8.1.

Table 8.1 Key Ethernet terms and concepts

Term	Description
Ethernet	Ethernet is a standardized networking technology that describes a way for computers and other devices to send information back and forth over a wired network.
Protocol	Protocols are established communication languages that allow devices to talk to one another. In order for two devices to communicate, they both must be speaking the same language, or protocol. For example, the Hypertext Transfer Protocol (HTTP) is a common protocol that you'll use to set up your Arduino as a web server. Using HTTP, you'll establish a language that allows the Arduino web server to understand messages and requests from web clients such as a computer's web browser.
MAC address	A Media Access Control (MAC) address is a unique identifier assigned to Ethernet and other networking devices. The MAC address allows the devices to be uniquely identified in order to communicate with other devices. Your Arduino shield will come with a sticker giving it a unique MAC address.
TCP/IP	Transmission Control Protocol (TCP) and Internet Protocol (IP) are internet protocols that pass messages over the global internet (the home of the "world wide web" we all know and love).
IP address	An IP address is a unique address that devices and servers use to identify themselves over the global internet. For example, when you go to a website, such as manning.com, the internet uses the Directory Name Service (DNS) to translate http://google.com/ to a numeric IP address, such as 209.85.148.139.
Local IP address	Local IP addresses are similar to regular IP addresses, but they're used specifically to communicate between computers and devices on a local network. For example, when you set up a network at home, each computer on the network is assigned a local IP address to communicate with the router and other computers on the network.

Although networking and Ethernet are complex topics that can take many years to fully understand, table 8.1 presents the fundamental terms you'll need to know in order to understand the rest of the chapter.

Now that you've reviewed the table, let's move on to the Ethernet library and see what it does.

8.1.1   *The Ethernet library*

The Ethernet library comes bundled with the Arduino IDE and allows you to configure your Arduino and Ethernet Shield to communicate with the outside world. You can configure up to four concurrent servers and clients (total). You set up the server such that it first accepts incoming connections from clients and then sends and receives data. In contrast, a client makes outgoing connections to the server first and then can send data to and receive it from the server.

More on this soon, but for now take a look at table 8.2, which provides an overview of the functions available in the Ethernet library.

Table 8.2   Overview of the `Ethernet`, `Server`, and `Client` class functions in the Ethernet library

Function	Description

`Ethernet.begin(mac)`
`Ethernet.begin(mac, ip)`
`Ethernet.begin(mac, ip, gateway)`
`Ethernet.begin(mac, ip, gateway, subnet)`
	Initializes the library, supplying the MAC address of the shield, and automatically configures your IP using DHCP. Optionally, supplies a manual IP address, gateway (typically your router's IP address), and subnet mask (default is 255.255.255.0, which tells the shield how to interpret IP addresses).

`Server(port)`	Creates a server to listen on a specific port.
`Server.begin()`	Starts the server listening for messages.
`Server.available()`	Returns a client if a client has data ready.
`Server.write()`	Sends data to all connected clients.
`Server.print()`	Prints data to all clients. Numbers print as a sequence of ASCII digits; for example, 123 becomes three characters, '1', '2', and '3'.
`Server.println()`	Same as `Server.print()` but with a newline character at the end of each message.
`Client(ip, port)`	Creates a client that can connect to the specified IP address and port.
`Client.connected()`	Returns whether or not the client is connected. If the connection is closed and some data is still unread, this will still return `true`.
`Client.connect()`	Starts the connection.
`Client.write()`	Writes data to the server.
`Client.print()`	Prints data to the server. Numbers print as a sequence of ASCII digits; for example, 123 becomes three characters, '1', '2', and '3'.

Table 8.2 Overview of the `Ethernet`, `Server`, and `Client` class functions in the Ethernet library *(continued)*

Function	Description
`Client.println()`	Same as `Client.print()` but with a newline character at the end of each message.
`Client.available()`	Returns the number of bytes available to be read (the number of bytes sent from the server).
`Client.read()`	Reads the next byte received from the server.
`Client.flush()`	Flushes any bytes that have been written to the client but have not yet been read.
`Client.stop()`	Disconnects from the server.

In addition to the `Ethernet`, `Server`, and `Client` classes, the Ethernet library also includes useful general-purpose User Datagram Protocol (UDP) networking classes to broadcast information over a network. When a server or client isn't required, the `UDP` class is what you'll use to broadcast data to or receive it from the Arduino. Table 8.3 details the functions in the `UDP` class.

Table 8.3 Overview of main `UDP` class functions in the Ethernet library

Function	Description
`EthernetUDP.begin(port)`	Initializes UDP object and specifies listening port.
`EthernetUDP.read(packetBuffer, MaxSize)`	Reads UDP packets from a buffer.
`EthernetUDP.write(message)`	Sends a message to the remote connection.
`EthernetUDP.beginPacket(ip, port)`	Must be called before sending a message, specifying the destination IP and port.
`EthernetUDP.endPacket()`	Must be called after the message is sent to end the message.
`EthernetUDP.parsePacket()`	Checks to see if there's a message to be read.
`EthernetUDP.available()`	Returns how much data has been received and is available to be read.

Now that we've covered the functions and classes in the Ethernet library, let's take a look at the Ethernet Shield. You'll use the shield to extend the hardware functionality of your Arduino so you can plug into a wired Ethernet network.

8.1.2 Ethernet Shield with SD data card

The original Ethernet Shield was a milestone for the Arduino platform, enabling projects to communicate over networks and over the internet. Powered by the WIZnet

W5100 Ethernet chip, it provides a network (IP) stack with both TCP and UDP, over a 10/100 Mb Ethernet connection. The shield has a standard RJ45 Ethernet jack allowing it to plug and play with your modem, router, or other standard devices.

The newer, widely-available Ethernet Shield improves upon the original by adding a microSD card slot on the shield itself. This means you can read and store files on your shield (by plugging in an SD card and using the SD library). But it's important to note that the W5100 chip and the SD card both communicate with the Arduino using the SPI bus (more information on SPI can be found in section 8.6). On most Arduino boards, this is on pins 11, 12, and 13, and on the Mega it's pins 50, 51, and 52. On both boards, pin 10 is used to select the W5100 and pin 4 to select the SD card. This is important because it means you can't use these pins as general-purpose I/O pins.

> **NOTE**   Because the W5100 chip and the SD card both use SPI, only one can be active at a time. To use the SD card, you only need to set pin 4 as an output and set it HIGH; for the W5100, set digital pin 10 as an output and set it HIGH. Also, the hardware SS pin (pin 10 on most Arduino boards and 53 on the Mega) might not be used, but it must be left as an output (default) for the SD and Ethernet libraries and SPI interface to work.

8.2   Arduino web server

With the basics of Ethernet, the Ethernet library, and the Ethernet Shield under your belt, you're ready to start your first Ethernet-powered project. For this project you're going to build an Arduino web *server,* a call-and-response system that can accept requests from *clients* and in turn send back data (as illustrated in figure 8.1). To do this, you'll use the Server and Client classes included in the Ethernet library.

8.2.1   Setting up the server

To set up the server, you'll need a few pieces of information.

First, you'll need to know the MAC address of the Arduino Ethernet Shield, which should be printed on a sticker on the shield. In the code you'll use for the server, you'll store the MAC address in a byte array, like so:

```
byte mac[] = { 0xDE, 0xAD, 0xBE, 0xEF, 0xFE, 0xED };
```

Remember, this is the unique hardware address that's used to talk directly to your shield over Ethernet.

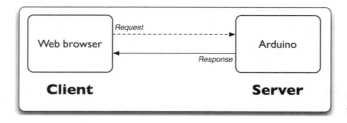

Figure 8.1   Overview of Arduino web server communication

If you have an older Ethernet Shield without the sticker, or you've lost your sticker, you can use the MAC address from the preceding example. The important thing is that if you have more than one device on the network, they all must have unique MAC addresses.

Next, you'll need your IP address. Since Arduino 1.0, the built-in Ethernet library supports Dynamic Host Configuration Protocol (DHCP), enabling Arduino to automatically discover your IP address. This will automatically configure your IP address whether you're connected directly to your modem or to a networked router, as long as they have DHCP enabled (which is typically the case).

You'll only need to find out the IP of your router and manually specify an IP address for your Arduino Ethernet Shield if your network isn't using DHCP, or if you're using a version of Arduino prior to 1.0. There are different techniques for doing so, depending on your setup.

If your Arduino is connected directly to your modem, the IP address will be supplied by your internet service provider (ISP). To find your IP address in this case, it may be easiest to connect a computer to your modem—there are many websites that can report your IP address. (A quick internet search for the term *IP lookup* should get you an address, or you can try www.whatismyip.com/.) Note that your IP address is automatically assigned by your ISP and may change from time to time.

If your Arduino is connected to your network via a router, you'll have to assign an unused local network IP address to your Ethernet Shield instead. To manually assign your Arduino an unused local IP, you'll need to know a bit more about your network's configuration. You can discover your router's IP address by using a web service via a computer connected to the network as described previously. Alternatively, you can go into your router's administration control panel. Normally, you can do this by opening your web browser and going to the default router IP, typically http://192.168.1.1 for Linksys and many other brands, or http://10.0.0.1. If your router's IP address is 192.168.1.1, you'll want to give your Arduino an IP address of 192.168.1.x, where *x* is any number from 1 to 255. Each computer or network device on your network will have a unique 192.168.1.x address, where the final number identifies the device on the network, so make sure your Arduino Ethernet Shield doesn't conflict with other devices. The same rules apply if your router is using another addressing pattern, such as the 10.0.0.x address.

If you do have to manually supply your IP address, you'll do so in an `IPAddress` object, like this:

```
IPAddress manualIP(192, 168, 1, 2);
```

The numbers in the preceding code line should be the IP address you want to set.

Finally, if you're on a network and using the router to connect to the internet, you may also need to specify your router as the gateway. Create a byte array and store the router's IP address to be used as the gateway. Here's an example:

```
byte gateway[] = { 192, 168, 1, 1};
```

Now that you know the IP configuration for your network, let's move on to the code.

8.2.2 *Sketch for creating a web server*

The following listing puts everything we've discussed into practice by creating a web server on the Arduino. The server will be given the task of getting online (or onto a local network), accepting incoming client connections (sent via a web browser), and responding with a custom message. This listing is a great template for starting almost *any* server-based application.

Listing 8.1 Arduino web server

```
#include <SPI.h>
#include <Ethernet.h>

byte mac[] = { 0xDE, 0xAD, 0xBE, 0xEF, 0xFE, 0xED };
IPAddress manualIP(192,168,1,120);

EthernetServer server(80);

boolean dhcpConnected = false;

void setup()
{
  if (!Ethernet.begin(mac)){
    Ethernet.begin(mac, manualIP);
  }

  server.begin();
}

void loop()
{
  EthernetClient client = server.available();
  if (client) {
    boolean currentLineIsBlank = true;
    while (client.connected()) {
      if (client.available()) {
        char c = client.read();

        if (c == '\n' && currentLineIsBlank) {
          client.println("HTTP/1.1 200 OK");
          client.println("Content-Type: text/html");
          client.println();
          client.println("Hi! I am your Arduino web server in Action!");

          break;
        }
        if (c == '\n') {
          currentLineIsBlank = true;
        }
        else if (c != '\r') {
          currentLineIsBlank = false;
        }
      }
    }
  }
  delay(1);
```

Annotations:
- **Assign unique MAC address**
- **Manually set IP if DHCP isn't enabled**
- ❶ **Initialize server**
- ❷ **Connect using DHCP**
- **Make manual connection if DHCP fails** ❸
- ❹ **Start server**
- **Listen for client connections**
- **Connect and read data from client**
- ❺ **End request by sending response to client**
- **Allow client time to receive data**

```
    client.stop();
  }
}
```

Close
connection

First, you initialize the server on HTTP port 80 **❶**. Once it's initialized, you can try to connect the Arduino to the Ethernet network using DHCP **❷**, or using a manual IP address if DHCP fails **❸**. Then you start the server and start polling in the main loop **❹**.

Once you've connected to a client and the data is received, a newline character delineates the end of a message, and you send a response back to the client **❺**.

8.2.3 Upload and test

Carefully copy the code from listing 8.1 into the Arduino IDE, and you're ready to upload the sketch to your Arduino.

Once you've uploaded the code and it's running, you can connect to the Arduino server remotely by opening up any web browser and going to http://*your_arduinos _network_ip_address*. Your web browser (the client) will send a connection request out to your Arduino web server, which will respond by sending back the message, "Hi! I am your Arduino web server in Action!" That's it.

Want to see real-time data? Try connecting a potentiometer or sensor up to analog input 0, and change the line

```
client.println("Hi! I am your Arduino web server in Action!");
```

to this:

```
client.println(analogRead(0));
```

We hope this has worked without a hitch, but if you aren't getting a response, please read the following brief troubleshooting section.

8.2.4 Troubleshooting

If you can't establish a connection, the first thing to double-check is your IP settings.

If you're positive that your settings are correct and you're on a home network, it's possible that you need to set up port forwarding on your router. Setting up port forwarding will tell your router to forward incoming messages specifically to your Arduino. Setting up port forwarding isn't difficult, but you'll have to do it through your router's configuration. See your router's documentation for more information on how to set up forwarding to your Arduino's IP address, and you should be good to go.

8.3 Tweet tweet: talking to Twitter

Creating a web server to communicate with the outside world is great, but another powerful option is to hook into other online services. One service that's great to tap into is Twitter.

The way Twitter works is simple. Once you have a Twitter account, you can broadcast tweets (messages) up to 140 characters long to the entire Twitter network. People can subscribe to your feed and automatically receive your tweet updates. Not only that, Twitter plays nicely with other services, meaning that you can automatically have your tweets post to your Facebook account as well.

Wouldn't it be great if you could set up a Twitter feed to automatically update when various things happen on your Arduino? You can. In this section, you'll learn how to set up your Arduino and Ethernet Shield to automatically send tweets to a Twitter feed when you press a button connected to your Arduino.

8.3.1   *Of Twitter and tokens*

If you don't already have a Twitter account, or you want to set up a new one for this project, go to www.twitter.com and create one now.

Next, you need to get a special "token" that will authorize the Arduino to send messages to your Twitter account. This token enables a middleware web service to mediate between your Arduino and Twitter. It's possible to communicate directly with Twitter, but going through a middleware service is useful because it'll prevent your code from breaking if or when Twitter updates its protocol and authorization. It also helps make the Twitter library more lightweight and saves memory space, which can be precious on the Arduino.

To get the token, go to http://arduino-tweet.appspot.com/ and click on the "Step 1: Get a token to post a message using OAuth" link.

Once your account is set up, it's time to take a closer look at the libraries you'll be using.

8.3.2   *Libraries and functions*

To communicate with Twitter, you'll need to install the Twitter library from www.arduino.cc/playground/Code/TwitterLibrary. Once you've downloaded it, place the library in your sketchbook or libraries folder.

Table 8.4 describes the Twitter library's functions.

Table 8.4   Overview of the Twitter library's functions

Function	Description
`Twitter(string token)`	Constructor takes in the authorization token.
`bool post(const char *message)`	Begins posting a message. Returns `true` if connection to Twitter is established, `false` if there's an error.
`bool checkStatus(Print *debug)`	Checks if the posting request is still running (can omit passing in the debug argument if no output is required).
`int status()`	Returns the HTTP status code response from Twitter, such as 200–OK. The status is only available after posting the message has completed and `checkStatus()` returns `false`.
`int wait(Print *debug)`	Waits until posting the message is done. Returns the HTTP status code response from Twitter.

8.3.3 Circuit diagram and connecting the hardware

Now that your Twitter and Arduino IDE are set up, let's build a simple circuit to send tweets whenever a user presses a button. Solder together the following simple button circuit, or assemble it on a breadboard.

Connect one leg of a push button to 5V and the other to GND through a 10k ohm pull-down resistor. Also connect that same leg (the one connected to ground) to digital input 2, as shown in figure 8.2.

8.3.4 Sketch for the Twitter button-press tweeter

Once you have the button wired up and the Ethernet Shield plugged in to your Arduino, copy the following code into the Arduino IDE and you're ready to go. Be sure to read the comments in the code carefully to make sure it's configured correctly for your network settings. If you need clarification on any of the networking concepts or terms, refer to section 8.1.

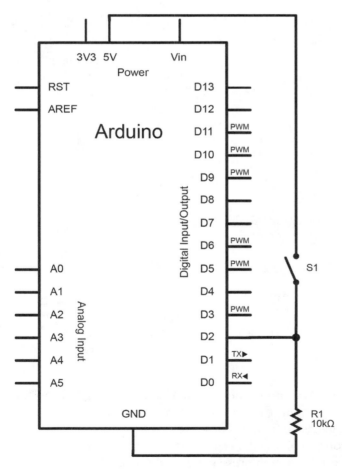

Figure 8.2 Simple button-tweeting circuit

Listing 8.2   Twitter button-press tweeter

```
#include <SPI.h>
#include <Ethernet.h>
#include <Twitter.h>

byte mac[] = { 0xDE, 0xAD, 0xBE, 0xEF, 0xFE, 0xED };
IPAddress manualIP(192,168,1,120);

int b1Pin = 2;
int pressCount = 0;

Twitter twitter("YOUR-TOKEN-HERE");

void setup()
{
  delay(1000);
  if(!Ethernet.begin(mac)){
    Ethernet.begin(mac, manualIP);
  }
  Serial.begin(9600);
}

void sendTweet(const char msgToSend[])
{
  Serial.println("connecting ...");
  if (twitter.post(msgToSend)) {
    int status = twitter.wait(&Serial);
    if (status == 200) {
      Serial.println("OK.");
    }
    else {
      Serial.print("failed : code ");
      Serial.println(status);
    }
  }
  else {
    Serial.println("connection failed.");
  }
}

void loop()
{
  if(digitalRead(b1Pin) == HIGH)
  {
    pressCount++;
    sendTweet("Times button pressed: " + pressCount);
    delay(2000);
  }
}
```

Assign unique MAC address

Set IP address manually if DHCP isn't enabled

Specify the button pin

Initialize Twitter token

1 Connect using DHCP

2 Connect manually if DHCP fails

3 Start serial connection

4 Format and send tweets

5 Check and send button press tweets

First, try to connect the Arduino to the Ethernet network using DHCP **1**, or with a manual IP address if DHCP fails **2**. Once it's connected, start your serial connection so you can print debug messages to the console **3**.

With everything connected, use the sendTweet function to format and send Tweets properly **4**. Then check for button presses and send tweets **5**.

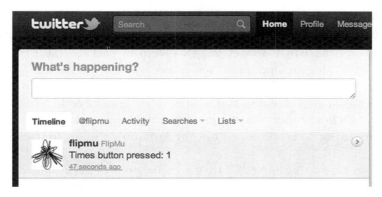

Figure 8.3   Screenshot of a Twitter button tweet

8.3.5   Upload and test

Once you're sure everything is correct, compile and upload the code to your Arduino. You're now ready to broadcast your button presses to Twitter. Check that you have the code running on your Arduino and that your Arduino is connected to the internet via an Ethernet cable, and you should be all set.

Press the button on your Arduino and log in to Twitter.com. You should see your last tweet, which says "Times button pressed: 1," as shown in figure 8.3. Each time you press the button, you'll see a new tweet pop up, incrementing the number of times the button has been pressed. Nice job.

> **NOTE**   Twitter blocks the same post from being sent consecutively within a short amount of time. In listing 8.2, the message changes each time the button is pressed (the number of times increments), so this isn't a problem. In most cases where messages are sent periodically or where they vary, this won't be a problem, but it's something to keep in mind.

As you can imagine, you can broadcast many other useful things besides a simple button press. Perhaps a sensor is triggered when the front door opens or closes at your house. Perhaps you tweet real-time data and visualize the information in your gallery installation—we're only scratching the surface here.

8.4   Wi-Fi

The Ethernet Shield will get your Arduino online in no time, but surely there will be times when being wireless would be useful. Perhaps you need to retrieve real-time data from a roaming rover-bot you've made, or your project needs to get online but isn't near a wired router or connection. Enter the official Arduino Wifi Shield, an elegant solution that will get your Arduino up and running on Wi-Fi networks.

> **NOTE**   If you own the SparkFun WiFly (a popular alternative to the official Arduino Wifi Shield), or need to use it in your project for other reasons, we adapted this section to work with the WiFly module. A web link to the adapted section can be found in appendix E.

8.4.1   *Arduino Wifi Shield*

The Arduino Wifi Shield will enable your Arduino to connect to any 802.11b/g wireless network. It uses the HDG104 wireless LAN system in package (SiP) from H&D Wireless, which provides an optimized, low-power wireless connection. This Wifi Shield is capable of communicating with both UDP and TCP, and using it is as easy as mounting it on top of your Arduino and writing a few lines of code using the WiFi library. The Wifi Shield's header pins also provide female connection points along the top, which makes it easy to retain access to your Arduino's pins, or to stack on additional shields.

In addition to supporting the 802.11b/g specification, the Wifi Shield supports both WEP and WPA2 personal encrypted networks. Once your sketch is uploaded and the Arduino is configured, your Arduino can be disconnected from the computer, powered externally, and serve two-way communications from anywhere within range of a wireless router.

Not only that, the Wifi Shield also provides an onboard microSD slot that can be used with both the Arduino Uno and Mega via the easy-to-use SD library. This is great if you want to store information and then send it out over the network, and in section 8.7 of this chapter you'll see exactly how to use the SD library.

Important information about I/O pins

The Arduino Wifi Shield and SD card reader communicate using the SPI bus (which is discussed further in section 8.6), which has a few important details regarding the use of your general I/O pins.

On the Arduino Uno, SPI communication is supported on digital pins 11, 12, and 13, and on the Mega, pins 50, 51, and 52. On both boards, pin 10 is used to select the HDG104 and pin 4 is used for the SD card reader. The hardware SS pin on the Mega (digital pin 53) isn't used by either the SD card reader or the HDG104, although it must be configured as an output for the SPI interface to work properly. Digital pin 7 is used as a handshake pin between the Wifi Shield and the Arduino, and it's vital that none of the mentioned pins be used for any I/O.

Lastly, because the shield's Wi-Fi chip (HDG104) and SD card reader both use the SPI bus, only one can be active at any given time. If both are being used, the SD and WiFi libraries automatically handle this for you, but if you're using just one, you must explicitly deselect the other (if you aren't using an SD card reader, you must manually deselect it), as you'll see in the example code.

The Wifi Shield has been well thought out and provides several useful features beyond the Wi-Fi connection. It's completely open source and has a Micro-USB port to support firmware updates in the future. It also has a series of status LEDs that report useful information, such as connection status (LINK/green), whether there are communication errors (ERROR/red), and whether data is being transmitted or received (DATA/blue).

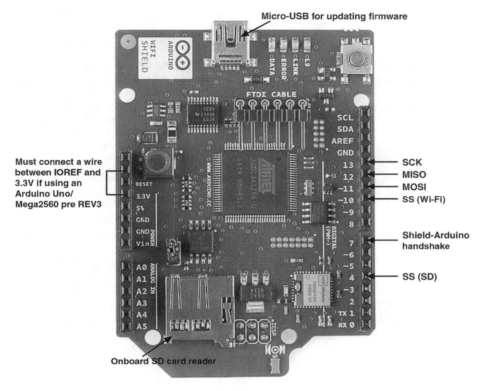

Figure 8.4 Overview of pins used by Wifi Shield.

USING YOUR WIFI SHIELD WITH OLDER ARDUINO BOARDS?
The Arduino Wifi Shield uses the IOREF pin available on newer Arduinos to sense the reference voltage for the I/O pins of the board it's connected to. This means that if you're using an Arduino Uno or Mega2560 earlier than REV3, you *must* connect a jumper wire between IOREF and 3.3V (as detailed in figure 8.4).

8.4.2 WiFi library and functions

To begin using your Wifi Shield, you'll use the WiFi library. Arduino plans to include the library with a future release of the IDE, but currently (version 1.0.1 or earlier) the library must be downloaded and installed from the Arduino website.

   The WiFi library handles all of the low-level networking communication for you and also provides support for many of the commands and functionality provided by the Wifi Shield.

   At this point, it would be good to familiarize yourself with table 8.5, which provides an overview of the main functions you'll use from the WiFi library.

   Once you've reviewed table 8.5, you're ready to move on to the example project, where you'll be sending out gestural sensor data over a wireless network.

Table 8.5   Overview of the `WiFi`, `WiFiServer`, and `WiFiClient` library functions

Function	Description

`WiFi.begin()`
`WiFi.begin(char[] ssid)`
`WiFi.begin(char[] ssid, char[] pass)`
`WiFi.begin(char[] ssid, int keyIndex, char[]key)`
	Initializes the WiFi library and begins communication with the device. You can join any open network, or provide the network's SSID, password for WPA encrypted networks, or `keyIndex` and key for WEP encrypted networks (WEP encryption can store up to four different keys, so a `keyIndex` must be supplied). This function returns the Wi-Fi status.

`WiFi.disconnect()`	Disconnects from the current network.
`WiFi.SSID()`	Gets the SSID of the current network and returns a `String`.
`WiFi.BSSID(bssid)`	Gets the MAC address of the router connected to and stores it in the 6-byte array passed in as an argument (for example, `byte bssid[6]`)
`WiFi.RSSI()`	Returns the signal strength of the connection as a `Long`.
`WiFi.encryptionType()` `WiFi.encryptionType(wifiAccessPoint)`	Returns the type of encryption of the current (or specified) access point. Returns as a `byte` value, where TKIP (WPA) = 2, WEP = 5, CCMP (WPA) = 4, NONE = 7, AUTO = 8.
`WiFi.scanNetworks()`	Returns the number of discovered networks as a `byte`.
`WiFi.getSocket()`	Returns the first socket available.
`WiFi.macAddress()`	Returns a 6-byte array representing the Wifi Shield's MAC address.
`WiFi.localIP()`	Returns the IP address of the shield (as an `IPAddress`).
`WiFi.subnetMask()`	Returns the subnet mask of the shield (as an `IPAddress`).
`WiFi.gatewayIP()`	Returns the gateway IP address (as an `IPAddress`).
`WiFiServer(int port)`	Creates a server to listen on a specific port.
`WiFiServer.begin()`	Starts the server listening for messages.
`WiFiServer.available()`	Returns a client if a client has data ready.
`WiFiServer.write(data)`	Sends data to all connected clients (either `byte` or `char`).
`WiFiServer.print()`	Prints data to all clients. Numbers print as a sequence of ASCII digits; for example, 123 becomes three characters, '1', '2', and '3'.

Table 8.5   Overview of the `WiFi`, `WiFiServer`, and `WiFiClient` library functions *(continued)*

Function	Description
`WiFiServer.println()`	Same as `WiFiServer.print()` but with a newline character at the end of each message.
`WiFiClient()`	Creates a client that can connect to the specified IP address and port defined in `connect()`.
`WiFiClient.connected()`	Returns whether or not the client is connected. If the connection is closed and some data is still unread, this will still return `true`.
`WiFiClient.connect(ip, port)` `WiFiClient.connect(URL, port)`	Starts the connection using the IP address and port specified. Will resolve the IP address from a URL.
`WiFiClient.write(data)`	Writes data to the server (`byte` or `char`).
`WiFiClient.print()`	Prints data to the client. Numbers print as a sequence of ASCII digits; for example, 123 becomes three characters, '1', '2', and '3'.
`WiFiClient.println()`	Same as `WiFiClient.print()` but with a newline character at the end of each message.
`WiFiClient.available()`	Returns the number of bytes available to be read (the number of bytes sent from the server).
`WiFiClient.read()`	Reads the next byte received from the server.
`WiFiClient.flush()`	Flushes any bytes that have been written to the client but have not yet been read.
`WiFiClient.stop()`	Disconnects from the server.

8.4.3   *Gestures: wireless accelerometers*

In this example, you're going to use a Wi-Fi-powered Arduino to send sensor data from an accelerometer wirelessly over a network. Accelerometers are fantastic sensors allowing all kinds of exciting gestural interactions. Perhaps you're interested in investigating new game-playing scenarios (as made popular by the Nintendo Wii), or putting accelerometers on a dancer's body to use their motion to control live visuals and sound, or using accelerometers in assistive aids for the physically impaired. As you can see, practical uses for wireless accelerometers abound, and we're sure you can think of more.

In this example, you'll need the following:

- An Arduino
- The Arduino Wifi Shield
- At least one accelerometer (such as the ADXL335)

You'll use the Processing language to create a server via which you can stream and parse the data from your wireless accelerometers.

8.4.4   *Connecting the hardware*

Connecting the Wifi Shield should be as simple as plugging it in directly on top of your Arduino. The steps for wiring up the accelerometer to your Arduino will differ depending on the particular model you're using.

If you're using the ADXL335 tri-axis accelerometer, which provides an independent analog output for each of its axes (x,y,z), please refer to figure 8.5 when making your connections. If you're using another accelerometer model, the connections may be similar or may use PWM pins instead of the analog inputs. Refer to your model's datasheet and documentation for the proper connections if you're using another type of accelerometer.

With the Wifi Shield and accelerometer connected, you're ready to rock and roll.

8.4.5   *Sketch for Bluetooth communication*

Let's use the WiFi library to get your Arduino to send the accelerometer data wirelessly to a server running on your computer. Wait—server on your computer? How do you do that?

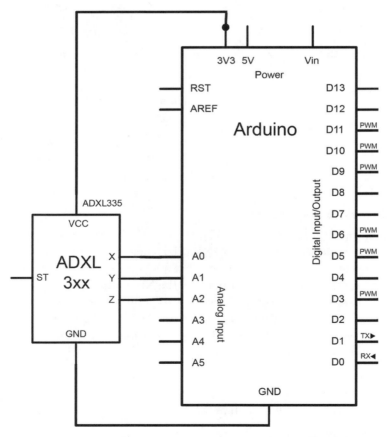

Figure 8.5   Connecting the ADXL335 analog accelerometer to the Arduino

You're going to use a programming environment called "Processing," so if you don't already have it on your computer, now would be a good time to go to processing.org and download the latest version. If you haven't used Processing before, don't worry; the code in listing 8.4 will look familiar to the code you've written before.

But first, let's get the Arduino side of things moving along with the following code.

Listing 8.3 Arduino accelerometer client

```
#include <WiFi.h>

char ssid[] = "network_name";
char pass[] = "network_key";
IPAddress server_address(192,168,0,1);
int server_port = 10000;
int status = WL_IDLE_STATUS;

WiFiClient client;

void setup() {
   Serial.begin(9600);
      connectToNetwork();
}

void connectToNetwork(){
  while ( status != WL_CONNECTED) {
    Serial.print("Attempting to connect to SSID: ");
    Serial.println(ssid);

    status = WiFi.begin(ssid, pass);
    delay(10000);
  }

  printWifiStatus();
}

void loop() {
  if(status == WL_CONNECTED){
    if(!client.connected())
    {
      client.connect(server_address, server_port);
      delay(1000);
    }
    else
    {
      Serial.print("Connected and sending data to ");
      Serial.println(server_address);
      client.print("x: ");
      client.print(analogRead(0));
      client.print(" y: ");
      client.print(analogRead(1));
      client.print(" z: ");
      client.println(analogRead(2));
    }

    delay(20);
  }
```

Set network name (SSID)

Set network passphrase (key)

Set server IP address

Set server port

❶ Wi-Fi client object

❷ Start serial connection

❸ Try to connect to network

❹ Join network

❺ Wait for network to join

❻ Test if network is connected

❼ Connect to server

❽ Read and send current accelerometer data

Wait 20 ms before retry

```
  else{
    Serial.println("wifi not up");
    connectToNetwork();
  }
}

void printWifiStatus() {
  Serial.print("SSID: ");
  Serial.println(WiFi.SSID());

  IPAddress ip = WiFi.localIP();
  Serial.print("IP Address: ");
  Serial.println(ip);

  long rssi = WiFi.RSSI();
  Serial.print("signal strength (RSSI): ");
  Serial.print(rssi);
  Serial.println(" dBm");
}
```

After importing the necessary libraries and supplying a few network and server details, you must create a `WiFiClient` object ❶. Then, in the setup routine you initialize the serial library for debugging ❷, before attempting to open a network connection using a method you create called `connectToNetwork` ❸. You attempt to join the Wi-Fi network using `WiFi.begin` ❹, and wait ten seconds to connect ❺. Next you enter the main loop, and if you successfully connected to the network ❻, but are not yet connected to the server ❼, you attempt to connect to the server. If you're already connected to the server, you read and send the current accelerometer values ❽.

In the next listing we jump into Processing and create a server that will accept incoming connections from clients (the Arduino) and display the messages it's receiving on the screen. For a bit more information on Processing, you can take a quick peek at section 13.2 in chapter 13.

Listing 8.4   Processing sketch to request accelerometer data from Arduino server

```
import processing.net.*;                          Import Processing
                                                  network library
int direction = 1;                    Set text direction
boolean serverRunning = false;
String currentData = "";                          Create string to store
                                                  accelerometer data
Server myServer;                          Create
                                          server
void setup()                              object
{
  size(400, 400);                                 Set window
  textFont(createFont("SansSerif", 16));          size
  myServer = new Server(this, 10000);
  serverRunning = true;                     Instantiate
  printData();                            ❶ server
}
```

```
void printData() {
  background(0);
  text("wireless accelerometer data: ", 15, 25);
  text(currentData, 15, 60);
}

void draw()
{
  Client thisClient = myServer.available();          ② Check for
  if (thisClient != null) {                              incoming
    if (thisClient.available() > 0) {                    clients
    currentData = "message from: " + thisClient.ip() + " : " +
    thisClient.readString();                           ③ Unpack and
      printData();                                        display data
    }
  }
}
```

After you set up the window and font for displaying your data in the setup function, you instantiate the server to start listening for incoming clients ①. The draw function is similar to the main loop in Arduino, and it continuously checks for incoming clients ②. If a client connects, you unpack the message (thisClient.readString()), append it with additional information such as the client's IP address, and display it in your window ③.

8.4.6 *Upload and test*

That's it. Click the play button on the Processing sketch, and Processing will open a window on your computer screen and the server will start. Upload the Arduino code to your Arduino, and as long as your network is properly configured (your Arduino and computer are on the same Wi-Fi network, and you've configured your Arduino with your computer's IP as the server), you should begin to see the accelerometer values displaying on your Processing program's window.

If you hunger for more, perhaps a good place to start would be to unpack the individual accelerometer data from the String you received, and visualize the three (x,y,z) axes on your display.

8.5 *Bluetooth wireless*

Wi-Fi isn't the only type of wireless communication you can have between the computer and your Arduino. Another viable option is Bluetooth, the wireless technology made popular by cellphone headsets and peripherals.

Bluetooth technology was developed by Ericsson as an open wireless technology that provides an alternative to traditional wired serial communication. Bluetooth is intended for near-field communication, meaning its range and speed are both limited. Nonetheless, it provides enough proximity, speed, resolution, and security for many scenarios and use cases. And because a Bluetooth device manifests itself as a virtual serial port (figure 8.6 shows a MacBook Pro's internal Bluetooth device as a regular serial device in the Arduino IDE's device list), sending data from your Arduino

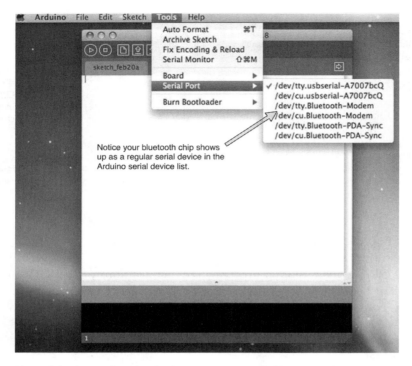

**Figure 8.6   Screenshot showing how your computer's Bluetooth chip acts as a
serial device**

over Bluetooth couldn't be any easier, utilizing the same commands as normal serial
communication. This means that whether your sketch sends to the computer via standard serial over USB or via Bluetooth, the code remains the same—and we love this
kind of portable code.

8.5.1   ArduinoBT

The ArduinoBT (pictured in figure 8.7) is an Arduino board with an embedded Bluetooth module for wireless communication. It can run on a minimum of 1.2 volts, making it battery-friendly in wireless scenarios. Compared to other models with similar
ATmega chips, the ArduinoBT has two additional analog inputs (8 total), but they
don't have header pins soldered in. In order to use the extra inputs, you can either
solder directly to the pads, or solder on two additional header pins (recommended).

> **NOTE**   Don't use pin 7; it's connected to the reset pin and should only be
> used for resetting the module.

8.5.2   Adding Bluetooth

If you don't have the ArduinoBT or your project requires one of the other models in
the Arduino line, you're in good company. There are many Bluetooth add-ons, such
as the BlueSMiRF line (recommended) available at SparkFun.

Figure 8.7 ArduinoBT, a Bluetooth-enabled Arduino board

The BlueSMiRF line connects to your Arduino's RX/TX serial lines, so wiring it up couldn't be easier. As described in figure 8.8, simply connect the VCC pin on the BlueSMiRF to 5V on your Arduino. Next, wire GND on the BlueSMiRF module to GND on your Arduino. Lastly, wire the communication lines by connecting RX on the BlueSMiRF module to TX on the Arduino, and TX on the BlueSMiRF module to RX on the Arduino.

> **NOTE** As the Bluetooth module takes control of the Arduino RX/TX lines, it must be disconnected when you're uploading sketches to the Arduino over USB.

8.5.3 Establishing a Bluetooth connection

The first step in Bluetooth communication is pairing your Bluetooth-enabled Arduino to your computer. During this step, your computer will create a virtual serial port between your computer and your Arduino over the Bluetooth connection. Many laptops today come with Bluetooth built in, but if your computer doesn't, you can easily buy a Bluetooth USB module for under $50—a great gift for any hobbyist or part-time Arduino hacker.

The process of pairing your ArduinoBT and computer varies depending on your operating system but the settings are the same. You're going to look for a device called ARDUINOBT if you're using an ArduinoBT or another self-describing name if you're using a third-party Bluetooth module, and connect using the passphrase 1234. That's it.

You should see your computer and Bluetooth-powered Arduino connected, and now you can return to the Arduino IDE as normal.

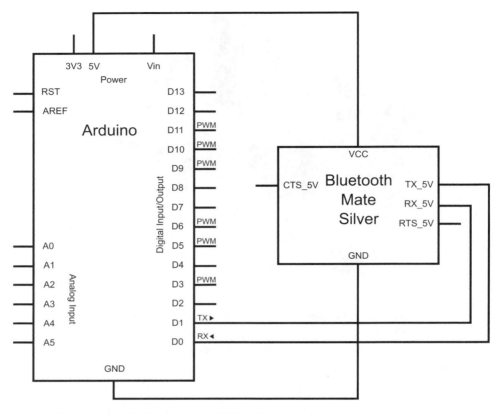

Figure 8.8   Connecting the SparkFun BlueSMiRF Silver to an Arduino

8.5.4   *Sketch for Bluetooth communication*

Writing code for our Bluetooth-powered Arduino is no different than for communicating over USB. Remember, the Bluetooth module shows up as a virtual serial port, so you can utilize the exact same Serial.print commands you're already familiar with.

The one catch to keep in mind is that the communication between the Arduino sketch and your Bluetooth module needs to be at the same baud rate—for the ArduinoBT, this will be 115,200 baud. In your setup function you need to make sure you set the correct baud rate when opening up the serial connection, such as Serial.begin(115200).

The code in listing 8.5 doesn't do anything fancy, but it shows what a simple Bluetooth sketch looks like. It properly configures the baud rate and then wirelessly broadcasts a random number every second over Bluetooth serial. The exciting thing is that getting this code going with your current project is as simple as modifying the print commands in the sketch to send out the readings from whatever sensor your project calls for.

Listing 8.5　Bluetooth test sketch

```
void setup(){
  Serial.begin(115200);
}

void loop(){
  Serial.print(random(1024));
  delay(1000);
}
```

NOTE If your messages don't seem to be sending correctly, double-check your baud rate. Some Bluetooth modules may communicate at 9,600 or other speeds.

Congratulations, you've now covered the most common ways to communicate with your Arduino over a network and wirelessly. The topic of communications, however, is broad, and remotely talking to your Arduino isn't the only type of communication possible. In the following section you'll learn about a nifty communication channel called serial peripheral interface; it's a powerful way to have your Arduino communicate with other devices.

8.6　*Serial peripheral interface (SPI)*

Serial peripheral interface (SPI) is a synchronous data protocol that enables multiple microcontrollers and peripheral devices to quickly communicate with one another over short distances. It follows a master-slave metaphor, where one device (usually a microcontroller) becomes the master, controlling all connected slave peripherals.

Normally SPI communicates over three channels:

- MISO—Master input, slave output
- MOSI—Master output, slave input
- SCK—Serial clock

The three lines' functions are relatively simple: MISO is the line for sending data from a slave to the master, MOSI is the line for sending data from the master to slave devices, and SCK (sometimes written SCLK or Clock) is a clock pulse that synchronizes the data transmission.

There's also a fourth slave select (SS) pin on each peripheral that you can use to select which device you wish to talk to. Setting the SS pin LOW tells the device to communicate with the master, while setting it HIGH tells it to ignore the master. By using the SS pin, you can have multiple devices utilizing the same three communication lines, and you can switch between devices one at a time by setting their pins LOW and HIGH respectively. A visual overview of the SPI communication channels is provided in figure 8.9.

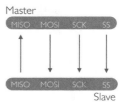

Figure 8.9　SPI communication channels

The other great thing about SPI is that because the MISO and MOSI lines are independent, you can use both at the same time (whereas other protocols, such as I2C, use one line for both directions of communication).

Please refer to table 8.6 when making SPI connections to the Arduino.

Table 8.6   Arduino SPI connection overview

SPI line	Arduino pin (non-Mega)	Arduino Mega
Slave select or chip select (SS/CS)	10	53
Master out, slave in or serial data in (MOSI/SDI)	11	51
Master in, slave out or serial data out (MISO/SDO)	12	50
Clock pulse (SCK/SCLK)	13	52

8.6.1   *SPI library*

To make things easier, the lovely people at Arduino have created an SPI library so you can get up and running quickly. Table 8.7 lists the library functions you'll use to get your devices talking over SPI.

Table 8.7   Arduino SPI library functions

Function	Description
begin()	Initializes the SPI bus setting SCK, MOSI, and SS to outputs (SCK and MOSI LOW, and SS HIGH)
end()	Disables SPI
setBitOrder(order)	Sets the order in which bits are shifted into or out of the SPI bus; will either be LSBFIRST (least-significant bit first) or MSBFIRST (most-significant bit first)
setClockDivider(amt)	Sets the SPI clock divider relative to the system clock; default is 4 (one quarter the system clock frequency) but can be 2, 4, 8, 16, 32, 64, or 128
byte transfer(val)	Transfers one byte over the SPI bus in both directions; val is the byte to send over the bus, and the function returns the byte read by the bus
setDataMode(mode)	Sets the clock mode (polarity and phase): SPI_MODE0, SPI_MODE1, SPI_MODE2, SPI_MODE3

Once you familiarize yourself with these functions, you can move on to wiring up a peripheral to your Arduino and communicating between the two over SPI.

8.6.2   *SPI devices and digital potentiometers*

There are many devices that communicate over SPI, ranging from color LCD screens to magnetometers to controllable RGB LED grids. In fact, the Ethernet Shield and SD card readers discussed earlier all use SPI to communicate with the Arduino. The basic principles of communicating with them are all the same, so to demonstrate basic use of SPI we're going to use the SPI-based AD5206 digital potentiometer by Analog Devices.

Digital potentiometers are very similar to their analog counterparts we use every day, except that they're adjusted electronically rather than by hand. The AD5206 digital potentiometer by Analog Devices has six independent pots built into it that you can access, and you can find digital potentiometers in many other configurations as well.

In this example, we're going to use four of the built-in potentiometers to control the brightness of four LEDs independently, but as you can imagine, the digital potentiometer can be used to control anything that requires a varying voltage.

Let's get right into it and look at connecting everything up.

8.6.3 *Circuit diagram and connecting the hardware*

The first thing you're going to do is look up the data sheet for the digital potentiometer you're using. SPI communication requires four communication pins (MOSI/SDI, MISO/SDO, SS/CS, and SCK), so you're going to locate them on the digital potentiometer using the data sheet.

The schematic in figure 8.10 shows the pin layout for the AD5206 digital potentiometer and how it connects to your Arduino and LEDs.

First you need to make your main power connections. On the AD5206, connect VDD to 5V on the Arduino and GND to GND. Next, connect VSS on the AD5206 to GND on the Arduino.

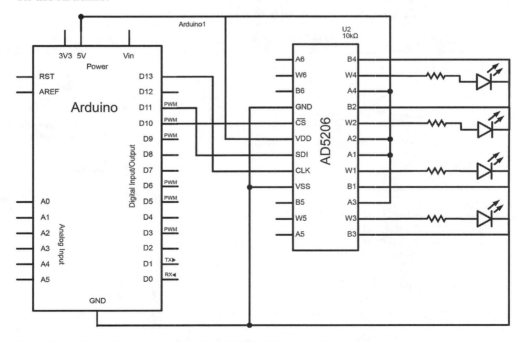

Figure 8.10 Four LEDs controlled by the AD5206 digital potentiometer

With the main power connections made, you can move on to the SPI connections. First, connect the CS pin (chip/slave select) to digital pin 10 on the Arduino. Next you'll connect the SDI (MOSI) pin to digital pin 11 on the Arduino. Since you'll be using MOSI, you won't have a MISO (SDO) pin to connect.

All that remains for SPI communication is the SCK pin, so go ahead and connect SCK to digital pin 13 on the Arduino.

That's it in terms of chip power and SPI communications. All that's left are the potentiometers. In figure 8.10, for each of the six potentiometers you'll see three pins, such as A1, B1, and W1. You can think of these as you do the legs on a regular potentiometer—connect all the A legs to 5V, all the B legs to GND, and all the W legs are your wipers. The W pins are where the varying voltage will come from, so you'll connect these to the Anode (positive) legs of your LEDs through a resistor (220 ohm should work, but you can calculate this specifically for the LEDs you're using for optimal brightness). Connect the cathode (negative) legs of the LEDs to GND and you're done!

Next we'll look at a simple sketch to dim the LEDs down and brighten them up, and we'll see the digital potentiometers in action.

8.6.4   *Sketch for a digital LED dimmer*

With everything connected, it's time to put the digital potentiometer to work. In the following sketch you'll loop through the LEDs and adjust their brightness. In doing so, you'll address the individual LEDs over SPI.

Carefully copy the following listing into the Arduino IDE.

Listing 8.6   SPI digital potentiometer LED dimmer

```
#include <SPI.h>                                    Import SPI
const int slaveSelectPin = 10;                      library
int numLeds = 4;                         Set slave
                                         select pin
void setup()
{
  pinMode(slaveSelectPin, OUTPUT);       ❶ Set slave select
  SPI.begin();                             as OUTPUT
}
                                         ❷ Start SPI
void setLed(int reg, int level)
{                                        ❸ Set slave          ❹ Choose
  digitalWrite(slaveSelectPin, LOW);       select LOW            register
  SPI.transfer(reg);
  SPI.transfer(level);
  digitalWrite(slaveSelectPin, HIGH);    ❺ Set data
}
                                         ❻ Set slave
void loop()                                select HIGH
{
  for(int i=0; i<numLeds; i++)
  {
    for (int j=50; j<=255; j++)
```

```
    {
      setLed(i,j);
      delay(20);
    }
    delay(500);

    for (int j=255; j>=50; j--)
    {
      setLed(i,j);
      delay(20);
    }
  }
}
```

After importing the SPI library and declaring your variables, you set your slave select pin as an output ❶. Next, you start SPI communication by calling begin ❷.

Setting an LED over SPI is a four-step process, so you create a subroutine called setLed() to perform the four steps each time:

1. You set SS LOW to choose the SPI slave to communicate with ❸. SPI will then expect two messages: one telling it which register to address, followed by a message setting a value.
2. The AD5206 has six registers, and your LEDs are connected to registers 0–3, so you can say SPI.transfer() and pass in the LED number (0–3) you wish to set ❹.
3. Call SPI.transfer() again and pass in a number (0–255) to set the brightness ❺. The AD5206 is an 8-bit digital potentiometer, which is why our maximum value for brightness is 255.
4. Now that the data is set, you can set SS HIGH and you're done ❻.

In the simple loop() function, you iterate through each LED and ramp the brightness up every 20 milliseconds, and then down every 20 milliseconds. Feel free to play around here and come up with other interesting ways to blink your LEDs.

That's it. Upload your sketch to your Arduino and you should see your LEDs animate by varying the voltage to the LEDs without you having to move your hands, and without using pulse width modulation.

Congratulations, you've just tackled one of the intermediate uses of the Arduino. Next we're going to take a look at another important area where you'll often use SPI to communicate: data logging.

8.7   *Data logging*

Sensors are a great way to get readings about something's *current* state. But how does that sensor reading change over time, and is that information useful?

Let's think about music for a moment. Music is a phenomenon that can be thought of as a sequence of events unfolding over a period of time. Each of these musical events can have many different properties such as pitch (how high or low a note is), amplitude (how loud), and timbre (quality), each giving a particular note or sound its "sound."

In isolation, these notes or events have no musical context. Once played in succession, however, in the context of the composition, different relationships form between the events. Melodies and rhythmic patterns emerge; higher-level structures build from thin air. Even non-musicians with "untrained" ears are great at recognizing these relationships. Even if we can't express these relationships in musical terms, we possess the ability to embody and feel them. This is because the human brain has long- and short-term memory that's able to store the relationships of the sounds as they're played, and even to compare the relationships to the library of sounds and tunes you've heard in the past. Our brains can recall and connect the dots for us!

Similarly, if you want to begin to understand the patterns and high-level relationships and information within your sensor data, you must collect the data over a period of time and look for these patterns. In this section, we're going to look at how you can start logging your data on your Arduino.

8.7.1   Types of memory

In order to log data locally on the Arduino, you need to store it somewhere. Usually this is done with some sort of external memory, like the memory in your computer, cellphone, or thumb drive. The great thing about external memory is that once the memory is stored, it remains even after the device is powered off. This is also true of the EEPROM, Arduino's built-in memory.

While the EEPROM can retain its memory even when the Arduino is turned off, its space is severely limited. Depending on your Arduino model, you'll only have between 512 and 4096 bytes of EEPROM memory. This makes the EEPROM good for storing variables and small amounts of data that need to persist between uses of the Arduino, but not very usable in most data-logging scenarios. Because of this, you'll often turn to other external memory solutions, such as Secure Digital (SD) cards and memory sticks.

8.7.2   SD cards and SD library

SD cards are one of the best ways to store data externally. You can get high-capacity SD cards that should have plenty of space not only for data logging but also hosting other resource files (such as sound files to play or pictures to display), and Arduino comes with an SD library, making reading from and writing to SD cards easy.

Table 8.8 provides an overview of the main SD class functions available in the SD library, but there are many more File class functions enabling you to read from and write to files. Table 8.9 provides a list of the main File class functions, but please refer to the online documentation for a full list of available functions at www.arduino.cc/en/Reference/SD.

Whether you're using one of the SD card shields or the SD card reader built into your Arduino Ethernet Shield, communicating with the SD libraries is always the same. If you're comfortable with the functions we covered previously, you're more than ready to write a sketch to log some real data.

Table 8.8 SD library `SD` class functions

Function	Description
`begin(chipSelect)`	Initializes the SD library and card, optionally passing in the chip select pin.
`exists()`	Tests if a file or directory is present on the SD card.
`mkdir("/directory/to/create")` `rmdir("/directory/to/remove")`	Creates or removes a directory on the card.
`open("file/to/open", mode)` `remove("file/to/remove")`	Opens or removes a file at the specified path. When opening, you can specify a mode (`FILE_READ` or `FILE_WRITE`) if you want to limit access to only reading, or to read and write to the file.

Table 8.9 SD library `File` class functions

Function	Description
`available()`	Checks for bytes available to be read from the file
`close()`	Closes a file, ensuring all data is written to the SD card
`flush()`	Ensures data is physically saved to the SD card; used by `close()`
`print()` `println()` `write()`	Prints or writes data to the file
`read()`	Reads a byte from the file

8.7.3 Sketch for an SD card sensor logger

In this section you're going to write a simple sketch to log sensor readings from one of your analog inputs (analog input 0) to a file on a SD card.

Listing 8.7 SD card data logger

```
#include <SD.h>                                    ◁──┐ Include SD
                                                       │ library
const int chipSelect = 4;

void setup()                                           Initialize serial
{                                                      for debugging      Set default
  Serial.begin(9600);                          ◁────                      chip select
  Serial.print("Initializing SD card...");                               to OUTPUT
  pinMode(10, OUTPUT);                                            ◁──

  if (!SD.begin(chipSelect)) {                                    ❶ Check for
    Serial.println("Card failed, or not present");                 SD card
    return;
  }
  Serial.println("card initialized.");
}
```

```
void loop()
{
  String dataString = "";

  int data = analogRead(0);
  dataString += String(sensor);

  File dataFile = SD.open("datalog.txt", FILE_WRITE);

  if (dataFile) {
    dataFile.println(dataString);
    dataFile.close();
    Serial.println(dataString);
  }
  else {
    Serial.println("error opening datalog.txt");
  }
}
```

2 Create a string to store data reading

3 Read sensor data and store in dataString

4 Open file, print data, and close

5 Print to serial for debugging

Logging your data couldn't be any easier. First you must check to make sure your SD card is present **1**. If it is, everything should open up properly; if not, you must return.

Once it's all set up, you can start your main loop, create a `String` to store your data **2**, and then read and store the current sensor reading into a `String` **3**. Next, you open the data file and print the data to the file before calling `close` **4**. You can also print the data to the console for debugging **5**.

You can connect any sensor you want to the analog input, whether it's a potentiometer, a temperature sensor, or an ultrasonic rangefinder. Once you have all your data, plug the SD card into your computer and open the file in your favorite text editor or programming environment. From there you can start graphing and visualizing your data and hopefully get a better understanding of its trends.

If you want to share your data logging with the outside, passing around your SD card isn't the best option. For that, you might want to use Cosm, an online resource for sharing live data feeds with others around the world.

8.8   Cosm

Cosm, formerly Pachube (pronounced *"patch-bay"*), is an exciting open source community for sharing live data feeds online. You can create both public and private feeds that servers and clients connect to in order to send and receive data from anywhere in the world. Data is sent in a human-readable format (XML), and Cosm provides interesting data visualizations of the feed that you can monitor via the web.

In this section, you're going to use an Ethernet-powered Arduino to send the values of a sensor to a Cosm feed, and also receive sensor data from another online feed. Let's get started.

8.8.1   Sign up for an account and get an API key

The first step is creating a Cosm account at www.cosm.com and getting an API key. The API key is what gives you access to create, delete, retrieve, edit, and update your Cosm feeds.

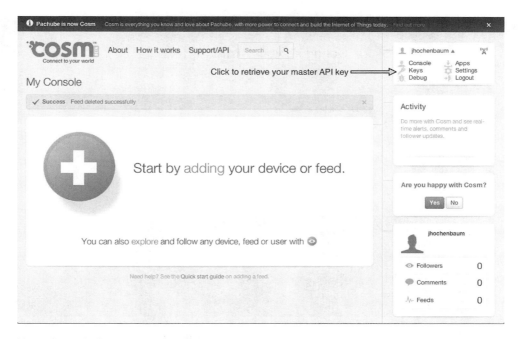

Figure 8.11   Main Cosm user interface

If you're sharing your project with others, you should keep your master API key private and instead use the Cosm user control panel to create a new secure sharing key for others to use. With sharing keys, you have full control over who has access and what functionality they have.

Once you've created an account, log in and go to the Keys page by navigating the main user menu (pictured in figure 8.11). There you'll see your Master API Key; write this down and keep it handy, as you'll need it later.

8.8.2   Creating a new data feed

You're going to create a new Cosm data feed that you'll send your sensor readings to.

If you're logged into your account, click the big blue + icon if this is the first Cosm feed you're creating, or the button that says +Device/Feed if you have already created other feeds. When prompted with the question, "What type of device/feed would you like to add?" select Arduino. You'll then be prompted with a display similar to figure 8.12. Give the feed a title and a few descriptive tags (you can, of course, change this later). Click Create, write down your Feed ID, and then click Finish— your new feed is all set.

> **NOTE**   By selecting Arduino as the device type, the feed is automatically set up to listen—this means the Arduino will be responsible for "pushing" data to your Cosm feed. You'll notice this option in the feeds control panel under General, or when creating a new feed and selecting the Something Else type.

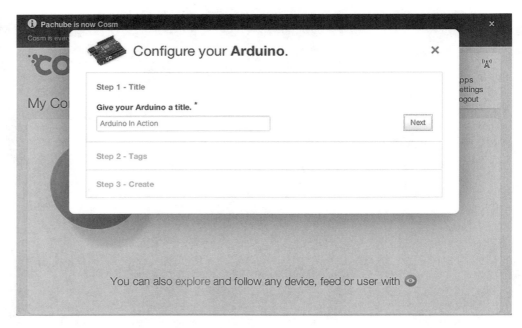

Figure 8.12   Creating a new Cosm feed to log sensor data

Your feed is now set up and it's ready to receive information. With your account, API key, and feed ID ready to go, you're set to get logging in section 8.8.3. If you forgot to write down your feed ID, you can retrieve it by browsing to your feed (simply click your feed name from the Cosm console).

8.8.3   Sketch for Cosm sensor logging

Talking to Cosm is easy. In this example, you'll log the readings from a potentiometer to a Cosm feed every ten seconds.

> **NOTE** In order to understand the workings of communicating with Cosm, you'll connect and send everything by hand in this example. Once you're familiar with how things work, you can save on a few lines of code—check out the wonderful Cosm Arduino library downloadable at https://cosm.com/support/libraries.

Enter the following code in the Arduino IDE.

Listing 8.8   Cosm sensor logging code

```
#include <SPI.h>
#include <Ethernet.h>

#define APIKEY        "YOUR API KEY GOES HERE"
#define FEEDID        12345
#define PROJECTNAME        "Arduino In Action"
```

❶ Configure Cosm feed settings

```
byte mac[] = {0xDE, 0xAD, 0xBE, 0xEF, 0xFE, 0xED};
IPAddress ip(192,168,0,120);
EthernetClient client;

long lastConnectionTime = 0;
boolean lastConnected = false;
const int postingInterval = 10000;

void setup() {
  if (!Ethernet.begin(mac)) {
    Ethernet.begin(mac, ip);
  }
  Serial.begin(9600);
}

void loop() {
  int sensorReading = analogRead(A0);

  if (client.available()) {
    char c = client.read();
    Serial.print(c);
  }

  if (!client.connected() && lastConnected) {
    Serial.println();
    Serial.println("disconnecting.");
    client.stop();
  }

  if(!client.connected() && (millis() - lastConnectionTime >
     postingInterval)) {
    sendData(sensorReading);
  }

  lastConnected = client.connected();
}

void sendData(int thisData) {
  if (client.connect("api.cosm.com", 80)) {
    Serial.println("connecting...");
    client.print("PUT /v2/feeds/");
    client.print(FEEDID);
    client.println(".csv HTTP/1.1");
    client.println("Host: api.cosm.com ");
    client.print("X-ApiKey: ");
    client.println(APIKEY);
    client.print("User-Agent: ");
    client.println(PROJECTNAME);
    client.print("Content-Length: ");

    int thisLength = 8 + getLength(thisData);
    client.println(thisLength);

    client.println("Content-Type: text/csv");
    client.println("Connection: close");
    client.println();

    client.print("sensor1, ");
    client.println(thisData);
  }
```

2 Configure network settings

Instantiate web client

Specify Cosm update interval

3 Open network connection

Open serial for debugging

4 Store current sensor data

5 Print incoming data for debugging

6 Stop client if no longer connected

7 Call sendData if it's time

Set Boolean to connected for interval timer

8 Connect to Cosm feed

9 Initiate PUT command and communication

10 Send API key

11 Send data to Cosm

```
    else {
      Serial.println("connection failed");
      Serial.println("disconnecting.");
      client.stop();
    }

    lastConnectionTime = millis();                          Store current
}                                                      ⑫   time
int getLength(int someValue) {
    int digits = 1;
    int dividend = someValue /10;
    while (dividend > 0) {
      dividend = dividend /10;
      digits++;
    }
    return digits;
}
```

First, you'll change the arguments for your Cosm feed settings ❶. Make sure your API key is in quotes, because it's supplied as a `String`. Next, configure your network settings by supplying the MAC address and manual IP address ❷, in case DHCP fails when connecting in setup ❸.

Next you enter the main `loop()` where you'll read the current sensor data ❹. You check to see if there is any incoming data, and print it to the console for debugging ❺. If you were previously connected but are no longer connected, you must stop the client ❻. Finally, if you're not connected and the interval time between sending messages has been met, you must connect and send the current data out ❼.

You actually call a subroutine called `sendData()`. This is a convenience function to establish a connection with the Cosm feed ❽ and send over your data. First, you must initiate the `PUT` command to talk to your feed ❾, and then supply your API key ❿. Then the function takes care of formatting the message (data) and passes along the data to Cosm ⓫. Finally, you store the time the message was sent ⓬ so you can calculate when to send the next message.

8.8.4   *Upload and test*

You can now connect your Arduino Ethernet Shield and USB cable and upload the code to your Arduino. You should be all set! Check your feed's page on Cosm, and you should see your sensor being logged online. If you don't see your sensor data, open up the Arduino IDE and click the Serial Monitor button to open up a serial connection for debugging.

8.9   *Summary*

In this chapter, you began to explore the broad spectrum of communications made possible with the Arduino. You started by getting your Arduino networked and on the internet. Using the Ethernet Shield, you turned your Arduino into a server ready to dish up information whenever a client has an appetite. Then you went a step further and patched your Arduino into Twitter, broadcasting button presses for the world to see. Because communicating with the Arduino wirelessly is useful in so many applications, we also explored communication with your Arduino both over Wi-Fi and Bluetooth technology.

The communication channels possible with your Arduino are far-reaching, and there are many ways you can communicate with other devices and peripherals. One such channel is called SPI, and in this chapter you learned how other devices and shields (such as the SD card and Ethernet Shields) use SPI to communicate with the Arduino. You even used SPI yourself to control digital potentiometers.

With all of these powerful means of communication at your disposal, we looked at data logging, an essential aspect of communication and interaction. Not only did we investigate storing information on local memory, but also storing it online using the powerful data logging service called Cosm.

How and what you choose to share is up to you; perhaps you want to have remote sensors in various environments that send their data to your feed, and are later sonified in a gallery installation. Perhaps you want to tap into other public feeds that are logging everything from seismic data to the temperature, humidity, dew point, and soil moisture of a garden in the UK, and use that to influence a virtual space. Whatever the scenario, there are virtually unlimited possibilities when it comes to the types of information your data feed can communicate, and the way you choose to interpret the information.

The applications discussed in this chapter are the tip of the iceberg. You can use the communication topics covered here in many ways, and it's this open-endedness that makes the Arduino such a powerful communication tool. Think about your project's goals and ask yourself whether putting your project online for the world to see or interact with would be useful. Could it tap into online resources? Does it need to communicate with other peripherals? Would it be useful to log certain data over time? With Arduino, the tools are in your hands.

But let's not stop there. Next, in chapter 9, we're going to look at how to interface the Arduino with game peripherals such as the Nintendo Wii Nunchuk and Xbox controller.

Game on

This chapter covers

- Connecting an Arduino to a Wii Nunchuk
- Arduino port manipulation
- Connecting an Arduino to an Xbox controller
- Using the USB Host Shield

It's time to dig out that old game controller that's lying unused in the cupboard, or alternatively, borrow one from your kids. Game controllers are a great way to control things on the Arduino. From robots to flying vehicles, they tend to be relatively low-cost because so many were mass-produced, and eBay and junk sales also offer a steady second-hand supply.

We'll start by looking at one of the controllers made for the Nintendo Wii games console—the versatile Nunchuk. Then we'll look at one of its main rivals, the Microsoft Xbox 360 and its USB controller. You'll learn how to get the controllers set up and running so you can use them in your own projects.

9.1 Nintendo Wii salutes you

Nintendo launched the Wii console to great acclaim late in 2006, although its graphics felt inferior to some of the existing games consoles, such as Microsoft's

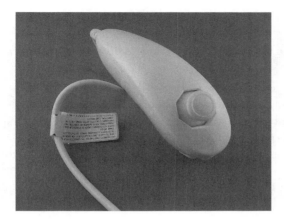

Figure 9.1   Wii Nunchuk

Xbox and Sony's PlayStation. The Wii had a unique games interface controller that was incredibly easy to use and communicated wirelessly with the main console. This controller, coupled with its family-themed games, made it a runaway success, with sales of over 90 million units. You'll find plenty of available games controllers.

The Wii is supplied with two main controllers, the Nunchuk, shown in figure 9.1, and the Wii remote. Let's look at the Wii Nunchuk and see how you can use it with the Arduino.

9.1.1   Wii Nunchuk

The Wii Nunchuk, shown in figure 9.1, is available from a wide range of suppliers, with prices from around $15 for an official version to $10 for one of the many compatible copies.

The Nunchuk packs in quite a few features: a built-in two-axis proportional analog joystick, two on-off buttons, and a three-axis accelerometer (more on this in a moment). Community projects have included controlling a motorized self-balancing skateboard (shown in figure 9.2), manipulating robot arms and servomotors, and designing small robots. The Nunchuk is also useful if you've built your own arcade games based on the Arduino. The video game shield kit designed by Wayne and Layne can use one or two

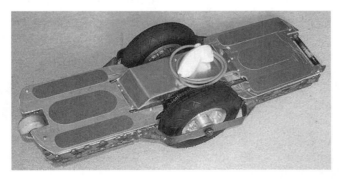

Figure 9.2   A self-balancing motorized skateboard built by John Dingley, UK

Nunchuks and is brilliant for anyone wanting to recreate the original Atari Pong or the classic Space Invaders.

Let's take a closer look at the individual components of the Nunchuk, starting with the three-axis accelerometer.

THREE-AXIS ACCELEROMETER

An accelerometer, as its name suggests, measures changes in acceleration.

The technical definition of acceleration is rate of change of velocity with respect to time. Or more plainly, it's how quickly something speeds up. For example, a car that reaches 60 mph in 5 seconds has greater acceleration than a car that reaches 60 mph in 10 seconds.

Accelerometers are used in all sorts of devices, including tablets and smartphones, where they're used to detect the angle at which you're holding or turning the screen, and air bags in cars, which are deployed when a car rapidly stops due to a collision.

The accelerometer contained in the Nunchuk and many other games controllers measures acceleration as the change in angular movement of the controller, and it can detect very small changes in angle. Many games controllers use one or more three-axis accelerometers and can detect small changes in the x, y, and z directions. Figure 9.3 shows this a little more clearly.

Accelerometers are used in Arduino-based projects in a multitude of ways: flying a remote-controlled plane or quadrocopter, playing digital musical instruments with gestural user input, and detecting if something is tilted or gets knocked.

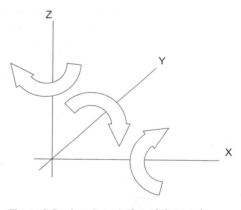

Figure 9.3   Angular rotation of three-axis accelerometer

In chapter 8 we looked at manually communicating the values from an accelerometer to the computer using Wi-Fi; now, we'll tap into the ultra-low-cost Wii Nunchuk controller, which not only gives us an accelerometer in an easy-to-grip form, but some extra modes of input that make it a versatile input controller for your projects.

JOYSTICK

The joystick on the Nunchuk is easily controlled with your thumb and is fully proportional, so it reports both the direction and how far you've moved the joystick. The Nunchuk fits nicely into your hand and the joystick is easily manipulated with your thumb.

The joystick returns numbers for the x and y axes, as shown in figure 9.4. As you can see, the joystick position can be anywhere within the circle.

BUTTONS

In addition to the joystick, the Nunchuk has two buttons at the front of the controller: a large one labeled Z and a smaller one labeled C. The buttons are simple momentary on-off switches, which means they report whether they're pressed or not.

NOTE By keeping track of button presses on the Arduino itself, it's easy to turn momentary buttons into toggle buttons if you so desire. If you get stuck, look at one of the many examples of doing this on the Arduino user forums, or download the toggle library called TButton, which also packs a few extra features.

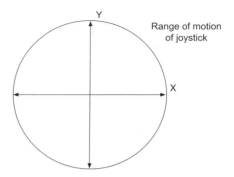

Figure 9.4 Range of motion of Nunchuk joystick

You've seen what a Nunchuk controller can offer, but how do you get access to all this functionality so you can use it with your Arduino projects?

9.1.2 Nunchuk connections

How do you connect your Arduino to a Nunchuk? Luckily Nintendo uses a well-known communication protocol called two-wire interface (TWI or I2C), which we looked at in chapter 4. To recap, the two-wire interface is used to communicate with low-speed devices and only requires two pins, as shown in table 9.1.

Table 9.1 Pin designations for the standard Arduino and the Mega for I2C

	Standard Arduino	Mega
SDA data line	Analog input pin 4	Digital pin 20
SCL clock line	Analog input pin 5	Digital pin 21

You're going to use your Arduino as a master device and the Nunchuk as its slave. We'll look in detail at the code required to communicate between the Arduino and Nunchuk shortly, but first we're going to look at how the Arduino can physically connect to a Nunchuk.

If you cut the end of the plug off your Nunchuk you would find four colored wires designated as in table 9.2.

NOTE You don't actually have to cut off the end of your Nunchuk—an alternative solution is shown here: www.flickr.com/photos/spyderella/6019588705.

Table 9.2 Color designations for wires in the Wii Nunchuk

Wire color	Designation
White	Ground
Red	3.3 Volts
Green	Data line
Yellow	Clock line

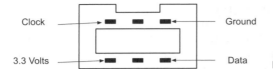

Clock

3.3 Volts

Ground

Data

Figure 9.5   Nunchuk end connector

NOTE The red 3.3 volt wire can be connected to 5 volts without apparent harm, although it may shorten the life of the Nunchuk.

You don't need to cut off the end of your Nunchuk to use it, as the end connector is female with six holes, only four of which are used. Figure 9.5 shows an end view of the connector. You can use jumper wires to connect from the connector to your Arduino.

An alternative that I like, as it gives a very good connection and is easy to use, is an adaptor or breakout board that can connect directly to the header on the Arduino (or to a breadboard) on one end, and to the Nunchuk plug on the other. Two low-cost breakout boards, available from a number of sellers, are the WiiChuck designed by Tod E. Kurt, shown in figure 9.6, and the NunChucky by Solarbotics, shown in figure 9.7. Both breakout boards are sold as small kits, so basic soldering skills are required.

So you have a couple of choices: you can either cut the plug off your Nunchuk cable and connect it directly to your Arduino using table 9.2 as a guide, or you can use a

Figure 9.6   WiiChuck designed by Tod E. Kurt

Figure 9.7   NunChucky breakout board from Solarbotics

breakout board like the NunChucky or WiiChuck. The breakout board can be plugged directly into the header on your Arduino as shown in figure 9.6 or to a breadboard.

That covers the main ways you can connect the Nunchuk to your Arduino. Let's move on to the code we're going to use to talk to it.

9.1.3 Wii will talk

The easiest way to get up and running with the Wii Nunchuk controller is to use one of the available libraries, such as Gabrial Bianconi's ArduinoNunchuk (www.gabrielbianconi.com/projects/arduinonunchuk/). Using this library, communicating with your Nunchuk can be done with ten lines of code or less. In this section, though, we're going to take a look at what goes on under the hood, in case you wish to dig a bit deeper into Arduino territory. As such, in this section we'll communicate with the Nunchuk from scratch and cover more advanced Arduino techniques such as port manipulation (more on this soon).

Techniques for communicating with a Nunchuk have evolved over a number of years, with contributions from Tod E. Kurt, who was responsible for some sections of the following code. We're going to break the code down into small chunks, explaining what each piece does before viewing the complete sketch. You can skip to listing 9.1 if you're desperate for a look now, but do come back to get an understanding of what each piece does.

CODE TO COMMUNICATE WITH THE NUNCHUK

You're going to communicate with the Nunchuk using TWI (I2C), so the first thing you must do is include the Wire library. Then you set up an `outbuf` array of six bytes to store the output from the Nunchuk. Finally, you set a `cnt` counter and set its value to 0. This will be used to keep track of the number of bytes read from the Nunchuk:

```
#include <Wire.h>

byte outbuf[6];                    ⟵——|  Array to store
int cnt = 0;                              Arduino output
```

The Nunchuk device sends a packet of data that's six bytes long, and this contains all the data from the accelerometer, the two-axis joystick, and the two buttons. The data is further summarized in table 9.3.

Table 9.3 Byte data returned from Nunchuk

Byte	Description	Typical values
1	*X*-axis joystick	35 (joystick fully left) to 228 (joystick fully right)
2	*Y*-axis joystick	27 (joystick fully back) to 230 (joystick fully forward)
3	*X*-axis acceleration	Roughly 300 (Nunchuk fully tilted left) to 740 (Nunchuk tilted right)
4	*Y*-axis acceleration	Roughly 320 (Nunchuk tilted backwards) to 810 (Nunchuk tilted forwards)

Table 9.3   Byte data returned from Nunchuk *(continued)*

Byte	Description	Typical values
5	Z-axis acceleration	Roughly 300 (Nunchuk upside down) to 720 (Nunchuk upright)
6	Button states (bits 0/1) Least significant bits (LSBs) of each accelerometer (bits 2–7)	Bit 0: Z-button (0 = pressed) Bit 1: C-button (0 = pressed) Bits 2–3: x acceleration LSBs Bits 4–5: y acceleration LSBs Bits 6–7: z acceleration LSBs

CODE TO SET UP AND POWER THE NUNCHUK

You've set your initial variables and allocated a buffer for the received data, so you can now move on to the setup function where you'll prepare the Arduino to work with the Nunchuk:

```
void setup ()
{
  nunchuk_setpowerpins();
  Serial.begin (19200);          Join I2C bus with
  Wire.begin();                  address 0x52
  nunchuk_init ();               Send initialization
}                                handshake
```

In the first part of this code, you call the nunchuk_setpowerpins() function. You then initialize the serial port with Serial.begin(19200), setting the baud rate to 19,200. You'll use the serial port to monitor the data sent from the Nunchuk.

Next it's time to initialize the Wire library with Wire.begin(). Finally, you call a function called nunchuk_init() to set up the Nunchuk so it will send back data when requested.

> **NOTE** You only need to call the nunchuk_setpowerpins() function if you're using a breakout board like the NunChucky or WiiChuck that's plugged directly into your Arduino's headers, or if analog pins A2 and A3 are being used for ground and power respectively. The nunchuk_setpowerpins() function isn't suitable and would need to be modified for use with an Arduino Mega, or if you're using the Arduino onboard 5 volts and ground to supply power.

Let's look at that first function called nunchuk_setpowerpins():

```
static void nunchuk_setpowerpins()
{
#define pwrpin PORTC3
#define gndpin PORTC2
  DDRC |= _BV(pwrpin) | _BV(gndpin);
  PORTC &=~ _BV(gndpin);              Wait for things
  PORTC |= _BV(pwrpin);              to stabilize
  delay(100);
}
```

At first glance this function looks fairly complicated, but we'll break it down to see what's going on. The function uses port manipulation to set analog pin 3 to power (5 volts), and analog pin 2 to ground.

Port manipulation

Arduinos based on the ATMega328 chip, such as the Uno, have three ports that provide fast low-level manipulation of the Arduino input/output pins. Each port gives access to a discrete set of pins:

- Port B gives access to digital pins 8–13
- Port C gives access to analog pins A0–A5
- Port D gives access to digital pins 0–7

Additionally, three registers control each port; the three registers are DDR, PORT and PIN:

- DDR register—This register sets individual pins as either input or output. The register state can be written to and read from.
- PORT register—This register sets the state of a pin's output: HIGH or LOW. The register state can be written to and read from.
- PIN register—This register can only be read from and provides the state of the inputs.

Each bit of each port controls a single pin. For example, the PORTC register controls port C. Port C consists of analog pins A0–A5 (A6 and A7 are only available on the Mini).

The bits in the DDRC register (the DDR register for port C) control whether a pin is an input or an output in PORTC. For example, the following command sets pins 1 and 3 as inputs and the rest as outputs:

```
DDRC = B11111010;
```

PORTC is the register for the state of the outputs. The following command sets pins 1 and 3–7 HIGH; these pins will only be set at 5 volts if they have previously been set as outputs by the DDR register:

```
PORTC = B11111010;
```

Reading the PINC register would allow you to read the state of all the PORTC pins simultaneously.

In the nunchuk_setpowerpins() function, the #define pwrpin PORTC3 and #define gndpin PORTC2 lines assign bit offsets, so PORTC2 is bit 2 of the PORTC register.

In the next line, you have this:

```
DDRC |= _BV(pwrpin) | _BV(gndpin);
```

DDRC is the direction register for port C, so this line sets the pwrpin and gndpin bits as outputs using the _BV macro.

The _BV macro

A macro is a method of performing a series of instructions with a single command, and the BV (bit value) macro is used to perform bitwise manipulation using bitmasks. Bitwise manipulation is the manipulation of the individual bits of a byte; a byte is made up of 8 bits numbered 0–7 with 0 being the least significant bit (LSB).

Operators can be used with the macro to operate on individual bits. These are some of the operators:

Operator	Description
|=	Sets bit
|	Logical or
&= ~	Clears bit

Here are a couple of examples. The following line sets bit 0 only:

```
PORTC |= _BV(0);
```

The next line clears bit 1 only:

```
PORTC &=~ _BV(1);
```

Using bit operators you can manipulate multiple bits at a time. The following line sets bits 0, 2, and 4:

```
PORTC |= _BV(0) | _BV(2) | _BV(4);
```

The next line clears bits 1 and 3:

```
PORTC &=~ _BV(1) | _BV(3);
```

Having set pwrpin and gndpin as outputs, the next line clears and sets the gndpin to LOW:

```
PORTC &=~ _BV(gndpin);
```

The following line sets the pwrpin to HIGH, 5 volts:

```
PORTC |= _BV(pwrpin);
```

The last line, delay(100);, is a 100-millisecond delay to allow the supply to stabilize.

Let's now have a look at the last function in the setup routine, nunchuk_init(), which sends a series of bytes commanding that the Nunchuk return its data, when asked, in an unencrypted format:

```
void nunchuk_init()
{
  Wire.beginTransmission (0x52);      <─── Transmit to device 0x52
  Wire.write ((byte)0xF0);            <─── Send memory address
  Wire.write ((byte)0x55);            <─── Initialization value 0x55

  Wire.write ((byte)0xFB);            <─── Send memory address
  Wire.write ((byte)0x00);            <─── Send initialization value 0
  Wire.endTransmission ();            <─── Stop transmitting
}
```

In this function, you set up the Nunchuk so that it's ready to send data. Each device on an I2C network has an ID or address. The Nunchuk has a device address of 0x52, so to send information to it, you start each transmission with `Wire.beginTransmission (0x52)`. You then prepare to send one or more commands or data packets to the address on the device. The data packets to be sent are queued in a buffer and are sent when the command `Wire.endTransmission()` is issued.

Having looked at the functions in the `startup` part of the sketch, we can now move on to the main `loop` function.

CODE FOR THE MAIN LOOP

You've set the initial variables and set up the Nunchuk and provided it with power. The main loop comes next, where you obtain the data from the Nunchuk and then process it:

```
void loop ()
{
  Wire.requestFrom (0x52, 6);          Request data
                                       from Nunchuk
  while (Wire.available ())
  {
    outbuf[cnt] = (Wire.read ());      Receive byte
    cnt++;                             as integer
  }

  if (cnt >= 5)                        If 6 bytes received,
  {                                    go print
    print();
  }

  cnt = 0;
  send_zero();                         Send request
  delay(100);                          for next bytes
}
```

In the loop, your first call is to request the data from the Nunchuk with `Wire.request-From(0x52, 6)`. This command has two parts: the address of the device, 0x52, and the number of bytes requested, 6. You next read in the 6 bytes with a `while` loop:

```
while (Wire.available ())
{
outbuf[cnt] = (Wire.read ());
cnt++;
}
```

The bytes read using `Wire.read` are stored in the `outbuf` array, with `cnt` being used to increment the index of the array. You check that you've received your 6 bytes and then print them with a `print()` function (more on that soon). In the loop, you call the `send_zero()` function, which requests the next set of bytes. Finally, you call a small 100-millisecond delay, `delay(100)`, before starting the loop again.

CODE TO PRINT THE OUTPUT

Let's investigate the main parts of the print function. Here's how it begins:

```
int joy_x_axis = outbuf[0];
int joy_y_axis = outbuf[1];
```

```
int accel_x_axis = outbuf[2] * 2 * 2;
int accel_y_axis = outbuf[3] * 2 * 2;
int accel_z_axis = outbuf[4] * 2 * 2;

int z_button = 0;
int c_button = 0;
```

Variables are initialized for the joystick's *x* and *y* axes and they're assigned values from the outbuf byte array. The accelerometer's *x*-, *y*-, and *z*-axis variables are similarly initialized and assigned values from the outbuf array. You multiply the last three variables by 2 * 2, because the acceleration data is 10 bits and you've only provided the most significant bits so far.

The remaining two bits for each acceleration value are obtained from the remaining byte, which also has the button state information for buttons C and Z:

```
if ((outbuf[5] >> 0) & 1)
  {
    z_button = 1;
  }
  if ((outbuf[5] >> 1) & 1)
  {
    c_button = 1;
  }

  if ((outbuf[5] >> 2) & 1)
  {
    accel_x_axis += 2;
  }
  if ((outbuf[5] >> 3) & 1)
  {
    accel_x_axis += 1;
  }

  if ((outbuf[5] >> 4) & 1)
  {
    accel_y_axis += 2;
  }
  if ((outbuf[5] >> 5) & 1)
  {
    accel_y_axis += 1;
  }

  if ((outbuf[5] >> 6) & 1)
  {
    accel_z_axis += 2;
  }
  if ((outbuf[5] >> 7) & 1)
  {
    accel_z_axis += 1;
  }
```

Each bit of the byte needs to be checked and its value added to the appropriate variable.

Finally the value of each variable is output to the serial port:

```
Serial.print (joy_x_axis, DEC);
Serial.print ("\t");
```

The `Serial.print("\t")` call adds a tab between each variable printed.

The last function we're going to look at is `send_zero()`.

CODE FOR SEND-REQUEST FUNCTION

The `nunchuck_send_request()` function is the final part of the puzzle. Having initialized the Nunchuk, powered it up, and printed the data received from it, you can now request more data with this function:

```
void nunchuck_send_request ()
{
  Wire.beginTransmission(0x52);
  Wire.write((byte)0x00);
  Wire.endTransmission();
}
```

This function transmits a value of 0 to the Nunchuk at address location 0x52; this is a "request to read" command that's sent to the Nunchuk.

THE COMPLETE SKETCH

That covers all the code we need for our sketch, so without further ado, here's the complete code listing.

Listing 9.1 Sketch to communicate with Nunchuk using I2C

```
#include <Wire.h>

byte outbuf[6];                         Creates buffer
int cnt = 0;                            for data

void setup ()
{
  nunchuk_setpowerpins();               Powers
  Serial.begin (19200);                 Nunchuk
  Serial.print ("Finished setup\n");
  Wire.begin();                         Initializes
  nunchuk_init ();                      Nunchuk
}

static void nunchuk_setpowerpins()      Powers
{                                       Nunchuk
#define pwrpin PORTC3
#define gndpin PORTC2
  DDRC |= _BV(pwrpin) | _BV(gndpin);
  PORTC &=~ _BV(gndpin);
  PORTC |= _BV(pwrpin);
  delay(100);
}                                       Initializes
                                        Nunchuk
void nunchuk_init ()
{
  Wire.beginTransmission (0x52);
  Wire.write ((byte)0xF0);
  Wire.write ((byte)0x55);

  Wire.write ((byte)0xFB);
  Wire.write ((byte)0x00);
```

```
    Wire.endTransmission ();
}
void loop ()
{
  Wire.requestFrom (0x52, 6);                      Gets data from
  while (Wire.available ())                        Nunchuk
  {
    outbuf[cnt] = (Wire.read ());
    cnt++;
  }

  if (cnt >= 5)
  {
    print ();                                      Prints
  }                                                data
                                  Requests
  cnt = 0;                        more data
  send_zero ();
  delay (100);
}
void print ()
{
  int joy_x_axis = outbuf[0];
  int joy_y_axis = outbuf[1];
  int accel_x_axis = outbuf[2] * 2 * 2;
  int accel_y_axis = outbuf[3] * 2 * 2;
  int accel_z_axis = outbuf[4] * 2 * 2;

  int z_button = 0;
  int c_button = 0;

  if ((outbuf[5] >> 0) & 1)
  {
    z_button = 1;
  }
  if ((outbuf[5] >> 1) & 1)
  {
    c_button = 1;
  }

  if ((outbuf[5] >> 2) & 1)
  {
    accel_x_axis += 2;
  }
  if ((outbuf[5] >> 3) & 1)
  {
    accel_x_axis += 1;
  }

  if ((outbuf[5] >> 4) & 1)
  {
    accel_y_axis += 2;
  }
  if ((outbuf[5] >> 5) & 1)
  {
    accel_y_axis += 1;
  }
```

```
  if ((outbuf[5] >> 6) & 1)
  {
    accel_z_axis += 2;
  }
  if ((outbuf[5] >> 7) & 1)
  {
    accel_z_axis += 1;
  }

  Serial.print (joy_x_axis, DEC);
  Serial.print ("\t");

  Serial.print (joy_y_axis, DEC);
  Serial.print ("\t");

  Serial.print (accel_x_axis, DEC);
  Serial.print ("\t");

  Serial.print (accel_y_axis, DEC);
  Serial.print ("\t");

  Serial.print (accel_z_axis, DEC);
  Serial.print ("\t");

  Serial.print (z_button, DEC);
  Serial.print ("\t");

  Serial.print (c_button, DEC);
  Serial.print ("\t");

  Serial.println();
}
void nunchuck_send_request()          ◁─── Requests
{                                           more data
  Wire.beginTransmission(0x52);
  Wire.write((byte)0x00);
  Wire.endTransmission();
}
```

You've now seen a couple of ways to connect a Nunchuk to the Arduino, and you've got the sketch to enter into the Arduino IDE. It's time to move on to testing.

9.1.4 *Wii will test*

Connect the Nunchuk to the Arduino using your preferred method, and then upload the sketch from listing 9.1. Open the serial monitor to observe the effects of moving the Nunchuk.

Try moving the Nunchuk about in various directions—tilt to the left and then to the right and observe how the *x*-axis acceleration alters. Move the Nunchuk forward and backward to observe the *y*-axis acceleration varying. Turn it upside down to see how the *z*-axis acceleration varies. Try moving the joystick and pressing the buttons. Some typical output to the serial monitor is shown in figure 9.8.

You've learned how to connect a Nunchuk to an Arduino and you've looked at the code involved in a typical sketch. You should now feel confident about using a Nunchuk in your own projects. Whether you want to use the joystick or accelerometers to control

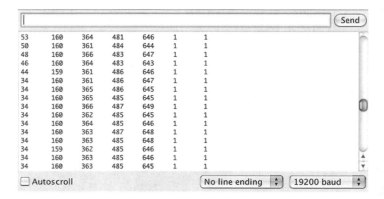

53	160	364	481	646	1	1
50	160	361	484	644	1	1
48	160	366	483	647	1	1
46	160	364	483	643	1	1
44	159	361	486	646	1	1
34	160	361	486	647	1	1
34	160	365	486	645	1	1
34	160	365	485	645	1	1
34	160	366	487	649	1	1
34	160	362	485	645	1	1
34	160	364	485	646	1	1
34	160	363	487	648	1	1
34	160	363	485	648	1	1
34	159	362	485	646	1	1
34	160	363	485	646	1	1
34	160	363	485	645	1	1

Autoscroll   No line ending   19200 baud

Figure 9.8   Typical output from Nunchuk to serial monitor

the position and tilt of a webcam using a servomotor, or you want to send the data into Processing to control a retro video game you've been working on, there are many unique applications for the affordable Nunchuk.

But although the Nunchuk is a fantastic game controller, it's by no means your only option when thinking about readily available controllers for your projects. Controllers come in many different shapes and sizes, and in the next section we're going to look at a controller from one of the Nintendo Wii's main competitors: Microsoft's Xbox 360.

9.2   *Release the Xbox*

Microsoft released the Xbox 360 game console in 2005 and at the time of this writing has sold over 57.6 million units. Figure 9.9 shows a typical controller.

The Xbox controller has the following buttons:

- 2 analog sticks
- 2 analog triggers
- 11 digital buttons
- 1 digital D-pad

Figure 9.9   Xbox 360 game controller

The wide range of buttons and joysticks on the controller make it ideal for controlling complex projects requiring multiple inputs, such as powered robots, complex light or sound displays, MIDI music instruments, or animatronics.

There are two versions of the Xbox controller, a wired and a wireless version. Both have the same functionality. We're going to concentrate on the wired controller in this chapter because it has a USB plug on it that, with the addition of a USB shield, can plug directly into an Arduino.

> **NOTE** The Xbox wireless controller also comes with a USB plug, but it can only be used to charge the controller's onboard batteries. It's possible to purchase an adaptor that has a USB connection and can also connect to a wireless controller. You can use techniques similar to the ones we'll discuss to connect to that version of the controller instead.

Having chosen the wired controller, let's take a look at what you need to connect it to your Arduino.

9.2.1 Getting connected

The Xbox controller communicates using a USB connection. A standard Arduino doesn't have an onboard USB connection suitable for plugging the games controller into, so you'll need to add a USB Host Shield.

In this example we're using version 2.0 of the USB Host Shield designed by Oleg Mazurov, available from Circuits@Home (www.circuitsathome.com/products-page/arduino-shields). The shield is shown in figure 9.10.

The USB Host Shield will allow you to connect to a range of USB devices, including mice, keyboards, and game controllers. In addition to the Host Shield, you'll need to download and install a software library.

9.2.2 USB Host library

To use the USB Host Shield, you'll need to download and install the USB Host Shield library from https://github.com/felis/USB_Host_Shield_2.0. Find the Downloads link

Figure 9.10   Version 2.0 of the USB Host Shield from circuitsathome.com

on the right, and click the "Download as zip" or "Download as tar.gz" button. Extract the contents to your Arduino/libraries folder.

Once the library is installed into the Arduino IDE, it will include some sample sketches. You'll use one of the sketches to discover information about the Xbox controller so that you can interface with it. The same techniques can be used with other USB devices to learn how to connect to them.

THE USB PROTOCOL

A thorough description of the USB protocol is beyond the scope of this book, as the protocol is complex and contains many parts. Full information and downloadable documents describing the protocol are available from the USB site (http://usb.org).

For an excellent overview and description of the main elements of the protocol, we highly recommend visiting the "USB in a Nutshell" explanation on the *Beyond Logic* website: http://www.beyondlogic.org/usbnutshell/. One of the main takeaways is that a USB device, when requested by a host device, should describe how it works and what is required to translate the information it provides. Unfortunately, as you'll see, this is not always the case in practice.

9.2.3   *Learning about the Xbox controller using the USB Host Shield*

The sample sketch you're going to use to connect to your controller in this section is called USB_desc, which can be found in the File menu, as shown in figure 9.11.

Connect the USB Host Shield to your Arduino, plug in the Xbox controller, load and run the example sketch, and open the serial monitor (setting the baud rate to 115,000 baud). The sketch issues a series of commands to the connected USB device—in this case your Xbox controller—and outputs the results to the serial monitor. The

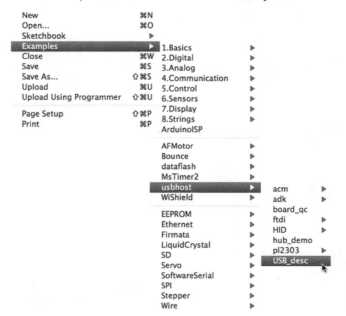

Figure 9.11   Select the USB_desc example sketch

sketch outputs a lot of data, but we'll look at the output a piece at a time to see what it tells you.

NOTE All values returned are hexadecimal values.

Take a look at the first piece of data as shown in figure 9.12.

The first piece of data shown in figure 9.12 provides the "device descriptor" and "configuration descriptor." A USB device can only have one device descriptor—it provides important information about the device, including the vendor ID, product ID, and the number of configurations available on the device. The majority of devices only have one configuration. In figure 9.12 you can see that the vendor ID is 045E (which corresponds to Microsoft), the product ID is 028E, and the number of configurations is 1.

The configuration descriptor provides information about the configuration of the device, such as the number of interfaces the device has and its maximum power consumption. All USB devices must have at least one interface, designated interface 0. An interface groups together information about endpoints; endpoints are addresses where data is transferred, and they can be either data providers or data consumers. Looking at the configuration descriptor in figure 9.12 for the Xbox controller, you can see "Num.intf: 04", meaning that the controller has 4 interfaces.

The interface descriptors make up the rest of the data output to the serial monitor by the USB_desc sketch. Each interface contains some common information, including the number of endpoints in that interface and the interface class, subclass, and protocol. It then goes on to describe each endpoint, including the endpoint address, its attributes, the maximum packet size for data, and the polling interval. We're going to concentrate on interface descriptor 00, as this is the main control and report interface for the Xbox controller.

Take a look at interface descriptor 00, as shown in figure 9.13.

You can see that figure 9.13 shows the description for interface number 00, and the interface has 2 endpoints at addresses

```
Device descriptor:
Descriptor Length:      12
Descriptor type:        01
USB version:            0200
Device class:           FF
Device Subclass:        FF
Device Protocol:        FF
Max.packet size:        08
Vendor  ID:             045E
Product ID:             028E
Revision ID:            0114
Mfg.string index:       01
Prod.string index:      02
Serial number index:    03
Number of conf.:        01

Configuration descriptor:
Total length:           0099
Num.intf:               04
Conf.value:             01
Conf.string:            00
Attr.:                  A0
Max.pwr:                FA
```

Figure 9.12 Device descriptor and configuration descriptor

```
Interface descriptor:
Intf.number:            00
Alt.:                   00
Endpoints:              02
Intf. Class:            FF
Intf. Subclass:         5D
Intf. Protocol:         01
Intf.string:            00
Unknown descriptor:
Length:       11
Type:         21
Contents:     0001012581140000000013010800000705

Endpoint descriptor:
Endpoint address:       81
Attr.:                  03
Max.pkt size:           0020
Polling interval:       04

Endpoint descriptor:
Endpoint address:       01
Attr.:                  03
Max.pkt size:           0020
Polling interval:       08
```

Figure 9.13 Description of interface 00 for the Xbox controller

81 and 01 (note that these are hex values, not decimal). Bit 7 of the address determines the direction of data for the endpoint, with 1 being "in" and 0 being "out." You can see that you have one endpoint in and one out, where hex 81 equals 10000001 binary. The maximum packet size is 0x20 bytes; packet sizes tend to be given in multiples of 8.

The endpoint attribute (attr.) indicates the type of endpoint. Endpoints with an attribute of 03 are classified as interrupt endpoints. The polling interval is the period of time between interrupt transfers in milliseconds.

> **NOTE** An endpoint interrupt isn't the same as the type of interrupt we learned about back in chapter 2, where an immediate response occurred in program execution. An endpoint interrupt is an indicator that informs the host device that it has data waiting when it's polled by the host.

Also in figure 9.13, the values for intf. class, intf. subclass, and intf. protocol are given by usb.org and can be used to specify supported classes. This allows many devices to be supported by a few class drivers instead of requiring individual drivers for each device. For example, a value of 03 for intf. class, according to the USB protocol, would represent a class interface for a human interface device (HID), like a mouse, keyboard, or joystick. For the Xbox controller, the value of FF means the class is vendor-specific, which potentially makes your job a little more complicated.

You've now learned about the Xbox controller's device and configuration descriptors, interface 00 and its associated data endpoints, how often the endpoints should be polled, and the maximum sizes for the packets of data. Next we'll look at the format of the data packets or reports.

9.2.4   *Xbox reporting for duty*

In a conventional USB device, we could delve to a deeper level and look at the data-packet report formats for each endpoint. But as we've seen, the Xbox controller masks that information and describes its interface classes as vendor specific. We need to look to other sources to get information about the report formats.

An excellent online source in this case is the Free60 GamePad page, at http://free60.org/GamePad. The input report format for interface 00 is summarized in table 9.4.

Table 9.4   Xbox input report for interface 00

Offset	Length (bits)	Description
0x00.0	8	Message type
0x01.0	8	Packet size
0x02.0	1	D-pad up
0x02.1	1	D-pad down

Table 9.4   Xbox input report for interface 00 *(continued)*

Offset	Length (bits)	Description
0x02.2	1	D-pad left
0x02.3	1	D-pad right
0x02.4	1	Start button
0x02.5	1	Back button
0x02.6	1	Left stick press
0x02.7	1	Right stick press
0x03.0	1	Left buffer (LB) button
0x03.1	1	Right buffer (RB) button
0x03.2	1	Xbox logo button
0x03.3	1	Unused
0x03.4	1	Button A
0x03.5	1	Button B
0x03.6	1	Button X
0x03.7	1	Button Y
0x04.0	8	Left trigger
0x05.0	8	Right trigger
0x06.0	16	Left stick, *x* axis
0x08.0	16	Left stick, *y* axis
0x0a.0	16	Right stick, *x* axis
0x0c.0	16	Right stick, *y* axis
0x0e.0	48	Unused

Message types with a value of 0x00 are normal input report messages. Those with a value of 0x01 are LED status messages. Eight-bit values are unsigned, and 16-bit values are signed little-endian. There are also other reports—messages that control the Xbox controller's LEDs and rumble motors—but we're going to concentrate on input reports with a message type of 0x00.

You've now gathered quite a lot of information about the Xbox controller, but what's the best way to use this information? You could write a driver from scratch, or you could build upon an existing sketch or library. A good place to start is by looking at the examples provided with the USB Host Shield; these are all very comprehensive and cover a variety of USB devices.

Big-endian and little-endian

Big-endian and little-endian describe the order in which a sequence of bytes representing a value is stored. Big-endian is where the "big end" (most significant value) is stored first. Little-endian is where the "little end" (least significant value) is stored first. In a big-endian computer, the two bytes required for the hexadecimal number FC62 would be stored as FC62. In a little-endian system, it would be stored as 62FC.

The big-endian and little-endian names derive from Jonathan Swift's *Gulliver's Travels*, in which the Big-endians were a political faction that broke their eggs at the large end and rebelled against the Lilliputian emperor who required his subjects, the Little-endians, to break their eggs at the small end.

You know that the Xbox controller is really a HID device. You also know that it doesn't provide a comprehensive description of its report format, but from research you do know what the format is. The closest examples provided with the USB Host Shield library are the boot keyboard and mouse examples. These use a known report format to parse the report messages sent by these USB devices.

9.2.5 *Let's boot it*

Mice and keyboards have a *default* or *boot* configuration that can be read. For example, all mice have a boot protocol of six bytes that provides information about which button has been pressed and the x and y coordinates of the mouse position. Similarly, keyboards have a default boot protocol, with the data returned providing information about which key has been pressed.

A default boot configuration enables the device to be easily read by a variety of host devices. Devices using a given configuration will all return at least this type of information, even though they may have more advanced capabilities, such as the sound controls on some keyboards or the scroll wheel on some mice.

You know the format of the reports and details for the interface produced by the Xbox controller, so you can do the same thing for the Xbox controller as for mice and keyboards—you can treat an Xbox controller as a boot device.

Let's now look at the steps involved in interfacing the Arduino with the Xbox controller.

9.2.6 *Interfacing with code*

The HID boot examples use a number of libraries. The library we're interested in is the hidboot library; this is made up of two files, hidboot.h and hidboot.cpp.

NOTE On Windows, the files are normally found in the My Documents/ Arduino/libraries/usbhost folder; on Mac OS X they're in the Documents/ Arduino/libraries/usbhost folder.

To dig deeper, carefully study these files, as the code you're going to use is closely based on them, with a few tweaks here and there. To keep the code listings shorter in the book, the code provided doesn't include error-checking, but it has been heavily commented to walk you through the important parts. To see good examples that include error checking, please examine the code library installed with the USB Host Shield.

The files you'll be using in this example are included in the source code for this book: the Xboxhidboot library (listing 9.2) and the Arduino sketch (listing 9.3). The Xboxhidboot library will handle lower-level communication, and we'll use it in conjunction with an Arduino sketch we'll look at shortly. Rather than write the Xboxhidboot library from scratch, we'll highlight the main functionality of the individual files in this section.

Let's start with Xboxhidboot.h, which will be the main communicator between the USB and the Xbox controller.

CODE FOR XBOXHIDBOOT.H

Xboxhidboot.h performs a number of tasks including setting the structure of the report, listing the functions for the individual Xbox controller controls, and initializing the Xbox controller when it's plugged into the USB Host Shield. It establishes communication with the controller and polls for reports, which are then parsed to establish which controls have been pressed.

CODE FOR XBOXHIDBOOT.CPP

Xboxhidboot.cpp, shown in the following listing, is the complementary file to Xboxhidboot.h and is the code that actually parses the returned report. In this section, we'll quickly look at how the data is parsed.

Listing 9.2   Xboxhidboot.cpp

```
#include "xboxhidboot.h"
void XboxReportParser::Parse(HID *hid, bool is_rpt_id, uint8_t
    len, uint8_t *buf)
{
    XBOXINFO    *pmi = (XBOXINFO*)buf;

    if (buf[2] != 0)                              ⟵─┐  Check byte for
    {                                               │  button data
        if ((buf[2] >> 0) & 1)
            onDPadUp(pmi);

        if ((buf[2] >> 1) & 1)
            onDPadDown(pmi);

        if ((buf[2] >> 2) & 1)
            onDPadLeft(pmi);

        if ((buf[2] >> 3) & 1)
            onDPadRight(pmi);

        if ((buf[2] >> 4) & 1)
            onStartButton(pmi);

        if ((buf[2] >> 5) & 1)
            onBackButton(pmi);

        if ((buf[2] >> 6) & 1)
            onLeftStickPress(pmi);
```

```
        if ((buf[2] >> 7) & 1)
            onRightStickPress(pmi);
    }
    if (buf[3] != 0)                                    ◁──┐ Check byte for
    {                                                      │ button data
        if ((buf[3] >> 0) & 1)
            onButtonLB(pmi);

        if ((buf[3] >> 1) & 1)
            onButtonRB(pmi);

        if ((buf[3] >> 2) & 1)
            onButtonLogo(pmi);

        if ((buf[3] >> 4) & 1)
            onButtonA(pmi);

        if ((buf[3] >> 5) & 1)
            onButtonB(pmi);

        if ((buf[3] >> 6) & 1)
            onButtonX(pmi);

        if ((buf[3] >> 7) & 1)
            onButtonY(pmi);
    }
    if (pmi->bmLeftTrigger != 0)                        ◁──┐ Check trigger
        onLeftTrigger(pmi);                                │ values
    if (pmi->bmRightTrigger != 0)                       ◁──┘
        onRightTrigger(pmi);

    if (prevState.xboxInfo.bmLeftStickXAxis != pmi->bmLeftStickXAxis
⇒      || prevState.xboxInfo.bmLeftStickYAxis != pmi->bmLeftStickYAxis)  ◁──┐
        onLeftStickMove(pmi);                                               │ Check for
                                                                            │ joystick
    if (prevState.xboxInfo.bmRightStickXAxis != pmi->bmRightStickXAxis      │ moves
⇒      || prevState.xboxInfo.bmRightStickYAxis != pmi->bmRightStickYAxis) ◁─┘
        onRightStickMove(pmi);

    for (uint8_t i=0; i<14; i++)
        prevState.bInfo[i] = buf[i];                    ◁──┐ Copy buffer to
};                                                         │ previous state
```

The code checks bytes two and three for button data. If data is present, it checks the byte bit by bit. Next it checks the values of the Xbox controller triggers, and then it checks the controller joysticks. Finally, the buf buffer is copied to the prevState buffer.

Now let's look at the sketch that brings this all together.

9.2.7   *Xboxhid.ino*

This is the sketch that brings everything together.

Listing 9.3   Xboxhid.ino complete listing

```
#include <avr/pgmspace.h>

#include <avrpins.h>
#include <max3421e.h>
```

```
#include <usbhost.h>
#include <usb_ch9.h>
#include <Usb.h>
#include <usbhub.h>
#include <avr/pgmspace.h>
#include <address.h>
#include <Xboxhidboot.h>
```

1 Include Xbox library

```
#include <printhex.h>
#include <message.h>
#include <hexdump.h>
#include <parsetools.h>
```

```
class XboxRptParser : public XboxReportParser
```

2 Declare parser class

```
{
protected:
    virtual void onDPadUp            (XBOXINFO *mi);
    virtual void onDPadDown       (XBOXINFO *mi);
    virtual void onDPadLeft        (XBOXINFO *mi);
    virtual void onDPadRight       (XBOXINFO *mi);
    virtual void onStartButton      (XBOXINFO *mi);
    virtual void onBackButton       (XBOXINFO *mi);
    virtual void onLeftStickPress    (XBOXINFO *mi);
    virtual void onRightStickPress    (XBOXINFO *mi);
    virtual void onButtonLB         (XBOXINFO *mi);
    virtual void onButtonRB         (XBOXINFO *mi);
    virtual void onButtonLogo       (XBOXINFO *mi);
    virtual void onButtonA          (XBOXINFO *mi);
    virtual void onButtonB          (XBOXINFO *mi);
    virtual void onButtonX          (XBOXINFO *mi);
    virtual void onButtonY          (XBOXINFO *mi);
    virtual void onLeftTrigger      (XBOXINFO *mi);
    virtual void onRightTrigger     (XBOXINFO *mi);
    virtual void onLeftStickMove     (XBOXINFO *mi);
    virtual void onRightStickMove     (XBOXINFO *mi);
};
```

3 Declare functions

```
void  XboxRptParser::onDPadUp (XBOXINFO *mi)
{
    Serial.println("D Pad Up");
};
void XboxRptParser::onDPadDown     (XBOXINFO *mi)
{
    Serial.println("D Pad Down");
};
void XboxRptParser::onDPadLeft        (XBOXINFO *mi)
{
    Serial.println("D Pad Left");
};
void XboxRptParser::onDPadRight       (XBOXINFO *mi)
{
    Serial.println("D Pad Right");
};
void XboxRptParser::onStartButton (XBOXINFO *mi)
{
    Serial.println("Start Button");
```

4 Button functions

```
};
void XboxRptParser::onBackButton    (XBOXINFO *mi)
{
    Serial.println("Back Button");
};
void XboxRptParser::onLeftStickPress    (XBOXINFO *mi)
{
    Serial.println("Left Stick Press");
};
void XboxRptParser::onRightStickPress    (XBOXINFO *mi)
{
    Serial.println("Right Stick Press");
};
void XboxRptParser::onButtonLB    (XBOXINFO *mi)
{
    Serial.println("Button LB Press");
};
void XboxRptParser::onButtonRB    (XBOXINFO *mi)
{
    Serial.println("Button RB Press");
};
void XboxRptParser::onButtonLogo (XBOXINFO *mi)
{
    Serial.println("Button Logo Press");
};
void XboxRptParser::onButtonA    (XBOXINFO *mi)
{
    Serial.println("Button A Press");
};
void XboxRptParser::onButtonB    (XBOXINFO *mi)
{
    Serial.println("Button B Press");
};
void XboxRptParser::onButtonX    (XBOXINFO *mi)
{
    Serial.println("Button X Press");
};
void XboxRptParser::onButtonY    (XBOXINFO *mi)
{
    Serial.println("Button Y Press");
};
void XboxRptParser::onLeftTrigger (XBOXINFO *mi)
{
    Serial.print("Left Trigger: ");
    Serial.println(mi->bmLeftTrigger, DEC);
};
void XboxRptParser::onRightTrigger (XBOXINFO *mi)
{
    Serial.print("Right Trigger: ");
    Serial.println(mi->bmRightTrigger, DEC);
};

void XboxRptParser::onLeftStickMove (XBOXINFO *mi)
{
```

4 Button functions

```
    Serial.print("Left stick X Axis  = ");
    Serial.print(mi->bmLeftStickXAxis, DEC);
    Serial.print(" Y Axis = ");
    Serial.println(mi->bmLeftStickYAxis, DEC);
};
void XboxRptParser::onRightStickMove (XBOXINFO *mi)
{
    Serial.print("Right stick X Axis  = ");
    Serial.print(mi->bmRightStickXAxis, DEC);
    Serial.print(" Y Axis = ");
    Serial.println(mi->bmRightStickYAxis, DEC);
};

USB      Usb;

HIDBoot<HID_PROTOCOL_KEYBOARD>     Xbox(&Usb);

uint32_t next_time;

XboxRptParser Prs;

void setup()
{
    Serial.begin( 115200 );
    Serial.println("Start Xbox");

    if (Usb.Init() == -1)
        Serial.println("OSC did not start.");

    delay( 200 );

    next_time = millis() + 5000;

    Xbox.SetReportParser(0, (HIDReportParser*)&Prs);
}

void loop()
{
    Usb.Task();
}
```

④ Button functions

Create USB instance

⑤ Initialize USB device

Set Xbox parser

Task loop

You first include the Xbox library you created in your sketch to get access to all the functions in that library **❶**. The report parser class is created **❷**, and the functions for the individual buttons and controls are declared **❸**. The functions are created **❹**, and in each function you print the status for the relevant button to the serial console monitor.

In the sketch's `setup` routine, the USB device, Xbox controller, is initialized and the report parser is set **❺**. In the sketch's `loop` routine, the USB device is called periodically by `Usb.Task` to check its state and return any report data.

That completes the software side of controlling an Xbox controller; let's now move on to testing it with the Arduino hardware.

9.2.8 *Hardware connections and testing*

Plug the USB Host Shield onto the Arduino and then plug in your Xbox controller, as shown in figure 9.14.

Figure 9.14   Xbox controller connected to USB Host Shield and Arduino

With everything plugged in, upload the Xbox-hid.ino sketch to the Arduino and open the serial monitor. Try pressing different buttons and moving the joysticks and D-pad, and observe the output in the serial monitor. Note that the monitor baud rate should be set to 115,200. Figure 9.15 shows some typical output.

You've now learned how to connect an Arduino to an Xbox controller using a USB Host Shield, and in the process you gained a basic grounding in working with USB peripherals. The software listings could be much improved by adding error-checking code, and maybe that could be your next step.

9.3   Summary

In this chapter, you've seen how to connect an Arduino to two types of game devices: a Wii Nunchuk and an Xbox controller.

The connection to the Wii Nunchuk was relatively straightforward, and in the process you saw a practical application of the Wire library.

The connection to the Xbox controller was much more complex, both from a hardware and a software point of view. You needed to use a USB Host Shield because the controller is a USB device. The host shield can be used to connect to a variety of other devices including mice, keyboards, USB-controlled cameras, and other peripherals.

```
0014000000000A640F07A680292F8000000000000
Left stick X Axis  = 16550 Y Axis = 31472
0014000000000A640AC79680292F8000000000000
Left stick X Axis  = 16550 Y Axis = 31148
0014000000000A6406878680292F8000000000000
Left stick X Axis  = 16550 Y Axis = 30824
00140000000001541747568 0292F8000000000000
Left stick X Axis  = 16661 Y Axis = 30068
0014000000000A640496E680292F8000000000000
Left stick X Axis  = 16550 Y Axis = 28233
0014000000000A6402964680292F8000000000000
Left stick X Axis  = 16550 Y Axis = 25641
00140000000001541B753680292F8000000000000
Left stick X Axis  = 16661 Y Axis = 21431
0014000000000B539B043680292F8000000000000
Left stick X Axis  = 14773 Y Axis = 17328
0014000000005E353D33D80292F8000000000000
Left stick X Axis  = 13662 Y Axis = 13117
Right stick X Axis  = 728 Y Axis = -1902
0014000000000F9208D0E680292F8000000000000
Left stick X Axis  = 8441 Y Axis = 3725
Right stick X Axis  = 616 Y Axis = -1902
0014000000008613E909680292F8000000000000
Left stick X Axis  = 4998 Y Axis = 2537
00140000000017133908680292F8000000000000
Left stick X Axis  = 4887 Y Axis = 2105
00140000000001713F506D80292F8000000000000
Left stick X Axis  = 4887 Y Axis = 1781
Right stick X Axis  = 728 Y Axis = -1902
0014080000000A8126107680292F8000000000000
D Pad Right
Left stick X Axis  = 4776 Y Axis = 1889
Right stick X Axis  = 616 Y Axis = -1902
00140800000017136107680292F8000000000000
D Pad Right
Left stick X Axis  = 4887 Y Axis = 1889
00140000000017136107680292F8000000000000
0014000000000A8126107680225F8000000000000
Left stick X Axis  = 4776 Y Axis = 1889
Right stick X Axis  = 616 Y Axis = -2011
```

Figure 9.15   Typical output from the Xbox controller

This is just the beginning! The real benefit of these controllers is that they're afford-able devices offering a number of easily manipulated controls at your fingertips. There's nothing stopping you from connecting a graphical LCD as discussed in chapter 7, and using the joysticks on the Xbox controller to make your own Etch-A-Sketch-type of device. In fact, using an accelerometer, you can even shake the devices to clear the screen, just like the real thing. Hopefully you see the potential.

Next, in chapter 10, we're going to look at how to connect the Arduino to iOS devices like the iPad, iPhone, and iPod Touch.

Integrating the Arduino with iOS

The focus of this chapter isn't iOS programming but instead the fundamentals of how to connect the Arduino to your iOS device. In this chapter, which is for those programming on a Mac only, we're going to look at using the Arduino with an iPhone or iPad.

We recommend several other Manning books for learning iOS programming. If you're new to coding, we suggest reading *iOS in Practice* by Bear Cahill. For more experienced programmers, we suggest either *iPhone and iPad in Action* by Brandon

Trebitowski, Christopher Allen, and Shannon Appelcline, or *Hello iOS Development* by Lou Franco and Eitan Mendelowitz.

Apple has sold over 400 million iOS devices since they first launched the iPhone in 2007. You may have an iPhone or iPod touch in your pocket right now, and you might be wondering if you can use it with an Arduino. Well, you're in luck! Previously if you wanted to connect an iOS device directly to an Arduino, the iOS device would need to be what is called "jail broken." This invalidates the warranty and can cause other problems. Fortunately, in 2011 Redpark Product Development released a serial cable approved for use by Apple. The Redpark serial cable can be used to connect directly to a range of iOS devices including the iPhone 3GS, iPhone 4, iPad 1, iPad 2, and iPod touch version 4 and above. For devices that use the Apple Lightning connector, adapters are available to connect them to the Redpark serial cable. At time of writing, Redpark was developing a serial cable that would directly connect to Lightning connector devices.

The Redpark serial cable has opened up many opportunities to use an Arduino with an iOS device. As of yet, few examples are available, but we expect to see many exciting projects appear as more people get the cable.

This chapter will discuss the basic tools you'll need and show you how to connect the Arduino to an iOS device. First, we'll see how to connect the cable to an Arduino and how to send commands from your iOS device to control devices connected to the Arduino. Then we'll demonstrate how data from a sensor connected to an Arduino can be sent to an iOS device and displayed on its screen.

iOS Developer Program

To complete and run the example code in this chapter you'll need to become a member of the iOS Developer Program for an annual fee of $99. Details can be obtained from http://developer.apple.com/programs/ios/.

To complete this chapter, you'll need the following:

- A Mac computer capable of running Xcode 4.0 or above
- An iOS device
- An Arduino
- A Redpark serial cable
- A Lightning adapter, if required
- The Redpark SDK
- A RS232 to TTL adapter
- Xcode 4.0 or above
- A breadboard
- A selection of jumper wires
- A colored LED

- A 200 ohm resistor
- A Sharp GP2D12 IR distance sensor

Let's get started by taking a detailed look at the most important part: the connection between an Arduino and your iOS device.

10.1   *Connecting your device to the Arduino*

In this section, we'll look mainly at the hardware and software needed to connect an Arduino to an iOS device. We'll start with the Redpark serial cable, which at one end plugs directly into an iOS device and at the other plugs into the RS232 to TTL adapter, which in turn connects to the Arduino. Once we've looked at what's required to physically connect an Arduino to an iOS device, we can have a more detailed look at the software side.

10.1.1   *The Redpark serial cable*

The Redpark serial cable, shown in figure 10.1, is available either directly from Redpark Product Development (http://redpark.com/) or from one of the suppliers listed on their website. After purchasing the Redpark serial cable you'll need to download the Redpark SDK from http://redpark.com/c2db9_Downloads.html.

The Redpark SDK download includes a readme file that tells you how to install the SDK. There's also a brief instruction manual giving details about the software library and its use. You can try out the example program that's included to test the cable's functionality with your device. The 1-meter-long cable can be used with devices running iOS 4.3.x or later and communicates serially at a maximum rate of 57.6 Kbps.

One end of the cable plugs into your iOS device, and the other is terminated with a DB-9 male connector, all pins connected. The pinout is shown in figure 10.2.

Table 10.1 gives a listing of all the pins for the DB-9 male connector. For this chapter, we only need to worry about the RX and TX pins.

Figure 10.1   The Redpark Product Development serial cable for use with older iOS devices

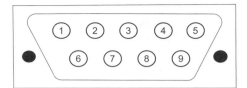

Figure 10.2   Pinout of male RS232 DB-9 connector

Table 10.1   Pinouts of RS232 DB-9 male connector

Pin	Name	Description
1	DCD	Data carrier detect
2	RX	Receive data
3	TX	Transmit data
4	DTR	Data terminal ready
5	GND	Ground
6	DSR	Data set ready
7	RTS	Request to send
8	CTS	Clear to send
9	RI	Ring indicator

The RS232 standard uses voltages of +12 volts and –12 volts, whereas the Arduino requires TTL-level voltages, 0 and 5, so you'll need to use a TTL to RS232 adapter. One example is the P4B, available from www.wulfden.org/TheShoppe/pa/index.shtml#P4 and pictured in figure 10.3. The P4B TTL to RS232 adapter is supplied as a kit requiring soldering, but it's very simple to assemble.

The female DB-9 connector plugs into the DB-9 male connector of the Redpark serial cable.

To complete the hardware setup, the TTL to RS232 adapter needs to be connected to the Arduino.

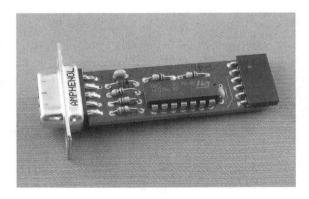

Figure 10.3   P4B TTL to RS232 adapter

Figure 10.4   P4B TTL to RS232 adapter connected to the Arduino

10.1.2 *The final connection*

You need to make the final connection between the TTL to RS232 adapter and the Arduino. This just requires four connections: 5 volts, ground, RX, and TX.

> **NOTE**   The RX of the adapter connects to the TX of the Arduino, and the TX of the adapter connects to the Arduino RX.

Figure 10.4 shows the Arduino connected to the TTL to RS232 adapter.

We've covered the hardware connections. Now it's time to have a look at the code and see how you can use the Redpark SDK to create your first iOS app.

10.2 *iOS code*

You've seen how an Arduino can be connected to your iOS device, and you've followed the readme to install the Redpark serial cable SDK. Now it's time to build your first app.

To program your iOS device, you'll need a copy of Xcode 4.0 or above. Xcode is the IDE provided by Apple to enable users to develop programs and applications for Apple products. To develop and deploy applications for iOS devices and to download the latest version of Xcode, you'll need to be a member of the iOS developer program, as mentioned in the introduction to the chapter.

Once you've got Xcode downloaded and installed, you can get started by opening up Xcode.

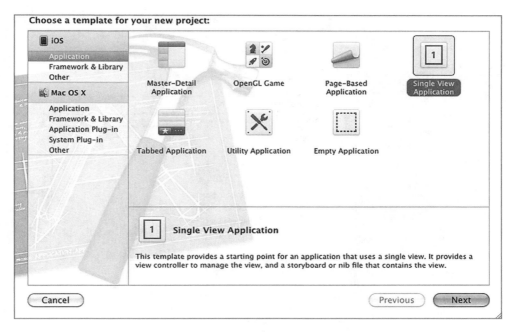

Figure 10.5 Select Single View Application

10.2.1 Creating a single-view application in Xcode

You're now going to create a single-view application, which is the simplest type of app you can create. For this example, you're going to create a universal project that can be deployed to either an iPhone or an iPad running iOS 5.0 or greater. The project will initially include a Switch object that can be used to turn an LED on and off.

In Xcode, select iOS Application and then Single View Application as shown in figure 10.5, and click Next.

> **NOTE** For more information on creating and building apps, check out Bear Cahill's *iOS in Practice* (Manning, 2012).

Complete the project details, as shown in figure 10.6, and click Next. We've called the project IOSArduino.

Select Create in the next dialog box. The basic project will now be generated, and you'll be shown the Xcode IDE.

Select MainStoryboard_iPhone.storyboard to get the initial view shown in figure 10.7.

Drag a Switch object from the object library onto the viewer, in the center, and set its state to Off, as shown in figure 10.8.

You next need to connect the Switch control to an outlet. From the menu, select View > Assistant > Show Assistant Editor. The editor should open ViewController.h. Ctrl-click on the Switch, select New Referencing Outlet from the context menu, drag

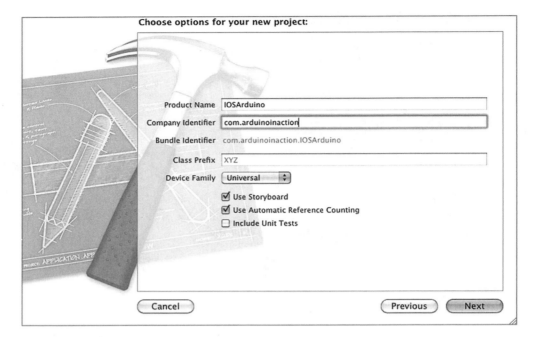

Figure 10.6   Complete the project details.

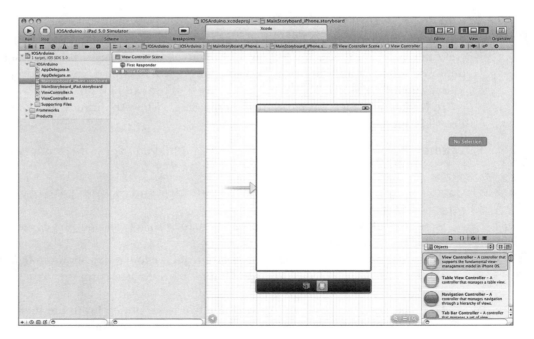

Figure 10.7   MainStoryboard_iPhone.storyboard view

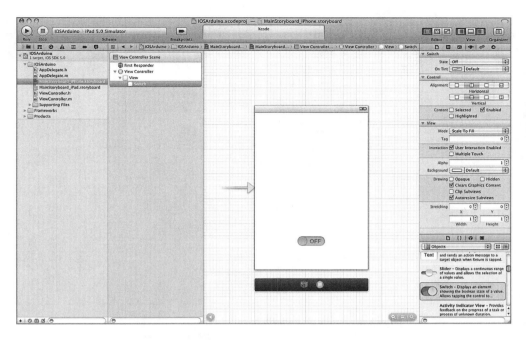

Figure 10.8   Switch object dragged onto the viewer with its state set to Off

to just above the @end in the editor window, and release. Name the outlet `toggle-Switch`, as shown in figure 10.9. Click Connect to complete adding the outlet.

You next need to add a new action by repeating the Ctrl-click on the Switch, selecting Value Changed from the context menu, and dragging it to @end. Name the action `toggleLED`, as shown in figure 10.10, and click Connect to complete the action.

The next step is to import the Redpark serial cable library. Select File > Add Files to IOSArduino, and navigate to the Redpark serial SDK folder. Ours was in the home folder, but it can be in root. Select the inc and lib folders, make sure the Copy Items into Destination Group's Folder (if Needed) option is selected (see figure 10.11), and click Add.

Next, you need to import the external accessory framework. Click the project in the left pane, select the Build Phases tab, and then open the "Link Binary With" section. Click + (as shown in figure 10.12), locate the external accessory framework, and add it.

That's the framework of the project set-up. Now you need to add some code to your view controller.

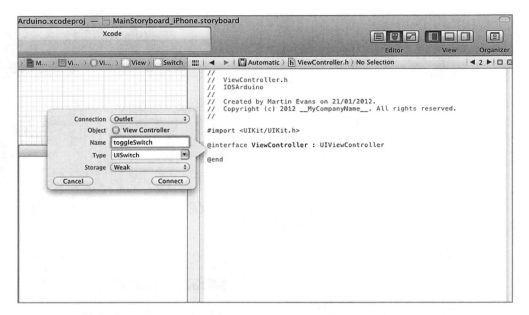

Figure 10.9   Name the outlet toggleSwitch.

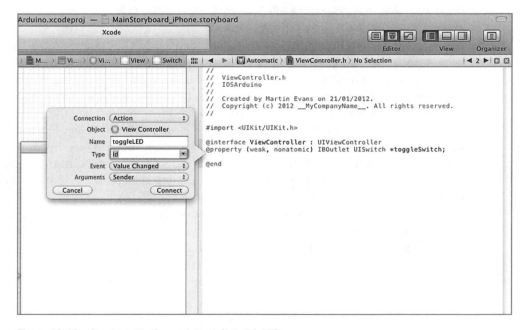

Figure 10.10   Create an action and name it toggleLED.

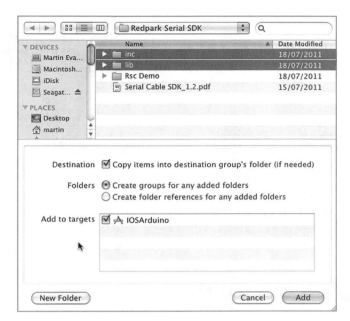

Figure 10.11 Import the Redpark serial SDK files.

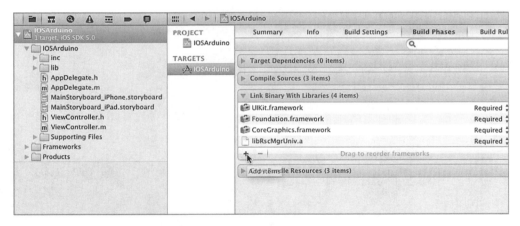

Figure 10.12 Add the external accessory framework to the project.

10.2.2 *Writing the code*

The code for the view controller, ViewController.h, is shown in the following listing.

Listing 10.1 ViewController.h

```
#import <UIKit/UIKit.h>
#import "RscMgr.h"

#define BUFFER_LEN 1024
```

❶ Import cable library and set buffer length

```
@interface ViewController : UIViewController
    <RscMgrDelegate> {

    RscMgr *rscMgr;
    UInt8 rxBuffer[BUFFER_LEN];
    UInt8 txBuffer[BUFFER_LEN];

    UISwitch *toggleSwitch;
}
@property (retain, nonatomic) IBOutlet
    UISwitch *toggleSwitch;
- (IBAction)toggleLED:(id)sender;

@end
```

> 2 Add delegate

> 3 Set variables for cable

> 4 Add variable for switch

> 5 Change "weak" to "retain"

You import the Redpark serial cable library and set the buffer length to 1024 bytes ❶, add a delegate to the interface ❷, set the serial cable variables ❸, add the switch variable ❹, and change weak to retain ❺.

The next step is to make some changes to the app delegate, ViewController.m, as shown in the next listing.

Listing 10.2   ViewController.m

```
#import "ViewController.h"

@implementation ViewController
@synthesize toggleSwitch;

- (void)didReceiveMemoryWarning
{
    [super didReceiveMemoryWarning];
}

#pragma mark - View lifecycle

- (void)viewDidLoad
{
    [super viewDidLoad];
    rscMgr = [[RscMgr alloc] init];
    [rscMgr setDelegate:self];
}

- (void)viewDidUnload
{
    [self setToggleSwitch:nil];
    [super viewDidUnload];
    }

- (void)viewWillAppear:(BOOL)animated
{
    [super viewWillAppear:animated];
}

- (void)viewDidAppear:(BOOL)animated
{
    [super viewDidAppear:animated];
}
```

> ❶ Cable set-up

```
- (void)viewWillDisappear:(BOOL)animated
{
    [super viewWillDisappear:animated];
}

- (void)viewDidDisappear:(BOOL)animated
{
    [super viewDidDisappear:animated];
}
    (BOOL)shouldAutorotateToInterfaceOrientation:
    (UIInterfaceOrientation)interfaceOrientation
{
    // Return YES for supported orientations
    if ([[UIDevice currentDevice] userInterfaceIdiom]
      == UIUserInterfaceIdiomPhone) {
        return (interfaceOrientation !=
    UIInterfaceOrientationPortraitUpsideDown);
    } else {
        return YES;
    }
}
- (IBAction)toggleLED:(id)sender {
    if (toggleSwitch.on) {
        txBuffer[0] = (int) '1';
    } else {
        txBuffer[0] = (int) '0';
    }

    [rscMgr write:txBuffer Length:1];
}
#pragma mark - RSC Interface

- (void) cableConnected:(NSString *)protocol {
    [rscMgr setBaud:9600];
    [rscMgr open];
}

- (void) cableDisconnected {

}

- (void) portStatusChanged {

}

- (void) readBytesAvailable:(UInt32)numBytes {
}

- (BOOL) rscMessageReceived:(UInt8 *)msg TotalLength:(int)len {
    return NO;
}

- (void) didReceivePortConfig {
}
@end
```

❷ Toggle LED method

❸ Cable delegate methods

When the app loads, the cable is set up ❶. The toggleLED method ❷ checks the position of the switch and sends a 1 to the Arduino if ON and a 0 if OFF. The subsequent methods

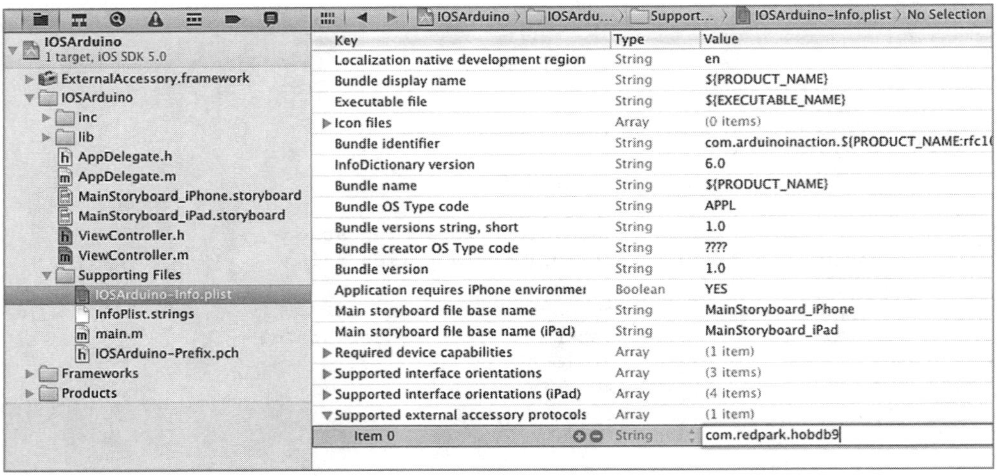

Figure 10.13   Declaring support for the Redpark serial cable

are required by the Redpark serial cable delegate ❸. Notice the `cableConnected` method, where the baud rate is set and the cable is prepared for communication.

The final step of the Xcode application, from a tip by Brian Jepson, is to declare support for the Redpark serial cable. In the project navigator, expand the Supporting Files group and click IOSArduino-Info.plist to open it. Right-click the bottom row, and from the context menu select Add Row. Select Supported External Accessory Protocols from the list. Click the triangle to the left of the key name to open up the list. In the value field for item 0, type `com.redpark.hobdb9` (see figure 10.13). Select File > Save from the menu to save the file.

Now you need to deploy the app to your iOS device. Connect your device to your development machine, and select iOS Device and Run. The Xcode IDE will run and build and then deploy the project to the iOS device.

So far in this chapter, you've learned how to connect an Arduino to an iOS device with the Redpark serial cable and an RS232 to TTL converter, and you've created a single-view application, IOSArduino, with a switch. Having completed the iOS device side of the project, you now need to develop a basic Arduino sketch that will respond to the switch in your app on the iOS device and physically switch an LED on or off on the Arduino.

10.3   *The Arduino gets involved*

It almost feels like we're back at chapter 1 where we switched an LED on and off, but you've come a long way since then. You've produced your first iOS program, but that's only half of the picture. Now you need to involve the Arduino. Let's start by looking at the Arduino sketch.

10.3.1 Sketch to switch LED from iOS device

To make things easier, this project won't introduce any new circuitry and will use the LED built into the Arduino that's connected to pin 13. Let's get started.

Open the Arduino IDE and type in the following sketch.

Listing 10.3 Switching LED from iOS device

```
void setup() {
  Serial.begin(9600);                    Set baud
  pinMode(13, OUTPUT);             ❶    rate
}

void loop() {
  if (Serial.available()) {
    byte inByte = Serial.read();
    if (inByte == '1') {
      digitalWrite(13, HIGH);
    }
    else {
      digitalWrite(13, LOW);
    }
  }
}
```

The sketch opens the serial port with a baud rate of 9,600, which matches the rate set by the iOS device ❶, and sets digital pin 13 as an output. In the main loop, the Arduino waits for a byte to be received at the serial port. If a byte is detected, the byte is read into the variable inByte. If the value of inByte is equivalent to 1, then the LED is switched on.

NOTE The maximum baud rate supported by the Redpark serial cable is 57,600.

We can now move on to testing the sketch.

10.3.2 Testing the sketch

Upload the sketch to the Arduino and then make the connections between the RS232 to TTL adapter shown previously in figure 10.4.

NOTE You'll need to upload the sketch when the RS232 to TTL adapter isn't connected to pins 0 and 1 of the Arduino, as this could prevent the upload occurring.

The final piece is to connect the iOS device, the Redpark serial cable, and the RS232 to TTL adapter together. It's probably best to power the Arduino from an external power supply, as shown in figure 10.14.

Start the IOSArduino app on your device and turn the switch on and off. If everything is connected correctly, the LED connected to pin 13 on the Arduino should turn on and off.

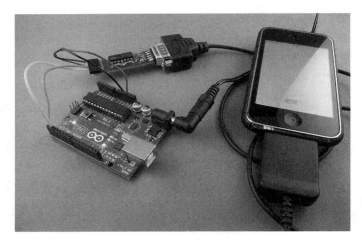

Figure 10.14 iPhone connected to Arduino, switching LED on and off

Now let's develop the iOS app further by adding a slider to control the brightness of an LED connected to the Arduino.

10.4 Doing more with Xcode

It's time to develop the IOSArduino app a little further by adding a Slider object to control the brightness of an LED connected to the Arduino. You're going to keep the Switch control, so you need a method of distinguishing whether it's the Switch or the Slider control that's sending a command from the iOS device to the Arduino.

You can start by adding a Slider control to the project.

10.4.1 Adding a Slider control

Open your IOSArduino project in the Xcode IDE, open the storyboard file, and drag a Slider control onto it, as shown in figure 10.15. In the Slider, set Minimum to 0, Maximum to 255, and Current to 0. In the View section, set Tag to 9. The tag will identify which Arduino pin you want to use.

You need to give a value to the tag for the existing switch as well, so select the Switch control and give Tag a value of 13, as shown in figure 10.16. The 13 indicates the pin that the Arduino LED is connected to.

You next need to connect the Slider control to an outlet. From the menus, select View > Assistant > Show Assistant Editor. The editor should open to display ViewController.h. Ctrl-click on the Slider, select New Referencing Outlet from the context menu, drag to just above the @end in the editor window, and release. Name the outlet moveSlider, as shown in figure 10.17. Click Connect to complete adding the outlet.

Next you need to add a new action by repeating the Ctrl-click on the Slider and dragging it to @end. Name the action brightnessLED as shown in figure 10.18, and then click Connect to complete the action.

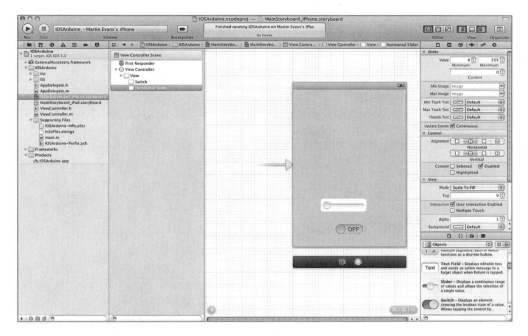

Figure 10.15   Adding a Slider control to the iPhone storyboard

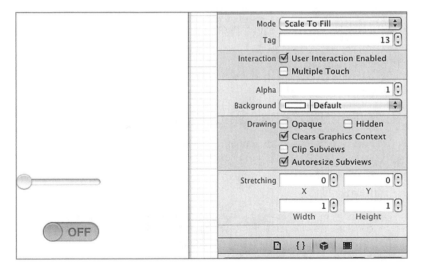

Figure 10.16   Add the Tag value 13 to the Switch.

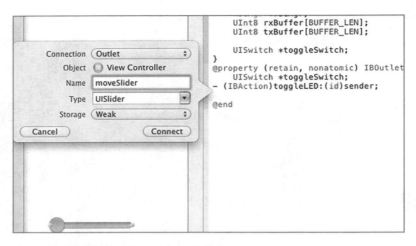

Figure 10.17   Add the `moveSlider` outlet.

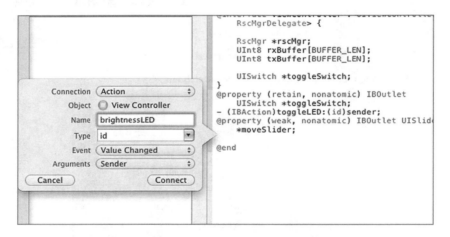

Figure 10.18   Add the `brightnessLED` action.

You now need to add some code to your view controller, ViewController.h, so that it matches the following listing.

Listing 10.4   ViewController.h

```
#import <UIKit/UIKit.h>
#import "RscMgr.h"

#define BUFFER_LEN 1024

@interface ViewController : UIViewController <RscMgrDelegate> {

    RscMgr *rscMgr;
    UInt8 rxBuffer[BUFFER_LEN];
    UInt8 txBuffer[BUFFER_LEN];
```

```
    UISwitch *toggleSwitch;
    UISlider *moveSlider;                        ←——  moveSlider
}                                                      variable
@property (retain, nonatomic) IBOutlet UISwitch *toggleSwitch;    "weak"
@property (retain, nonatomic) IBOutlet UISlider *moveSlider;  ←—  changed to
                                                                 "retain"
- (IBAction)toggleLED:(id)sender;
- (IBAction)brightnessLED:(id)sender;        ←——  brightnessLED
                                                   action
@end
```

You've added a new outlet and a new action to ViewController.h. The next step is to make some changes to the app delegate, so that when you move the Slider control a value is sent to the Arduino. Change ViewController.m so that it matches the following listing.

Listing 10.5 ViewController.m

```
#import "ViewController.h"

@implementation ViewController
@synthesize moveSlider;
@synthesize toggleSwitch;

- (void)didReceiveMemoryWarning
{
    [super didReceiveMemoryWarning];

}

#pragma mark - View lifecycle

- (void)viewDidLoad
{
    [super viewDidLoad];
    rscMgr = [[RscMgr alloc] init];
    [rscMgr setDelegate:self];
}

- (void)viewDidUnload
{
    [self setToggleSwitch:nil];
    [self setMoveSlider:nil];
    [super viewDidUnload];
}

- (void)viewWillAppear:(BOOL)animated
{
    [super viewWillAppear:animated];
}

- (void)viewDidAppear:(BOOL)animated
{
    [super viewDidAppear:animated];
}

- (void)viewWillDisappear:(BOOL)animated
{
    [super viewWillDisappear:animated];
}
```

```objc
- (void)viewDidDisappear:(BOOL)animated
{
    [super viewDidDisappear:animated];
}

- (BOOL)shouldAutorotateToInterfaceOrientation:
  (UIInterfaceOrientation)interfaceOrientation
{
    if ([[UIDevice currentDevice] userInterfaceIdiom]
    == UIUserInterfaceIdiomPhone) {
        return (interfaceOrientation !=
    UIInterfaceOrientationPortraitUpsideDown);
    } else {
        return YES;
    }
}
```

1 Tag added to method

```objc
- (IBAction)toggleLED:(id)sender {
    txBuffer[0] = [sender tag];
    txBuffer[1] = [(UISwitch *)sender isOn];
    [rscMgr write:txBuffer Length:2];

}
```

2 New method for Slider control

```objc
- (IBAction) brightnessLED:(id)sender {

    int brightness = (int)[(UISlider *)sender value];
    txBuffer[0] = [sender tag];
    txBuffer[1] = brightness;
    [rscMgr write:txBuffer Length:2];
}

#pragma mark - RSC Interface

- (void) cableConnected:(NSString *)protocol {
    [rscMgr setBaud:9600];
    [rscMgr open];
}

- (void) cableDisconnected {

}

- (void) portStatusChanged {


}

- (void) readBytesAvailable:(UInt32)numBytes {
}

- (BOOL) rscMessageReceived:(UInt8 *)msg TotalLength:(int)len {
    return NO;
}

- (void) didReceivePortConfig {
}

@end
```

In this listing, a new method is added to the original toggleLED method ❶, brightness-LED ❷. You need to distinguish which method is sending data to the Arduino, so you use the Switch's and the Slider's Tag properties to store the pin number. Each method sends two bytes to the Arduino, the first identifying the pin and the second the value.

Build the project to check for any errors. If everything builds okay, you can deploy it to your iOS device.

It's now time to look at the Arduino side of things, beginning with a sketch, and then building a circuit with an LED connected to pin 9.

You can probably see a pattern here: we're building a project and making changes a little at a time. First we work on the Xcode side and then the Arduino, testing and then returning to Xcode again. We find this helps when building more complex projects. Doing incremental development simplifies the debugging as you only need to look at the last small piece of code you added.

10.5 Arduino sliding

In this section, you're going to use the messages received from an iOS device to control switching the LED connected to pin 13 on or off and to control the brightness of an LED connected to pin 9. Listing 10.6 shows the sketch you're going to use. Although you're only adjusting the brightness of an LED in this example, a similar technique could easily be used to control the speed of a motor, as shown in chapter 5, or to control similar devices that respond to a PWM signal.

Listing 10.6   Sketch for iOS Slider control

```
#define LENGTH 2
const int ledPin = 13;
const int brightnessPin = 9;

int rxBuffer[128];
int rxIndex = 0;

void setup() {
  Serial.begin(9600);
  pinMode(ledPin, OUTPUT);
  pinMode(brightnessPin, OUTPUT);
}

void loop (){
  if (Serial.available() > 0) {

    rxBuffer[rxIndex++] = Serial.read();
    if (rxIndex == LENGTH) {

      byte pinNumber = (int)rxBuffer[0];
      byte pinValue = (int)rxBuffer[1];

      if (pinNumber == ledPin){
        if (pinValue == 1) {
          digitalWrite(ledPin, HIGH);
        }
```

```
      else {
        digitalWrite(ledPin, LOW);
      }
    }
    else if (pinNumber == brightnessPin){
      analogWrite(brightnessPin, pinValue);
    }
    rxIndex = 0;
  }
  delay(10);
  }
}
```

The sketch reads two bytes of data sent from the iOS device. The first byte identifies the pin number to be operated on. The second byte is the value to send to the identified pin. Either the ledPin is switched HIGH or LOW, or the brighnessPin's value is set to alter the brightness of the attached LED.

Let's move on and build the test circuit.

10.5.1   *Arduino slider circuit*

You're now going to build a circuit using a colored LED and a 200 ohm resistor. The LED will be connected to pin 9 of the Arduino, which will respond to commands from the iOS device and be used to vary the brightness of the attached LED. Connect the circuit together as shown in figure 10.19.

Having constructed the circuit, the next task before linking the RS232 to TTL adapter to the Arduino is to upload the sketch from listing 10.6.

10.5.2   *Testing the circuit*

With the sketch uploaded to the Arduino, you can go ahead and connect the RS232 to TTL adapter to the Arduino. Plug in the Redpark serial cable to your iOS device and the adapter.

Figure 10.19   LED connected to pin 9 on the Arduino

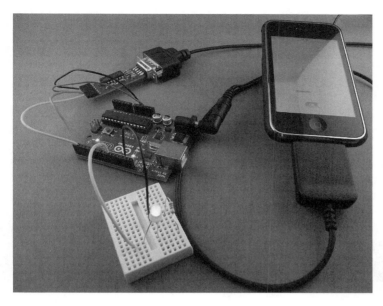

Figure 10.20 Complete setup: iPhone controlling LED's brightness

Start up the IOSArduino app and notice that when you move the slider from side to side, the LED connected to pin 9 should alter its brightness. Likewise, moving the switch between on and off should turn the onboard LED connected to pin 13 on and off. The complete setup is shown in figure 10.20.

So far, we've looked at sending data from an iOS device to an Arduino that responds to commands by either altering the brightness of an LED or switching an LED on or off. Next we're going to look at communication going the other way, sending information from the Arduino, via the serial port, and displaying it on the iOS device.

10.6 Moving data to the iOS device

So far we've explored how to control the Arduino from an iOS device, but how about reading data from a sensor and using an iOS device to display it? In this section, we're going to add a GP2D12 IR distance sensor, which you first encountered in chapter 6.

Let's complete the iOS side of the project.

10.6.1 Xcode coding

Start up Xcode and load the IOSArduino project. You want to add two labels to your project: one that displays the static text "Distance" and another that displays the distance value.

Start by dragging a Label object onto the view, and set its text value to Distance. Next, drag a second Label next to the first and set its text value to 0.00. Your view should now look like figure 10.21.

Figure 10.21 Labels added to the view

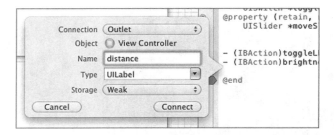

Figure 10.22   Adding the distance outlet

You next need to connect the second label to an outlet. Select View > Assistant > Show Assistant Editor from the menus. The editor should open in ViewController.h. Ctrl-click on the label and drag to just above the @end in the editor window, and release. Name the outlet distance as shown in figure 10.22. Click Connect to complete adding the outlet.

You now need to add some code to your view controller, ViewController.h, so that it matches the following listing.

Listing 10.7   ViewController.h

```
#import <UIKit/UIKit.h>
#import "RscMgr.h"

#define BUFFER_LEN 1024

@interface ViewController : UIViewController <RscMgrDelegate> {

    RscMgr *rscMgr;
    UInt8 rxBuffer[BUFFER_LEN];
    UInt8 txBuffer[BUFFER_LEN];

    UISwitch *toggleSwitch;
    UISlider *moveSlider;
    UILabel *distance;                                 ❶ Label variable
}
@property (retain, nonatomic) IBOutlet UISwitch *toggleSwitch;
@property (retain, nonatomic) IBOutlet UISlider *moveSlider;
@property (retain, nonatomic) IBOutlet UILabel *distance;      New outlet

- (IBAction)toggleLED:(id)sender;
- (IBAction)brightnessLED:(id)sender;

@end
```

This version of ViewController.h adds a new label variable ❶ so you can display the distance, as well as a new outlet. Note the change from weak to retain.

The next step is to make changes to ViewController.m by adding some code to the readBytesAvailable method of the Redpark serial cable delegate. Make the changes so that they match the following listing.

Listing 10.8   ViewController.m

```
#import "ViewController.h"

@implementation ViewController
@synthesize distance;
```

```objc
@synthesize moveSlider;
@synthesize toggleSwitch;

- (void)didReceiveMemoryWarning
{
    [super didReceiveMemoryWarning];
}

#pragma mark - View lifecycle

- (void)viewDidLoad
{
    [super viewDidLoad];
    rscMgr = [[RscMgr alloc] init];
    [rscMgr setDelegate:self];
}

- (void)viewDidUnload
{
    [self setToggleSwitch:nil];
    [self setMoveSlider:nil];
    [self setDistance:nil];
    [super viewDidUnload];
}

- (void)viewWillAppear:(BOOL)animated
{
    [super viewWillAppear:animated];
}

- (void)viewDidAppear:(BOOL)animated
{
    [super viewDidAppear:animated];
}

- (void)viewWillDisappear:(BOOL)animated
{
    [super viewWillDisappear:animated];
}

- (void)viewDidDisappear:(BOOL)animated
{
    [super viewDidDisappear:animated];
}

- (BOOL)shouldAutorotateToInterfaceOrientation:
    (UIInterfaceOrientation)interfaceOrientation
{
    if ([[UIDevice currentDevice] userInterfaceIdiom] ==
        UIUserInterfaceIdiomPhone) {
        return (interfaceOrientation !=
            UIInterfaceOrientationPortraitUpsideDown);
    } else {
        return YES;
    }
}

- (IBAction)toggleLED:(id)sender {
    txBuffer[0] = [sender tag];
```

```
    txBuffer[1] = [(UISwitch *)sender isOn];
    [rscMgr write:txBuffer Length:2];

}

- (IBAction) brightnessLED:(id)sender {

    int brightness = (int)[(UISlider *)sender value];
    txBuffer[0] = [sender tag];
    txBuffer[1] = brightness;
    [rscMgr write:txBuffer Length:2];
}

#pragma mark - RSC Interface

- (void) cableConnected:(NSString *)protocol {
    [rscMgr setBaud:9600];
    [rscMgr open];
}

- (void) cableDisconnected {

}

- (void) portStatusChanged {

}

- (void) readBytesAvailable:(UInt32)numBytes {
    NSString *string = nil;
    [rscMgr read:rxBuffer Length:numBytes];
    for (int i=0; i < numBytes; ++i){
        if (string) {
            string = [NSString stringWithFormat:@"%@%c",
    string, rxBuffer[i]];
        } else {
            string = [NSString stringWithFormat:@"%c", rxBuffer[i]];
        }
        self.distance.text = string;
    }
}

- (BOOL) rscMessageReceived:(UInt8 *)msg TotalLength:(int)len {
    return NO;
}

- (void) didReceivePortConfig {
}

- (IBAction)switchOnOff:(id)sender {
}
- (IBAction)controlSlider:(id)sender {
}
@end
```

❶ **readBytesAvailable method**

Notice the new code added to the readBytesAvailable method ❶. This is a callback function that's called when data is received by the iOS device. The method reads the bytes as a string and outputs the result to the distance label.

Figure 10.23 GP2D12 infrared sensor added to circuit

That completes the iOS part of the code, and it can now be uploaded to your iOS device. We're next going to look at the Arduino side of things.

10.6.2 *The GP2D12 IR distance sensor*

Now you're going to use the GP2D12 IR distance sensor that was discussed in chapter 6. The sensor only requires three connections: ground, 5 volts, and signal, which is connected to analog pin 0 on the Arduino (as was shown in circuit diagram 6.7 in chapter 6).

Add the sensor to your existing circuit. The completed circuit is shown in figure 10.23.

We now need to look at the Arduino sketch. You can use some of the code from chapter 6. The complete sketch is shown in the following listing. Enter the sketch into the Arduino IDE and upload it to the Arduino.

Listing 10.9   Sketch to read distance from GP2D12 sensor

```
#define LENGTH 2
const int ledPin = 13;
const int brightnessPin = 9;
const int RANGER_PIN = A0;

int rxBuffer[128];
int rxIndex = 0;                                    ❶ Function to
                                                      read distance
float read_gp2d12_range(byte pin) {
  int dist = analogRead(pin);
  if (dist < 3)
    return -1;
  return (6787.0 /((float)dist - 3.0)) - 4.0;
}
```

```
void setup() {
  Serial.begin(9600);
  pinMode(ledPin, OUTPUT);
  pinMode(brightnessPin, OUTPUT);
}

void loop (){
  float distance = read_gp2d12_range(RANGER_PIN);
  delay(400);
  if (distance != -1) {
    Serial.println(distance);
  }

  if (Serial.available() > 0) {
    rxBuffer[rxIndex++] = Serial.read();

    if (rxIndex == LENGTH) {
      byte pinNumber = (int)rxBuffer[0];
      byte pinValue = (int)rxBuffer[1];

      if (pinNumber == ledPin){
        if (pinValue == 1) {
          digitalWrite(ledPin, HIGH);
        }
        else {
          digitalWrite(ledPin, LOW);
        }
      }
      else if (pinNumber == brightnessPin){
        analogWrite(brightnessPin, pinValue);
      }

      rxIndex = 0;
    }
    delay(10);
  }
}
```

❷ **Call read distance function**

❸ **Print distance**

The primary addition to the existing sketch is the read_gp2d12 function ❶, which reads the input from the analog A0 pin and converts it to a distance. In chapter 6 you learned that the distance isn't linear, so you have to perform a fancy mathematical conversion on it before returning the distance. The distance function is called from within the main loop ❷. The returned distance value is printed to the serial port ❸, and it's then received by the iOS device connected to it.

> **NOTE** We found that a delay of 400 milliseconds after reading in the distance was required to display correct values on iOS. We found values as low as 250 milliseconds worked, but not consistently, so you may have to play around with this figure a little.

Once you've uploaded the sketch, it's time to put everything together.

Figure 10.24 The completed circuit with GP2D12 sensor connected to Arduino and iPhone

10.6.3 *Testing*

Connect your iOS device to the Redpark serial cable and then to the Arduino. The completed setup is shown in figure 10.24. Start the IOSArduino app and then power up the Arduino.

Try steadily moving the sensor about and notice the values for distance changing. Figure 10.25 shows the IOSArduino app running on an iPhone.

10.7 *Summary*

In this chapter, you learned how to use the Arduino with an iOS device both to control devices connected to the Arduino and to receive information from connected sensors. We concentrated on the raw mechanics of sending data to and from an Arduino using the Redpark serial cable and an RS232 to TTL adapter. You can now use your own Objective-C programming skills to present the sent or received data in interesting and novel ways, from complex tables to brightly colored graphics.

In chapter 11 we're going to look at ways of making wearables and how you can carry an Arduino around with you.

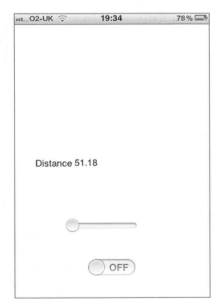

Figure 10.25 The complete IOSArduino app running on an iPhone

Making wearables

11

The term "wearable" generally refers to clothing and accessories that incorporate computer and advanced-electronic technologies. The designs often incorporate practical functions and features as well as make a statement or establish a technological look.

Another way of imagining a wearable is that it's a dynamic surface around your body that is capable of connecting you to devices around you, people, and places. These days most people carry a mobile phone, always on them and always on, but it's not hard to imagine a near future in which most of our communication tools will be even smaller, perhaps even integrated into clothing or accessories that we carry with us. Wearables can be clothing like jackets or sweaters, accessories like hats or scarves, or objects that are worn or carried like necklaces or headphones.

All of these are rich areas to explore. Another mode of wearable computing that you may consider is wearable technology that can be integrated with a mobile phone or laptop using radio frequencies or Bluetooth.

In this chapter we'll examine two platforms for creating wearable applications: the LilyPad and the Arduino Pro Mini. Each has different strengths and weaknesses, and each requires a slightly different development mentality.

The Arduino Pro Mini is a very stripped-down and simple board for more advanced Arduino users. It comes in two different versions: a lower-power version that runs at 8 MHz and a higher-power version that runs at 16 MHz. It draws slightly less current than the LilyPad and is cheaper, but it's a little trickier when you're just getting started.

The LilyPad is more oriented toward the development of wearables. Its connections are slightly unorthodox loops drilled into the board that are perfect for holding a thread, particularly conductive thread. It also has a large community that provides a lot of ideas and help.

We'll start with the LilyPad.

11.1 Introducing the LilyPad

The LilyPad Arduino was designed and developed by Leah Buechley in tandem with SparkFun Electronics. The LilyPad Arduino is a microcontroller board designed for wearables and e-textiles. It can be sewn to fabric and similarly mounted power supplies, sensors, and actuators with conductive thread.

There are two versions of the LilyPad that you can choose from: one based on the ATmega168, and a higher-powered version based on the ATmega328. The differences between them are slight, but significant if you need higher power.

The LilyPad Arduino is a circle, approximately 50 mm (2 inches) in diameter. It can be powered via the USB connection or by an external power supply. If an external power supply is used, it should provide between 2.7 and 5.5 volts. This can come either from an AC-to-DC adapter (a wall-wart) or a battery. The pins of the LilyPad are shown in figure 11.1.

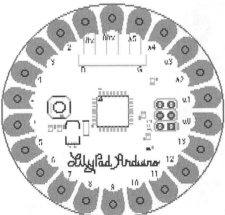

Figure 11.1 The pins of the LilyPad

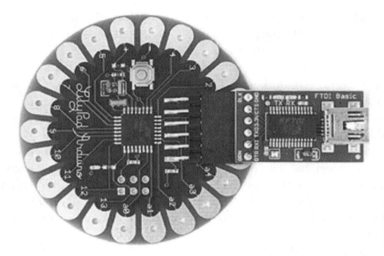

Figure 11.2   Connecting the SparkFun FTDI breakout board to the LilyPad for programming

You can program the LilyPad using SparkFun's FTDI breakout board, as shown in figure 11.2, or you can use an encapsulated FTDI cable. With a cable, the green wire goes in the right pin of the LilyPad socket (note the G in the wiring diagram in figure 11.1), and the black wire goes in the left (at the B in the wiring diagram). It's very important to keep the FTDI cable attached correctly, or you run the risk of damaging the LilyPad.

As you can see, the LilyPad has 6 analog in pins, 14 digital in/out pins, and 2 pins to provide power and ground for the board. It also has a reset button and a six-pin header to attach a programmer, like the FTDI breakout board shown in figure 11.2.

In addition to the main board just outlined, the LilyPad is also available in a Simple version, shown in figure 11.3. The LilyPad Simple has fewer input and output pins, but it includes an on/off switch to make turning projects on and off easier. It's also slightly less expensive than the regular versions.

Figure 11.3   The LilyPad Simple

Figure 11.4   LilyPad Temperature Sensor and LilyPad Vibe Board from SparkFun Electronics

11.1.1 *LilyPad accessories*

The LilyPad comes with lots of different kinds of accessories. Figure 11.4 shows the Temperature Sensor and the Vibe Board, both of which are made by SparkFun.

   How you power your LilyPad project is a very important consideration. Because LilyPad projects are almost always worn or carried on the body, they don't have an external power supply. You should give careful thought to the power requirements of your application. Consider how long you want it to last, whether it can be turned on and off, and how the power supply can be accessed and charged or changed.

   Figure 11.5 shows two easy ways of powering your LilyPad. On the left is the AAA Battery Holder that holds a single AAA battery and provides an easy interface to connect to the LilyPad. On the right is the LiPo Holder that allows you to connect a lithium polymer battery with a two-pin adapter, which is the standard adapter for LiPo batteries. Because these are a part of the LilyPad series, they are both available almost anywhere that stocks LilyPad boards and components.

   The length of time that either of these will power a LilyPad project depends on the application, which components you're using, and how careful you are to prevent your circuits and connections from leaking current. Conductive fabric and thread can be a serious current drain if you're not careful.

   Let's look at conductive fabric and thread and see how to use them properly.

11.1.2 *Conductive thread and fabric*

Your LilyPad can be connected to its circuits using wires or conductive thread. The advantage of thread is that it allows you to sew your components into the wearable itself, making a stronger bond with the fabric and the surface of the garment. The

Figure 11.5   Two different LilyPad power boards: the AAA Battery Holder, and the LiPo Holder, which allows you to connect a lithium polymer battery

Figure 11.6   Conductive ribbon

disadvantage is that conductive thread has a much higher resistance than wire, meaning that your signals will be weaker, and precise communication like I2C or SPI can be affected. Our general approach is to use insulated wires in combination with conductive thread when practical. Figure 11.6 shows some conductive ribbon and table 11.1 outlines some types of conductive thread.

Table 11.1   Types of conductive thread

Name	Resistance	Notes
Shieldex sewing thread, size 33	40 ohms/meter	Has to be hand-sewn
Shieldex sewing thread, size 92	300 ohms/meter	Can be used in industrial sewing machines
Conductive ribbon	0.3 ohm/meter	1 mm thick Can carry three signals

Conductive fabrics are different from conductive threads but the theory is the same: they provide a medium that you can attach to the fabric of your wearable and to which you can connect components. Extremely flexible and nearly transparent circuits can be made using conductive fabrics. Copper-based conductive fabrics can be painted or drawn on with a resistant material like Vaseline and then etched like a standard circuit board. Conductive glue or conductive thread is then used to attach the components to the fabric circuit board.

A few types of fabric, along with their resistivity, thickness, and a thoroughly unscientific assessment of their comfort level as a fabric, are listed in table 11.2. The resistance is measured as a ratio; it's proportional to the length and inversely proportional to the width. If you have a piece that is 1 x 1 inches, then you'll have 1 ohm resistance in either direction; a piece that is 3 x 1 inches will have 3 ohms resistance lengthwise and 0.3 ohms resistance widthwise.

Table 11.2   Types of conductive fabric

Name	Resistance	Thickness	Comfort
Shieldex	0.3 ohms/sq	0.1 mm	Somewhat uncomfortable
MedTex 180	< 1 ohm/sq	0.55 mm	Fairly comfortable against the skin
Nickel mesh	0.1 ohm/sq	.08 mm	Uncomfortable

You can solder to some fabrics, though you need to be very careful when doing so.

There are also several types of conductive glues that are readily available if you don't want to sew a component or a circuit into place. These usually hover around 300 ohms of resistance and can hold a few grams, but nothing extremely heavy or anything that will be stressed greatly. A quick search for wire glue or conductive adhesive should help you locate some options.

Adhesive or glue is good for attaching ends of components to conductive fabric or small mounting brackets, but it's permanent, so be sure about the placement and arrangement before breaking out the glue.

Now we'll look at building with the Arduino.

11.2 Creating a turn-signal jacket

This section shows you how to make a simple turn-signal jacket that allows the wearer to activate turn signals by pressing small flex sensors at the cuffs to turn the signals on and off. For this example, you'll need the following:

- Two flex sensors
- A LilyPad
- Four LEDs
- Three meters of conductive thread

This project is not terribly inventive—it was done by Leah Buechley as one of the first demonstrations of how to use the LilyPad. But it's an excellent demonstration project. In her example, Buechley used pushbutton switches, which we find slightly more difficult to use while cycling than a flex sensor. A small flex sensor, like the one pictured in figure 11.7, allows the user to easily turn the signal on and off.

The flex sensor is not easy to sew into fabric, so our suggestion is to place a piece of fabric over the top of the flex sensor and sew that into the cuff of the jacket on the inside. Fabric in front of the sensor won't affect its operation or readings at all, so it's perfectly safe.

Figure 11.7 Flex sensor

You can wire the jacket however you'd like, but figure 11.8 shows a wiring diagram that we've tested out and that has been robust so far. Figure 11.9 shows how the sensors can be attached to the jacket itself.

The code for the application is quite simple (see listing 11.1). You read the analog value from the flex sensor, and if the change in the value is above a certain amount, the LEDs are lit for 10 seconds. This change in the value means that gradual pressure can be applied to the sensor without triggering it—handy for bike riding when you may brush or press against things.

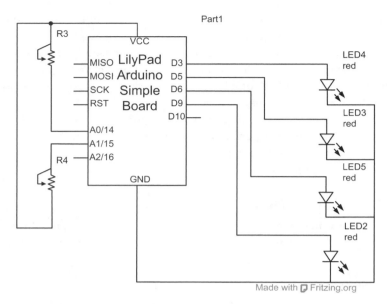

Figure 11.8   Connecting the LilyPad, LEDs, and flex sensors

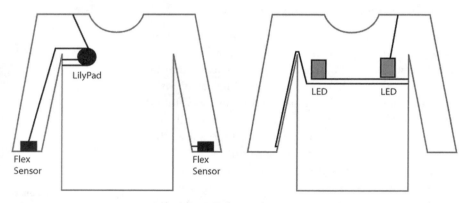

Figure 11.9   Sewing the components into the jacket

Listing 11.1   TurnSignals.ino

```
const int LFORCE = 0;
const int RFORCE = 1;

const int pressLength = 10000;

const int LTURNSIGNAL = 2;
const int RTURNSIGNAL = 3;

int lPrevious, rPrevious;

boolean leftOn, rightOn;

int pressTime;
```

◁ — Each "signal" has two LEDs for better visibility.

```
void setup()
{
  pinMode(LTURNSIGNAL, OUTPUT);
  pinMode(RTURNSIGNAL, OUTPUT);

  leftOn = false;
  rightOn = false;
}

void loop()
{
  int lCurr = analogRead(LFORCE);
  int rCurr = analogRead(RFORCE);
  if( lCurr - lPrevious > 200) {
    pressTime = millis();
    leftOn = true;
  }
  lPrevious = lCurr;

  if( rCurr - rPrevious > 200) {
    pressTime = millis();
    rightOn = true;
  }
  rPrevious = rCurr;

  if(leftOn) {
    digitalWrite(LTURNSIGNAL, HIGH);
    if( millis() - pressTime > pressLength) {
      leftOn = false;
    }
  }

  if(rightOn) {
    digitalWrite(RTURNSIGNAL, HIGH);
    if( millis() - pressTime > pressLength) {
      rightOn = false;
    }
  }

}
```

> **Only listen for changes.**

> **Turn off after a while.**

One thought for improving the jacket might be to add a sound from a speaker or a buzz from a vibration motor to indicate to the user when the turn signals are on. Let's move on to another project to explore attaching a small speaker to a jacket.

11.3 Creating a wearable piano

Another classic example of garment-sized wearables is a musical instrument outfit. For this example you'll need the following:

- A LilyPad Arduino
- A 0.25 W speaker
- 10 thin pieces of copper
- 5 thin pieces of rubber foam
- Thread

We'll examine a simple synthesizer that uses soft buttons to trigger different notes. These buttons can be attached however you'd like, but our preference is to attach them vertically at the breast-pocket level using two layers of thin copper separated by foam and encased in fabric (see figure 11.10). These can then be sewn onto the garment.

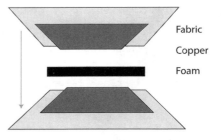

Figure 11.10 **Creating a simple soft button**

The example in listing 11.2 requires five buttons. It can be modified to use more or less depending on how you decide to configure your synthesizer or whether you want more or fewer notes. In the `loop()` method you'll notice that some of the buttons are used in combination to trigger other notes.

Listing 11.2   WearablePiano.ino

```
#define   CNOTE      3830      // 261 Hz
#define   DNOTE      3400      // 294 Hz
#define   ENOTE      3038      // 329 Hz
#define   FNOTE      2864      // 349 Hz
#define   GNOTE      2550      // 392 Hz
#define   ANOTE      2272      // 440 Hz
#define   BNOTE      2028      // 493 Hz
#define   CNOTE2     1912      // 523 Hz

const int key1 = 2;
const int key2 = 3;
const int key3 = 4;
const int key4 = 5;
const int key5 = 6;

void setup()
{
  pinMode(key1, INPUT);
  pinMode(key2, INPUT);
  pinMode(key3, INPUT);
  pinMode(key4, INPUT);
  pinMode(key5, INPUT);
}

void loop()
{
  if( digitalRead( key2 ) && digitalRead( key1 )) {
    tone(9, ANOTE);
  }else if( digitalRead( key2 ) && digitalRead( key3 )) {
    tone(9, BNOTE);
  }else if( digitalRead( key3 ) && digitalRead( key4 )) {
    tone(9, CNOTE2);
  } else if( digitalRead( key1 ) ) {
    tone(9, CNOTE);
  } else if( digitalRead( key2 )) {
    tone(9, DNOTE);
```

Check the keys for the note to play.

```
    } else if( digitalRead( key3 )) {
      tone(9, ENOTE);
    } else if( digitalRead( key4 )) {
      tone(9, FNOTE);
    } else if( digitalRead( key5 )) {
      tone(9, GNOTE);
    }

}
```

Check the keys for the note to play.

The series of if statements in the loop() method checks each button or pair of button combinations to play the eight notes. If you want to play more notes you can simply add more button combinations to check, though keep in mind that it might be hard for users to remember which button combinations create which notes.

The wiring diagram for this application is shown in figure 11.11.

To develop this further you may want to add a flex sensor or other analog input device to control how long the notes are played. You can also add a headphone jack instead of a speaker to play back the sounds, which makes the wearable more private but less enjoyable for the public.

For the next project we'll use something smaller—the Arduino Pro Mini—to make a more-miniaturized wearable.

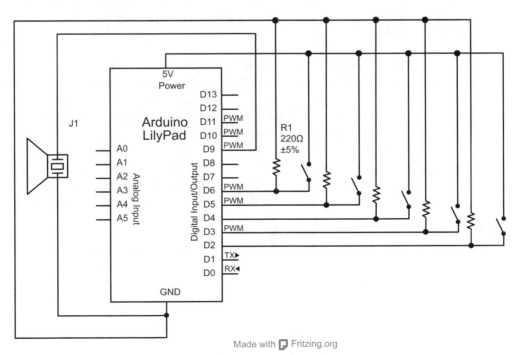

Made with Fritzing.org

Figure 11.11 Connecting the buttons and speaker to the LilyPad Arduino

Figure 11.12   The Arduino Pro Mini

11.4   *The Arduino Pro Mini*

There's more than one way to create a wearable, and more than one controller you can use to create one. The Arduino Pro Mini is a microcontroller board based on the ATmega328. As mentioned earlier in the chapter, there are two different versions of the Pro Mini: a lower voltage one that runs at 3.3V and 8 MHz, and a higher voltage one that runs at 5V and 16 MHz. Both versions have 14 digital input/output pins (of which 6 can be used as PWM outputs), 6 analog inputs, an onboard resonator, a reset button, and holes for mounting pin headers. A six-pin header can be connected to an FTDI cable or SparkFun breakout board to provide USB power and communication to the board.

The Arduino Pro Mini shown in figure 11.12 is intended for semi-permanent installation in objects or exhibitions, but it's also excellent for wearables. The board comes without premounted headers, allowing you to use various types of connectors or to solder wires to it directly. The Arduino Pro Mini is designed and manufactured by Spark-Fun Electronics, but it's available from hobbyist electronics shops all over the world.

The Pro Mini connects directly to the FTDI basic breakout board that you can see in figure 11.2. When the Pro Mini is used with this breakout board it supports auto-resetting after you load a new sketch to the board. It also works with the FTDI cable, but note that the FTDI cable doesn't allow you to use the auto-reset feature.

11.5   *Creating a smart headphone*

One of our favorite project ideas is making a pair of headphones that pause the music on your computer when you take them off. To detect when your headphones are off we'll use the QRE1113, which is a small IR-reflectance sensor (see figure 11.13).

The sensor shines an IR LED out and allows you to determine how much of that light bounces back using a phototransistor. There are four pins on the QRE1113: two control the IR-emitting LED, and the other two are the collector and emitter of a phototransistor. In the application code, you watch for a sudden change in the value returned from the QRE1113 and

Figure 11.13
The tiny QRE1113
IR-reflectance sensor

send a signal to the parent computer if one is received. The serial message is received by a small program that monitors the serial communication and pauses the iTunes player if any signal is received.

At its simplest, this program requires that an FTDI cable is used to connect the Arduino Pro Mini to the parent computer. For this example you'll need the following:

- A pair of headphones
- An Arduino Pro Mini
- A QRE1113
- A computer to connect to the Arduino

The .ino file to run on the Arduino Pro Mini is shown in the next listing.

Listing 11.3   headphones.ino

```
const int QRE1113_Pin = 0; //connected to analog 0
boolean isConnected;

void setup(){
  Serial.begin(9600);                          Start as
  isConnected = false;                         disconnected
}

void loop(){

  int QRE_Value = analogRead(QRE1113_Pin);     Check QRE1113
                                               for presence
  if(isConnected) {
    if(QRE_Value > 900) {
      Serial.print("X");
    }
  } else {
    if(QRE_Value > 300) {
      isConnected = true;
    }
  }
}
```

Now it's time to pause the music on the computer when receiving data from the Arduino. There are a great number of music players for computers and we can't specify how to pause all of them, so we'll just demonstrate iTunes on Windows and OS X. Both of these use Python, the language outlined in chapter 12.

The code for the Windows Python program is shown in the following listing.

Listing 11.4   win.py

```
import win32com.client
import serial

itunes = win32com.client.Dispatch("iTunes.Application ")

arduino = serial.Serial(
    port='/dev/ttyUSB1',                       Connection to
    baudrate=9600,                             the Arduino
)
```

```
arduino.open()
arduino.isOpen()

out = ''
while arduino.inWaiting() > 0:
    out += arduino.read(1)

    if out != '':
        itunes.Pause()
```

The code for OS X looks a bit different because it uses AppleScript, a scripting language for OS X that's included with the operating system (see the next listing).

Listing 11.5   osx.py

```
import subprocess
import serial

cmd = """osascript -e 'tell app "iTunes" to pause'"""          ← The AppleScript
                                                                   command
arduino = serial.Serial(                                       ←
    port='/dev/ttyUSB1',
    baudrate=9600,                                                 Connection to
)                                                                  the Arduino

arduino.open()
arduino.isOpen()

out = ''
while arduino.inWaiting() > 0:
    out += arduino.read(1)

    if out != '':
        subprocess.call(cmd, shell=True)
```

If you'd like to make this into a more lightweight and less intrusive program you could consider altering this project so that the Arduino communicates with the parent computer over Bluetooth using a Bluetooth module such as the Bluetooth Mate Silver shown in figure 11.14. None of the code needs to change, but you'll need to configure the connection to the Bluetooth channel on your headphones.

In the next example we're going to create a compass with a real-time readout that's sewn into a jacket. Although you can get this functionality from a smartphone, the

Figure 11.14   A Bluetooth Mate Silver transmitter

Figure 11.15   The HMC5883L magnetic compass

advantage of adding it to a garment is that it can be visible all the time without needing to pull a phone out of a pocket and start an app.

11.6   *Creating a jacket with a compass*

In this section we're going to look at connecting a user display directly to the wearable and to a magnetometer. A *magnetometer* is an instrument used to measure the strength or direction of a magnetic field, like Earth's magnetic field. Magnetometers can identify your orientation with respect to the North Pole in one, two, or three axes, and they're usually precise enough for simple applications. You've probably used or seen one of these in a smart phone.

For this example we'll use the HMC5883L created by Honeywell (see figure 11.15). These are very small, and it's recommended that you get a breakout board to simplify connecting it to your Arduino.

For the readout from the magnetometer we'll use a 7-segment serial-enabled display from SparkFun. Although a serial-enabled 7-segment display is an expensive way of creating a 7-segment display, it's also easy to connect and simplifies construction and troubleshooting. If you'd like to, you can create your own 7-segment display and connect the controls for each segment directly to your Arduino.

The SparkFun 7-segment display draws a good amount of current and is more expensive than other options, which is a definite downside. The upside is how simple it makes the code. The SparkFun 7-segment display is shown in figure 11.16.

To complete this project you'll need the following:

- An Arduino Pro Mini
- An HMC5883L
- A 7-segment serial display
- Three meters of conductive thread

Figure 11.16   The SparkFun 7-segment serial display

Now let's move on to the code. The magnetometer is complex and requires a good amount of setup to initialize correctly and correct for errors and drift. All of this is done over I2C using the Wire library, which you were introduced to in chapter 9. You'll notice a lot of register addresses in the code that will be used to initialize the different settings in the HMC5883L that you'll be using.

Because the magnetometer communicates using I2C and the 7-segment display uses serial communication you need to use wires or conductive ribbon to ensure that the communication isn't disturbed by the resistance of the conductive thread. Another consideration is that the 7-segment display should be visible but needs to be protected from moisture. Putting it behind a film of plastic might be advisable, though it's not absolutely necessary.

The `writemem()` method in the following code listing is a simple way to send a command to the magnetometer using the `Wire` library and to check the value of the call to `endTransmission()`. This method is broken out to conserve space.

Listing 11.6   compass.ino

```
#include <Wire.h>

const int magnetometer_address = 0x1E;          ◁── HMC5883L
int magVals[3];                                       address

float magx_scale, magy_scale, magz_scale, magx_max, magy_max, magz_max;

#define HMC_POS_BIAS 1
#define HMC_NEG_BIAS 2
#define HMC58X3_R_XM 3

#define HMC58X3_R_CONFA 0          ◁── HMC5883L
#define HMC58X3_R_CONFB 1               register map
#define HMC58X3_R_MODE 2
#define HMC58X3_R_XM 3
#define HMC58X3_R_XL 4
                                                   Start transmission
                                                       to device
void writemem(uint8_t dev_address, uint8_t _addr, uint8_t _val) {
  Wire.beginTransmission(dev_address);        ◁──
  Wire.write(_addr);                    ◁──    Send register
  Wire.write(_val);                     ◁──    address
  Serial.print(Wire.endTransmission());  ◁──
}
                                                   Send value to
                                                   HMC5883L
void initMag()
{                                                  End
  Serial.print(" init mag ");                      transmission
  writemem(magnetometer_address, HMC58X3_R_CONFA, 0x70);
  writemem(magnetometer_address, HMC58X3_R_CONFB, 0xA0);
  writemem(magnetometer_address, HMC58X3_R_MODE, 0x00);
}

void calibrateMag(unsigned char gain) {
  magx_scale=1;
  magy_scale=1;
  magz_scale=1;
```

**Start
calibration**

```
writemem(magnetometer_address, HMC58X3_R_CONFA, 0x010 + HMC_POS_BIAS);
writemem(magnetometer_address, HMC58X3_R_CONFB, gain << 5);

float x, y, z, mx=0, my=0, mz=0, t=10;

for (int i=0; i<(int)t; i++) {
  writemem(magnetometer_address, HMC58X3_R_MODE, 1);
  delay(100);

  readFromMagnet();
  if (magVals[0] > mx) mx = magVals[0];
  if (magVals[2] > my) my = magVals[2];
  if (magVals[1] > mz) mz = magVals[1];
}

float max=0;
if (mx>max) max=mx;
if (my>max) max=my;
if (mz>max) max=mz;

magx_max = mx;
magy_max = my;
magz_max = mz;
magx_scale = max/mx;
magy_scale = max/my;
magz_scale = max/mz;
writemem(magnetometer_address, HMC58X3_R_CONFA, 0x010);
delay(10);

unsigned char mode = 0;
writemem(magnetometer_address, HMC58X3_R_MODE, mode);
delay(100);
}
void readFromMagnet()
{
  Wire.beginTransmission(magnetometer_address);
  Wire.write(HMC58X3_R_XM);
  Wire.endTransmission();

  Wire.beginTransmission(magnetometer_address);
  Wire.requestFrom(magnetometer_address, 6);
  if(6 == Wire.available()) {
    magVals[0] = (Wire.read() << 8) | Wire.read();
    magVals[2] = (Wire.read() << 8) | Wire.read();
    magVals[1] = (Wire.read() << 8) | Wire.read();

    magVals[0] /= magx_scale;
    magVals[2] /= magy_scale;
    magVals[1] /= magz_scale;
  }
  Wire.endTransmission();
}

void setup()
{
  //magnetometer startup
  initMag();
  calibrateMag(4);
}
```

⟵ **Get the
highest value**

⟵ **Calculate
scales**

Set the mode

⟵ **Start from
most-significant bit**

⟵ **Magnetometer
will automatically
wrap around**

```
void loop()
{
  readFromMagnet();
  char str[3];
  itoa(magVals[2], str, 10);
  Serial.print('x'); // print a 0
  Serial.print(str[0]);
  Serial.print(str[1]);
  Serial.print(str[2]);
  delay(100);
}
```

<--| **Print ASCII**

The preceding application is complex but its functionality is fairly straightforward: turn on the magnetometer, initialize it correctly, and compensate for the scale that it returns. Once that's completed, the loop() method simply reads the values from the HMC5883L and writes them to the 7-segment display using the hardware serial connection on the Arduino Pro Mini. The calibration routine is necessary to ensure that the compass isn't overly influenced by noise in the environment or its default settings.

If you're interested in how the HMC5883L actually understands each command you can check out the datasheet for it, which is available at the Honeywell website: http://honeywell.com/.

11.7   *Summary*

In this chapter you learned how to use two new Arduino-compatible controllers, and also learned about an entire new range of applications for your Arduino skills. The possibilities of using microcontrollers to add computational capability to a small unobtrusive object worn on the body is one of the most exciting ways of working with the Arduino and of thinking about how to add intelligence and functionality to our lives.

You've seen two different Arduino-compatible boards that are small, lightweight, and easily powered by small batteries, all of which are important considerations when making a wearable. The Arduino LilyPad is larger, but it's built specifically for attaching conductive thread and has a large community of users creating wearables. The Arduino Pro Mini is a small board that's very lightweight, but it's slightly more difficult to use with conductive thread, lacking the easy-to-sew eyelets of the Arduino LilyPad. It is, however, significantly smaller and provides more pins for you to use in your projects.

In the next chapter you'll learn about connecting your Arduino to other applications written in a variety of programming languages, which will allow you to make larger and more complex projects than you would be able to with just an Arduino.

Adding shields 12

This chapter covers

- What Arduino shields are
- Using libraries with shields
- Making your own shields

Up to this point, you've used shields in several examples, but this chapter will focus on what a shield is, how shields are made, what they're supposed to do, and how you can make your own. Shields are boards that can be plugged into the Arduino board to extend its capabilities. Making a shield means collecting a discrete set of components for a specific task, like playing back MP3 files or communicating with a GPS device, and then fitting the components to the form factor of the Arduino device and adding pins so that they can be easily snapped into place or removed without soldering.

12.1 Shield basics

Almost of all of the Arduino shields follow the same philosophy as the original toolkit: they are easy to mount and friendly to work with. Figure 12.1 shows a motor shield developed by Adafruit that allows you to easily control up to two servomotors, four DC motors, or two stepper motors.

Figure 12.1   The Adafruit motor shield—the first motor shield we will be using in this chapter. Image from http://www.adafruit.com/products/81.

This shield, which we'll examine in greater detail later in this chapter, provides several very nice features in a convenient form factor, including pull-down resistors that keep motors disabled during power-up, terminal block connectors to easily hook up connections and power, and internal kickback protection diodes that allow you to use larger voltages for larger motors. That's just the start. The main advantage of using this shield is that it puts all of the functionality for working with several different kinds of motors into a single board that doesn't need to be set up again each time your configuration changes.

Shields also often come with libraries and examples, which are great ways to learn how to work with the components that the shield contains. For instance, the Adafruit shield can be used with the AFMotor library, which is written for the Arduino. This library contains a wealth of knowledge about how to control the different kinds of motors for which the shield provides functionality and numerous examples of controlling motors.

Shields can be bought assembled or you can assemble your own. Often self-assembly is far cheaper than having them assembled for you, but self-assembly also introduces the possibility of making mistakes. It is, however, far more fun and educational to put things together than to have them put together for you.

12.2   *The Adafruit motor shield*

The motor shield from Adafruit, which was discussed in the previous section, is one of the most popular Arduino shields because of what it enables you to do easily: connect multiple motors and external power sources to the Arduino without worrying about over-powering or over-drawing current from the Arduino.

The motor shield allows you to connect four bidirectional DC motors or two stepper motors, and it also has two connections for 5V servos. Without some serious power behind it the shield is probably not going to work if you connect all of them at the same time, but it does allow you to work with multiple large motors at the same time quickly and easily. Now let's look at the library that works with the shield.

12.2.1 *The AFMotor library*

Like many shields, the motor shield comes with a library that allows you to easily control the shield and, by extension, any motors attached to it. The library can be downloaded from https://github.com/adafruit/Adafruit-Motor-Shield-library. Let's examine that library and see how to use it.

To control a DC motor, you need to construct an instance of the AF_DCMotor class, passing it the number of the motor being attached. If the motor is *not* going to communicate with a 34.8 kHz PWM signal, you also need to pass in the frequency of the motor.

For example, if the motor is going to communicate with a 34.8 kHz PWM signal you only need to specify the motor driver on the board that the motor is attached to:

```
AF_DCMotor motor(2);
```

How do you know the frequency of the motor that you have? Check the data sheet. So many small DC motors are 34.8 kHz that the makers of the shield set that as the default, but there are plenty of motors with different frequencies, so it's best to check. If you do have a motor with a different frequency you can set it like this:

```
AF_DCMotor motor(2, MOTOR12_19KHZ);
```

Once you've created the motor, you can start it, setting the speed in a range from 0 to 255. Then call run() and pass either FORWARD or BACKWARD to the method:

```
motor.setSpeed(100);
motor.run(FORWARD);
```

To stop the DC motor call run() and pass RELEASE to the method:

```
motor.run(RELEASE);
```

The Stepper library works a little differently. You first create the AF_Stepper instance by passing the number of steps the motor takes for a complete circle and the connection number on which the stepper is connected. The number of degrees in a step can usually be found in the datasheet. It may be listed as the number of degrees that the stepper makes per step, in which case you can divide 360 by the number of degrees to get the number of steps. If the stepper motor is connected to motor ports 1 and 2 the connection number is 1. If the stepper motor is connected to motor ports 3 and 4 the connection number is 2:

```
const int STEPS = 360/1.8;
AF_Stepper stepperMotor(STEPS, 1);
```

To advance the motor call `step()` with the number of steps and the direction that you want to turn the stepper:

```
stepperMotor.step(1, FORWARD);
```

You can also set the type of step that you want the stepper motor to turn. These are the available options:

- `SINGLE`—Single-coil activation
- `DOUBLE`—Two coils activated at once for slightly higher torque
- `INTERLEAVE`—Alternates between single- and double-coil activation to get twice the resolution but half the speed
- `MICROSTEP`—Attempts to turn the stepper smoothly to its next position using a PWM signal

Not all steppers can perform all of these actions, so you'll want to check the data sheet and perhaps the Adafruit forums for info on your particular motor.

12.2.2 *Using the motor shield with a stepper motor*

For this example you'll need the following:

- An Arduino
- An Adafruit motor shield
- A 5V stepper motor
- Two AA batteries or a power source sufficient to drive the stepper motor
- Two buttons
- Two resistors (5k ohms or similar)

This application uses the two buttons to control the direction of the stepper. Each button acts as a toggle to turn the stepper on and off and determine in which direction it will turn, if it turns at all.

The connections are shown in figure 12.2. Note the battery pack attached to the motor shield to power the stepper motor. The two buttons have pull-down resistors on them to ensure that they only read HIGH when pressed.

You'll also need to install the AFMotor library, which you can download from GitHub at www.github.com/adafruit/Adafruit-Motor-Shield-library. Here's the code that will drive the stepper motor.

Listing 12.1   MotorDriving.pde

```
#include <AFMotor.h>

AF_Stepper stepper(48, 1);

const int STEPPER_BWD_BUTTON = 2;
const int STEPPER_FWD_BUTTON = 13;

const int BACKWARDS = 2;
const int FORWARDS = 1;
```

```
const int STOPPED = 0;

int motorState;

void setup() {
    }

void loop() {

    int fwd = digitalRead(STEPPER_FWD_BUTTON);
    int bwd = digitalRead(STEPPER_BWD_BUTTON);

    if(fwd == HIGH) {
        if( motorState == FORWARDS ) {
            motorState = STOPPED;
        } else {
            motorState = FORWARDS;
        }
    }

    if(bwd == HIGH) {
        if( motorState == BACKWARDS ) {
            motorState = STOPPED;
        } else {
            motorState = BACKWARDS;
        }
    }

    if(motorState == FORWARDS) {
        stepper.step(1, FORWARD, INTERLEAVE);
    } else if(motorState == BACKWARDS) {
        stepper.step(1, BACKWARD, INTERLEAVE);
    }

}
```

Toggles directions

12.2.3 *Using the motor shield with a DC motor*

Controlling a DC motor is equally simple: create an instance of the AF_DCMotor class and set the controller block it's attached to in its constructor. For instance, a DC motor connected to the second motor block (marked with M2) would be declared like this:

```
AF_DCMotor motor(2);
```

For the next project we'll control a motor's speed with a potentiometer and control its direction with a pair of buttons. For this project you'll need the following:

- An Arduino
- An Adafruit motor shield
- A small DC motor
- Two buttons
- Two resistors (5k ohms or similar)
- A servomotor
- Two AA batteries or a power source sufficient to drive the motor
- One potentiometer

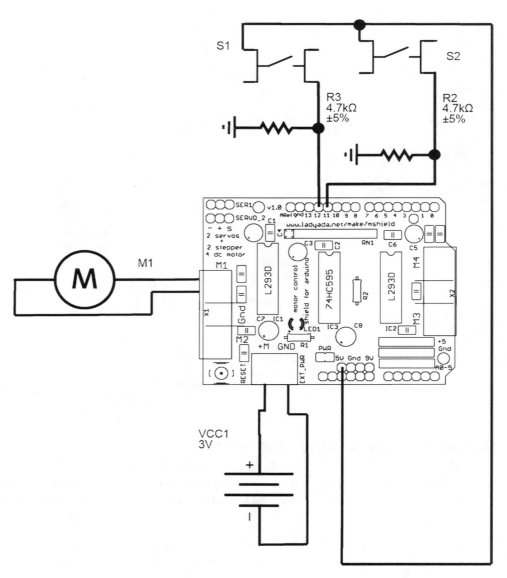

Figure 12.2   The connections for listing 12.1

Sometimes you can get away with powering a stepper motor from the Arduino itself, but with a DC motor you'll definitely need a separate power source, as shown in figure 12.3.

The code for this example requires the AFMotor library and the Servo library, so make sure that you have them both installed on your computer (see the following listing).

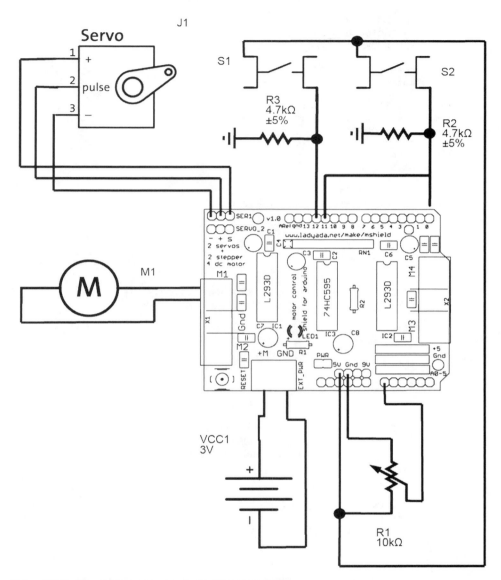

Figure 12.3   **Connecting a servomotor to the motor shield**

Listing 12.2   PotToMotors.pde

```
#include <AFMotor.h>
#include <Servo.h>

AF_DCMotor motor(1);
Servo servo;
```

**Servo connection
I is Arduino D9**

```
const int MOTOR_FWD_BUTTON = 2;
const int MOTOR_BWD_BUTTON = 13;
const int POTENTIOMETER_PIN = 0;

int motorSpeed;
int motorState;

const int BACKWARDS = 2;
const int FORWARDS = 1;
const int STOPPED = 0;

void setup() {
  servo1.attach(9);

  pinMode(MOTOR_FWD_BUTTON, INPUT);
  pinMode(MOTOR_BWD_BUTTON, INPUT);

}

void loop() {

    int tmp = analogRead(POTENTIOMETER_PIN);

      int fwd = digitalRead(MOTOR_FWD_BUTTON);
    int bwd = digitalRead(MOTOR_BWD_BUTTON);

    if(fwd == HIGH) {
        if( motorState == BACKWARDS || motorState == STOPPED) {
            motorState = FORWARDS;
                        motor.run( FORWARD );
        }
    }

    if(bwd == HIGH) {
        if( motorState == FORWARDS || motorState == STOPPED) {
            motorState = BACKWARDS;
                        motor.run( BACKWARD );
        }
    }
      if( tmp != motorSpeed / 4) {                  // Only set speed if
        motorSpeed = tmp;                          //    it has changed
        motor.setSpeed(  motorSpeed / 4);
      }

      if( motorState == FORWARDS ) {
        servo.write( motorSpeed / 1024. * 90 + 90 );
      } else {
        servo.write( 90 - (motorSpeed / 1024. * 90) );
      }

}
```

This code listing is a bit lengthy, but what it does is quite simple: it controls motor speed and direction using simple components and it gives some visual feedback using a servomotor. Now you have a project with a controllable motor and a speedometer.

12.2.4 *Getting a motor shield*

There are two options for getting a motor shield: you can buy it assembled, or you can assemble it yourself. Buying it assembled saves you some time and costs you some money; buying it unassembled saves you some money and gives you a chance to hone your soldering skills.

If you go the latter route, the kit will arrive with all the pieces in a bag, and you'll have to take a look at the directions on the Adafruit site to put it together. To avoid needless repetition, we won't list the directions here, but they're fairly self-explanatory. The biggest things to watch out for are getting the right capacitor in the right place and orienting the polarity of the capacitors correctly.

We recommend putting it together yourself, but if you want to be absolutely sure that the shield will be assembled correctly you can buy it preassembled.

12.3 *Creating your own shield*

At some point, you'll make something that works so well that you'll want to use it over and over again in different projects without needing to set it all up again on a breadboard. This is where the idea of making a shield using a project board comes in handy. Figure 12.4 shows a project board (sometimes also called a perfboard).

A project board is a little more permanent than a breadboard because you solder the components into place. This ensures that no noise is conducted through the board that might affect your circuit and that components can't be jostled out of place. You can get many different kinds of project board, some with rails on the side,

Figure 12.4   A project board, sometimes called a perfboard (source: SparkFun)

some with strips connecting all the perforations in a single line, and some with configurations for specific components.

12.3.1 *Memory*

Ah, memory. Compared to the microcontrollers of 10 years ago, or even regular computers of 30 years ago, the Arduino has a remarkable amount of memory, but even that fills up quickly when you're trying to log GPS coordinates or keep track of environmental indicators over days or weeks. That's why computers have hard disks, and it's also why cameras have flash memory; it's the latter of these that we're going to emulate. The SD card in the standard digital camera is a marvel: it's small, light, and easy to operate, it has no moving parts, and it has a robust storage system.

The most common type of memory card is the SD card, and these generally come in two formats: microSD and SD. These two types differ not only in protocol and capacity, but also in the physical size of the card: one is larger and the other is much smaller. There's another important difference between these two cards: microSD generally uses a format called FAT32, whereas SD cards use FAT16. The differences between these formats are in how files are allocated and stored. This isn't important for you at the moment, but it's good to know which variety you're getting because the storage system will affect how you read data from and write it to the card.

In this example we're going to focus on the regular SD card because it's easier to work with by hand. As we write this book, the capacity of SD cards ranges from 64 MB all the way up to 32 GB, but by the time you read this they may be even larger.

Connecting an SD card to an Arduino presents a few problems. As you may recall from chapter 9 where you were introduced to I2C, the I2C protocol transmits data between the component and the Arduino using short bursts of digital information that represent the bits of each byte. SD cards operate at 3.3V, and that means that they need to be powered with 3.3V and they also need to be communicated with at 3.3V. This is a problem for the Arduino, because the digitalRead() method sometimes won't register a 3.3V signal as HIGH when performing a digital read. You might guess where this is going: we need a way to turn the signals from the Arduino into 3.3V signals, and the signals from the SD card to 5V signals. Luckily, there's a component that does it for us.

12.3.2 *Level shifters*

A level shift does one thing well: it shifts any level received on one of the input pins down to whatever voltage is received on the voltage-in pin. Applying 3.3V to the level shifter means that any signal sent through it will come out at 3.3V, which is exactly what you want to avoid damaging your SD card.

There are a lot of level shifters available with varying precision and different numbers of inputs and outputs. For this example, you really only need two level shifters to communicate safely with the SD card, but one of the most readily available and cheapest level shifters has six outputs. It's the 74HC4050 from NXP Semiconductors, and the pinout is shown in figure 12.5.

The voltage level pin determines the voltage that all the output current will be stepped down to, the ground grounds the current, and the rest of the pins are either input, output, or don't connect (marked here as DNC).

That's the first challenge of the SD card shield handled. Now how do you connect the SD card to the shield so that it can be easily inserted and removed without trouble? The answer is an SD card holder.

12.3.3 *The SD card holder*

You've probably used a card holder for an SD card before, but you may not have gotten a good look at it because they're usually hidden inside a camera or a computer

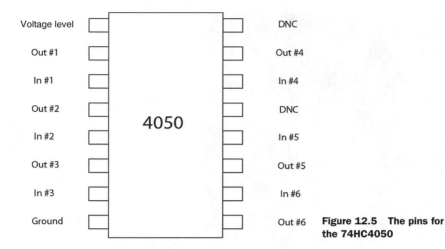

Figure 12.5   The pins for the 74HC4050

case. The card holder allows you to connect the card to the shield without needing to actually alter the card itself. This is important, because it ensures that you can have the Arduino write data to the SD card, and then take the card out of the holder and read it on a computer with a card reader.

As you can see in figure 12.6, the card holder has pins that can be soldered into a project board and a small latch at the top to hold the card in place when it's in use.

Now that you know how to put the SD card onto the shield, let's look at how to connect the card to the Arduino.

12.3.4 Connecting the SD card to the Arduino

You can probably get an idea of how the SD card is connected to the Arduino by examining figure 12.7, but keep in mind that the card will be placed facedown into the

Figure 12.6   An SD card holder that can be soldered into a project board

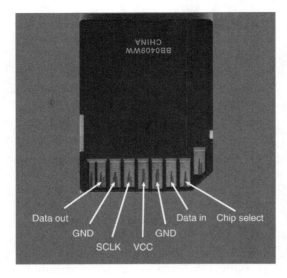

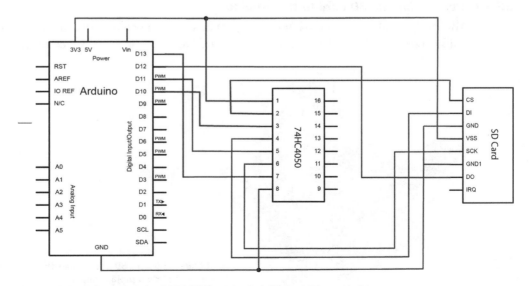

Figure 12.7   **The various connections for an SD card**

holder. The I2C pins that send data from the Arduino are all run through the level shifter and then to the SD card. The pin that sends data from the SD card to the Arduino can connect directly to the Arduino without any problems. The VCC is connected to 3.3V and the ground is connected to, unsurprisingly, the ground of the Arduino.

Let's look at the wiring diagram to see how this will look on the board (figure 12.8). As you can see, the level shifter sits between the SD card and the Arduino, ensuring that no 5V signals are sent to the SD card.

With the schematic out of the way it's time to start making the board itself.

Figure 12.8   **Connecting the 74HC4050 to the Arduino and SD card holder**

12.3.5 *Preparing the perfboard*

You're ready to start making your board. You'll need the following:

- A perfboard (preferably double-sided)
- An Arduino
- Four female header strips (long pin) *or* three female header strips and one Arduino offset header
- An SD card holder
- An SD card
- A 74HC4050 level shifter

The next step is an important one, so please don't skip it: the pins must be modified so that they'll fit into the headers on the Arduino. If you don't modify the pins, the shield won't fit onto the Arduino. You have two options: use standard female headers or use Arduino offset headers. The two different types are shown in figure 12.9.

You might be wondering why the pins in the Arduino offset header (on the right in figure 12.10) are bent slightly. The answer is that the perfboard has a grid of small holes separated by 0.1 inches (2.54 mm), which is to say that the holes are laid out in 0.1 inch spacing. The Arduino doesn't use 0.1 inch spacing. This is not out of malice or a desire to make you buy more shields—it was an error in a very early edition of the Arduino that, for compatibility reasons, has been preserved. The bent pins on the Arduino offset header allow you slide the pins into the Arduino's pins REF and D8 or D7 and D0 and use non-bent pins to connect to the other digital pins on the Arduino. These offset header pins are available at several retailers, including Adafruit and SparkFun.

If you don't want to buy pre-bent pins, why not bend your own? Get a pair of needle-nose pliers and a row of five long-pin female headers and bend each pin slightly. It might take several tries to get it right, but it should be doable.

If you don't want to buy bent pins or bend your own long pins, you have another option: take the perfboard and drill holes in between the existing holes so that they match up with the digital pins of the Arduino. To drill the holes you'll need a 0.8 mm drill bit. You'll then need to scrape away some of the copper from the sides of the board to avoid accidental shorts between pins. Figure 12.10 shows the holes carefully drilled in a piece of perfboard.

You'll need to ensure that the board fits properly before soldering the pins in place, but once you've confirmed that everything will fit, go ahead and secure the pins

Figure 12.9   The two types of header pins: standard female header on the left, and Arduino offset header on the right

Figure 12.10   You can drill additional 0.8 mm holes into the perfboard if you don't have pre-bent pins or don't want to bend them yourself.

with a healthy amount of solder. If it works, all is well; if not, you may need to unsolder one or more of the headers and try to gently tweak some of the pins with a pair of needle-nose pliers.

Done? Good. With that out of the way, you're ready to start connecting the female headers to the board. You're going to use these headers to connect to the pins of the Arduino and to connect to the 74HC4050 and SD card, allowing you to still access all the pins of the Arduino and provide the power and I2C that the SD card requires. Your goal is to end up with something that looks like figure 12.11.

Notice how the headers on the board match the pins on the Arduino. One nice thing about the SD card shield you're creating here is that you don't need to lose any

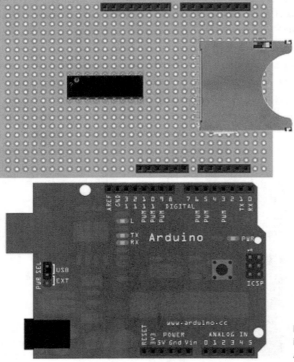

Figure 12.11   The SD card shield is ready to be connected to the Arduino board.

pins. This is one of the great advantages of I2C: additional components can be attached to the I2C pins of the Arduino without interfering with any other I2C as long as they're using a separate address for communication.

Now you can solder the 74HC4050 to the perfboard. You can put a 16-pin socket on there if you want to change the level shifter out at some point, but it's not necessary. Whether you're using a socket or not, you can place the component in the center of the board.

Next it's time to place the SD card holder—it will need to be tweaked a little bit to fit on a standard perfboard. Make sure you know which direction the 74HC4050 is facing. The level shifter has a small indent indicating the top. It doesn't matter which way the top is facing, but it does matter which connections you attach to the Arduino and the SD card holder.

First, if your SD card holder has mounting strips like those shown on the left in figure 12.7, you'll need to cut them off so the holder can lie flat on the board. If they're plastic, you can do this with a knife. If they're metal, you may need a pair of snips or a small grinder, depending on how thick they are. Next you'll need to very gently shift the position of the last pin on the right, as shown in figure 12.7, so that it can fit the holes on the board.

Now you're ready to start connecting the SD card holder to the perfboard. Our approach is to solder insulated jumper wires into place where you're going to attach the SD card holder, and then to connect the pins on the SD card holder directly to one side of each jumper wire. You'll want to be liberal with the solder, because it's all that's going to hold the SD card holder in place, unless you add a little bit of hot glue around the sides.

Now it's time to connect the 74HC4050 to the SD card holder. Figure 12.12 shows the connections between the level shifter and the SD card holder.

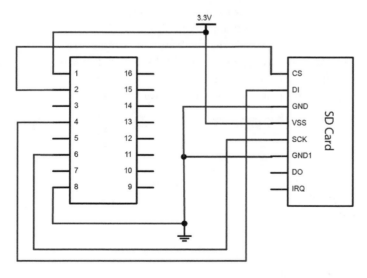

Made with **Fritzing.org**

Figure 12.12   Connecting the level shifter to the SD card holder

You *can* run the jumper wires over the top of the board, but it's probably better to run them under the board where they'll be out of the way. If you're running the wires on the top of the board, thread the wire through the board and bend the non-insulated end to contact the jumpers from the SD card and the 74HC4050, and then solder them into place. If you're running them along the bottom of the board, lay them so that they connect to the ends of the jumpers for the SD card and the level shifter, and then solder them into place. Be sure to clip away any extra length of the jumper wire.

Now run jumper wire between the headers connected to the I2C pins on the Arduino and the level shifter. Again, you can run them over the top of the board or along the bottom.

Now you have a shield that you can use with an SD card and that can be controlled from the Arduino using simple components. If everything has been connected correctly you should be able to plug your new shield into the Arduino and run a test that monitors a button. That's what we'll do next.

12.3.6 *Testing the shield*

Now that you have your shield assembled, it's time to test it.

For this example you'll need the following:

- An Arduino
- Two buttons
- Two resistors (5k ohms or similar)
- An SD card shield (which you just made)

You'll also need to download the SDFat library for the following example. This library allows you to communicate with an SD card using a filesystem called FAT16, which is what we'll use to create files and store data on the SD card.

In the next listing you'll write code to store button presses on an SD card that you've attached to the Arduino using your new shield. When the button is pressed it should write the time of the button press to a text file. The advantage of using a text file is that it can be opened on just about any computer or operating system.

Listing 12.3   SDShieldWriter.pde

```
#include <SdFat.h>

SdFat sd;
SdFile myFile;

const int chipSelect = 2;
const int READ_BUTTON = 3;
const int WRITE_BUTTON = 4;

void setup() {

  Serial.begin(57600);
  if (!sd.begin(chipSelect, SPI_HALF_SPEED)) //
    sd.initErrorHalt();
```

Start card reading

```
    pinMode(READ_BUTTON, INPUT);
    pinMode(WRITE_BUTTON, INPUT);
}

void loop() {
    if( digitalRead( WRITE_BUTTON )) {
        if (!myFile.open("logger.txt", O_RDWR | O_CREAT | O_AT_END)) {
        sd.errorHalt("opening logger.txt for write failed");
        return;
      }
      myFile.print(" tapped the button at ");
      myFile.print( millis() );                          Always close
      myFile.print( " milliseconds since starting ");    the file
      myFile.close(); //
    }

    if(digitalRead( READ_BUTTON) ) {                      Check for
       if (!myFile.open("logger.txt", O_READ)) {//        errors when
          sd.errorHalt("opening logger.txt for read failed");  opening file
          return;
       }

       int data;
       while ((data = myFile.read()) > 0) {
         Serial.write(data);
       }                                       Always close
       myFile.close();//                        the file
    }
}
```

The error checking in this code when opening the file is important to ensure that any problems reading from or writing to the card and the filesystem don't crash your program. The calls to the SDFat library's errorHalt() method ensure that the filesystem on the card won't be corrupted, and it returns the error message.

You now have a way to store text data for access later on and to read it back. You can even send it to a host computer using the serial port. If you've made it all the way through this section of this chapter you've also built your own shield, a not-inconsiderable accomplishment.

12.4   Summary

In this chapter you've learned what shields are, what they do, and the small positioning details that make them unique to the Arduino. You've also explored one of the better-known shields available—the motor shield from Adafruit. You've seen how to connect multiple motors and motor types to that shield and how to control them very precisely. You also built a shield from scratch that allows you to connect an SD card to the Arduino and store information. Finally, you learned how to use the SDFat library to write files to and read files from an SD card with the Arduino.

Software integration 13

This chapter covers

- Using serial ports to communicate with applications
- Connecting an Arduino board to a Processing application
- Connecting an Arduino board to a Python application

The Arduino is a potent tool on its own, but it becomes all the more powerful when you connect it to a full-featured computer, like a laptop or a desktop computer. In fact, you do this whenever you connect the Arduino to your computer with a USB cable to upload code from the Arduino IDE to your Arduino board. The reason you take this step when you're programming the Arduino is to take advantage of the power of your desktop or laptop to compile your code and run the Arduino IDE.

You may be thinking of the other powerful things your desktop computer can do that your Arduino can't: computer vision, audio synthesis, network communications, and so on. But your computer is unmistakably a computer, and that's the advantage of the Arduino: it allows you to create a new interface to your computer that doesn't need to look or feel computer-like.

You can set up an Arduino and another computer to speak to one another using serial communication, sometimes called RS232. You've seen it in action if you've used the `Serial.print()` method to send messages from the Arduino to the Arduino IDE for debugging. But the Arduino IDE isn't the only device that can receive messages from and send them to your Arduino. In this chapter, we'll show you how your Arduino can communicate with several different programming platforms on a desktop computer to make new interfaces between your computer and your Arduino.

13.1 The serial channel

You've already used the serial channel to send debugging messages to the Arduino IDE using the `Serial.print()` method. Lots of devices other than the Arduino use serial communication to communicate with a parent computer: Bluetooth-enabled devices, GPS sensors, older printers and mice, barcode scanners, and, of course, the Arduino board. As a communication protocol, it's rather low-level and can be quite simple or quite complex, depending on what you need from it.

Connecting the Arduino to a computer with a USB cable announces to your computer's operating system that you've connected a serial device. When you install the Arduino IDE, you also install several drivers that allow the Arduino to be recognized as a device that communicates over a serial connection. Once your computer's operating system recognizes the Arduino any programming language can be set up to listen and send data over the serial channel.

The important thing to remember is that, as with the Arduino IDE, the program listening on your computer needs to be communicating at the same baud rate as your Arduino. If your Arduino is using 9,600 the program on your computer needs to be set the same way. Another element you need to consider is that the 9,600 may be acceptable for some purposes, but for an application that requires faster communication between your controllers and your computer you might want to use a faster baud rate.

When the serial channel is set up at 9,600 bps 12 bytes of data takes about 1/100 sec. to transfer. The fastest transfer rate currently is 115,200 bps, which means those same 12 bits take about 1/1000 sec., which works out to a rate of 1 kHz. This rate is sometimes unnecessary, but in extremely time-critical applications (tangible musical interfaces are a great example), that sort of speed can be important in creating greater fidelity for the person using your application.

Once your Arduino has broadcast your message you'll need to receive it. Most programming languages, and we do mean almost all of them, provide ways for you to send and receive messages on the serial port of the machine they're running on. This means that anything your computer can do, you can network with your Arduino, and anything that your Arduino is capable of can be controlled or networked with your computer.

You can use several different strategies to set up serial communication between your Arduino and a computer. In the next few sections we'll outline some of the more common strategies and look at some example code for each. First, we'll use face tracking in Processing to control servomotors connected to an Arduino in order to ensure that a detected face stays in the center of the frame.

13.2 *Servos for face tracking*

Processing is one of the most influential and oldest creative code projects. Originally developed at MIT by Ben Fry and Casey Reas, it's now maintained by a larger team. It's written in Java, so anyone familiar with Java will understand the platform instantly. It's also designed to be friendly to designers and artists who don't have deep technical backgrounds so that they can begin making visual or interactive projects. It's open source, free to download, and has versions for all the major platforms, so it's easy to get up to speed and easy to port your projects from computer to computer or even onto the internet.

We don't want to dig too deeply into how Processing works in this chapter, but you'll notice a few similarities between projects in the Arduino IDE and almost all Processing applications right away. For example, the Arduino setup() and loop() methods become setup() and draw() in Processing. The IDEs look more or less the same, and the libraries are organized similarly. The two projects share a lot of history as well as a design attitude that allows for exploration and quick prototyping.

SERIAL COMMUNICATION IN PROCESSING

Processing has a library that allows serial communication, and it's called, unsurprisingly, Serial. The following code lets you easily import this library into your project:

```
import processing.serial.*;
```

To create a serial connection you'll want to create an instance of the Serial class:

```
Serial arduinoPort;
```

Next you need to set up the communication between the Arduino and the Processing application. In the setup() method of your application, where your application is initialized, you initialize the Serial instance:

```
arduinoPort = new Serial(this, "", 9600);
```

The constructor for the Serial class looks like this:

```
Serial(this, port, rate)
```

Let's break this down further:

- this—The application that will run the Serial instance
- port—The name of the serial device that represents the connected Arduino
- rate—The baud rate that the communication will use

If you don't know the name of the port off the top of your head you can call Serial.list(). It'll return an array of the names of all devices attached to the serial ports of the computer as Strings which will allow you to easily do something like the following:

```
arduinoPort = new Serial(this, Serial.list()[0], 9600);
```

This selects the first `String` representing the name of a serial device. For instance, you might want to use the third serial device, so you'd pass the third item from the result of `Serial.list()` as the second argument to the `Serial` constructor:

```
arduinoPort = new Serial(this, Serial.list()[2], 9600);
```

To send a message to the serial port call the following method:

```
arduinoPort.write();
```

To read data from a serial port, you check whether there's any data available in the serial buffer and read from it until none is left. This works because each call to `read()` pulls the byte out of the buffer so that it's only read once. The buffer shrinks as you read each byte:

```
while(Serial.available() > 0) {
    print(arduinoPort.read());
}
```

Now that you've seen how a Processing application can interact with an Arduino you're ready to look at a project that leverages both of these tools.

13.2.1 Assembling the face-tracking hardware

One of the things that Processing makes easy and painless is interfacing with peripheral devices, such as a camera. Reading data from a webcam attached to your computer can be a hassle in C++ or other programming languages, but in Processing it's a breeze. The same goes for doing complex computer vision tasks like detecting faces. You might be getting some idea of where this is going: in this example we're going to build a simple face tracker using Processing and an Arduino.

For this project you'll need the following:

- Two servo motors
- A pan and tilt kit for the servos, or materials to make your own
- A breadboard and jump wires
- An Arduino
- A desktop or laptop computer with Processing installed on it
- A USB webcam

Let's assemble and wire the structure that the Arduino will use to position the webcam at the center of the detected face. The basic idea is that one servomotor should control the *x* rotation of the servo and the other should control the *y* rotation of the servomotor. There are kits that allow you to do this quickly, such as the Lynx Pan and Tilt kit shown in figure 13.1.

If you don't want to get a Lynx you can easily create a simple mount for your servomotor out of acrylic, metal, or even light wood, and then attach it to the servo disk with hot glue or screws. As long as the *x*-axis servo is facing upright and the *y*-axis servo is facing sideways you'll have full 180-degree rotation across a hemisphere. The trick then becomes attaching the camera atop the servo that's providing the *y*-axis

Figure 13.1   The Lynx Pan and Tilt kit

rotation. As long as your camera is light enough any mount that provides a 90-degree angle should work. Once you have the camera in place you're ready to position the image with signals from the Processing application.

To ensure that your camera will properly track faces, make sure that the tilt motor (*y*-axis) is mounted at the 90-degree position of the pan motor (*x*-axis) and that the camera is mounted at the 90-degree position of the tilt motor. This way, the middle point of your combined servo motors will correspond to what the Processing application is sending. Figure 13.2 shows how to connect the two servos to the Arduino board. The camera will be connected directly to the computer that is running your Processing sketch.

13.2.2 *Code for face-tracking*

This example uses OpenCV, the most comprehensive and powerful open source computer vision library available. The OpenCV library for Processing was built by Douglas Edric Stanley and Stephane Cousot by compiling the original C++ code and then creating a Java library that can link to the Processing frameworks. This means that you can use the OpenCV library without needing to compile all the C++ code that comprises it, but it also means that the install process for this library is a little more involved than usual.

You can find the OpenCV libraries and instructions for installation at ubaa.net/ shared/processing/opencv/, but here they are summarized briefly:

1 Download the files for your OS.
2 Run the installer.
3 Move the library to the libraries folder of your Processing home folder.

You should now be ready to start working with the OpenCV libraries.

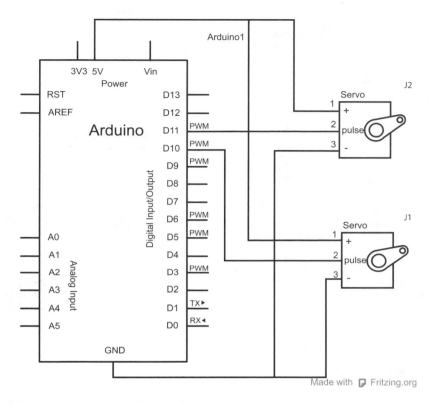

Figure 13.2   Connecting the servomotors to the Arduino

Now let's look at the Arduino code in listing 13.1. The general idea is that the Processing application will send the coordinates for the center of the detected face to the Arduino. These are sent as normalized screen coordinates, which means it uses numbers from 0 to 1.0. The Arduino then smoothly moves the two servos toward that center. Because the camera is mounted on the servos, you don't have to worry about centering the image in the Arduino, only moving them to the location sent from the Processing application.

Listing 13.1   Face tracking using OpenCV in Arduino

```
#define DSERVO_TWO_X_PIN 10
#define DSERVO_TWO_Y_PIN 11

#include <Servo.h>

const float ratio = 0.7058;
Servo vert;
Servo horz;
byte target[2];
byte current[2];
```

Value 180/255 used
to change unsigned
char into degrees.

```
void setup() {
  horz.attach(DSERVO_TWO_X_PIN );
  vert.attach(DSERVO_TWO_Y_PIN );

  memset(target, 0.5, 2);
  memset(current, 122, 2);

  Serial.begin(9600);

}
void loop() {
    if(Serial.available() > 1) {
        target[0] = Serial.read();
        target[1] = Serial.read();
    }

    if(abs(target[0] - current[0]) > 1) {
      horz.write(lerp(0.5, current[0], target[0]) * ratio);
      current[0] = target[0];
    }

    if(abs(target[1] - current[1]) > 1) {
      vert.write(lerp(0.5, current[1], target[1]) * ratio);
      current[0] = target[1];

    }
}
byte lerp(float t, byte a, byte b)
{
  return a + t * (b - a);
}
```

If we've got new positions, store them.

If the x position needs to be updated, lerp to it.

If the y position needs to be updated, lerp to it.

On the Processing side, there may be some strange new things in the code that you haven't seen before, and you don't need to understand all of it to use the face-detection functionality in OpenCV. The overview is that OpenCV can read in XML files that describe the characteristics of certain kinds of shapes: a car, a person, or a face. The data structure described in that XML file is called a *Haar Cascade.* By loading that XML file a data structure is created that the OpenCV library can compare each incoming frame against. If the information in the frame is a close-enough match to the XML description file, the library reports the location of the detected shape.

In this example we'll be using a prepared XML file that describes faces. This comes with the Processing OpenCV library, so you don't need to prepare anything extra; just add the path to it, stored in the OpenCV library as OpenCV.CASCADE_FRONTALFACE_ALT, and go.

The general flow of the Processing application is as follows:

1 Start the camera.
2 Read in the Haar Cascade XML file.
3 Start reading in each frame from the camera.
4 Convert the frame to grayscale to save on memory.
5 Check for matches against the face Haar Cascade pattern.
6 If a match is found send the Arduino the screen-normalized location of the face.

It sounds complex, but as you can see in the following listing the Processing code isn't remarkably long for how powerful it is.

Listing 13.2   Face tracking in Processing

```
import hypermedia.video.*;
import java.awt.Rectangle;
import processing.serial.*;

OpenCV opencv;
Serial arduinoPort;

int contrast_value    = 0;
int brightness_value  = 0;

void setup() {
    size( 320, 240 );
    opencv = new OpenCV( this );
    opencv.capture( width, height );
    opencv.cascade( OpenCV.CASCADE_FRONTALFACE_ALT );
    arduinoPort = new Serial(this, Serial.list()[0], 9600);

}

public void stop() {
    opencv.stop();
    super.stop();
}

void draw() {
    opencv.read();
    opencv.convert( GRAY );
    opencv.contrast( contrast_value );
    opencv.brightness( brightness_value );

    Rectangle[] faces =
     opencv.detect( 1.2, 2, OpenCV.HAAR_DO_CANNY_PRUNING, 40, 40 );

    image( opencv.image(), 0, 0 );
    boolean foundFace = true;

    Rectangle bestFace = new Rectangle();
    if(faces.length > 1) {
      for(int i = 0; i < faces.length; i++) {
        if( (faces[i].height * faces[i].width)  >
                   (bestFace.height * bestFace.width)) {
          bestFace = faces[i];
        }
      }
    } else if(faces.length > 0) {
      bestFace = faces[0];
    } else {
      foundFace = false;
    }

     if(foundFace)
    {
      noFill();
```

Load detection description from "haarcascade_frontalface_alt.xml"

Grab a new frame and convert to gray

Find the largest face

```
        stroke(255,0,0);
        for( int i=0; i<faces.length; i++ ) {
            rect( bestFace.x, bestFace.y,                    ┐  Draw face
                  bestFace.width, bestFace.height );    ◁───┘  area(s)
        }

        arduinoPort.write( 255*(bestFace.x -
                              (bestFace.width/2)) / width);   ◁──┐ Send
        arduinoPort.write( 255*(bestFace.y -                      │ coordinates to
                              (bestFace.height/2)) / height);     │ the Arduino
    }

}

void mouseDragged() {
    contrast_value   = (int) map( mouseX, 0, width, -128, 128 );
    brightness_value = (int) map( mouseY, 0, width, -128, 128 );
}
```

Now you have a somewhat sophisticated face-tracking system that responds to its environment and adjusts accordingly. This is only the beginning of the fun that you can have with paired servomotors and Processing. If you look around online you'll find everything from pet toys, to home-security implementations, to practical jokes that use the same system.

13.3 Using Firmata to create an equalizer

One thing that Processing does easily that the Arduino doesn't is audio analysis. The processor on the Arduino is just not powerful enough to analyze and extract information about audio data as it plays, but your computer is. In this example we'll create an extremely simple equalizer display using Processing and the Arduino, running Firmata to send an analysis of the audio currently playing from an MP3 file. It's simple but it's fun, and it shows the basics of working with Firmata as well.

Firmata is a project initiated by Hans-Christoph Steiner that acts almost as a stripped-down operating system for the Arduino, driven completely by serial communication. You load Firmata onto your Arduino, and then from another programming language you can check the values of pins, perform complex communication with components, and set the values of pins without needing to update your Arduino code at all. You can use Firmata in Processing, openFrameworks, Cinder, Python, Ruby, Pd, and several other programming platforms.

13.3.1 Using Firmata in your application

First we'll go over the simple part so you can see how similar using Firmata in Processing is to programming the Arduino.

If you load Firmata onto your Arduino and then want to set digital pin 12 to HIGH from a Processing application, you'd simply create an instance of the Arduino class (in this case named arduino) and then call the digitalWrite() method:

```
arduino.digitalWrite(12, Arduino.HIGH);
```

To read values you simply use the methods `analogRead()` or `digitalRead()`, passing the appropriate pin numbers as parameters.

These methods are properties of the Arduino instance that you create, so the method calls are always going to look like the following:

```
int an1Value = arduino.analogRead(1);
```

or:

```
int dg13Value = arduino.digitalRead(13);
```

Firmata requires that you set the digital pins that you want to use to be output or input pins. This is similar to what you do when you write a sketch for the Arduino using the Arduino IDE, except that, again, you're calling the methods on the Arduino object in Processing.

Now we're getting to the slightly harder part: how do you make an Arduino object that your Processing application can use to do all this stuff on the Arduino? The trick is to construct an instance of the `Arduino` class and pass in all the appropriate data when the object is created. Here's the constructor:

```
Arduino(parent, name, rate)
```

In this constructor `parent` is always the Processing application that's going to use the Arduino instance. `name` is the serial device that you want to connect to, and it's something like COM1 on Windows or /dev/tty.usbmodem411 on OS X or Linux. Finally, `rate` is the baud rate that you want to communicate with the Arduino at. By default the Firmata library is set up to use the fastest baud rate available, 115,200, so unless you've changed that in the Firmata library you'll want to use the default.

A complete constructor call will look something like this:

```
Arduino arduino = new Arduino(this, "/dev/tty.usbmodem411", 115200);
```

You'll typically want to do this in the `setup()` method of your Processing application, or in the initialization of whatever other application you're using. Once you've created an instance of the Arduino you can begin sending and receiving information from the Arduino itself.

Firmata also allows you to read and write over the I2C protocol, as well as control servomotors and query the state of all the digital pins on the Arduino. While it's somewhat limited at this time (SPI or pulseIn/pulseOut aren't currently supported), Firmata does allow you to control your Arduino from a host computer with a minimum of configuration and a great deal of control.

13.3.2 *Audio analysis in Processing*

First let's look at the audio analysis we're going to do. When you want to figure out how loud different frequency ranges in audio data are, most commonly you'll use what's called a fast Fourier transform (FFT). This is a technique that maps the raw numbers of audio data to the audible frequency spectrum and provides that data in an array representing the volumes in a given range of frequencies. Anyone who's ever seen an equalizer will have an intuitive sense of what this looks like. The spectrum does not represent individual frequencies, but frequency bands centered on particular frequencies.

To do this FFT in Processing we'll use Minim, an audio library that uses the Java Sound API, a bit of Tritonus, and JavaZOOM's MP3SPI. This audio library is easy for people developing in the Processing environment to use. The underlying philosophy of Minim is to make integrating audio into a Processing application as simple as possible while still providing computational power to do real-time audio processing.

Minim comes installed with Processing so you don't need to do anything to start using it, other than to add the import statement to the top of your application.

13.3.3 Assembling the equalizer hardware

This example will not have any Arduino code, because you'll be loading the Firmata library onto the Arduino and then allowing that to handle all the communication with the Processing application. But you'll need a few simple hardware components:

- Five LEDs
- Five 4.7k resistors
- An Arduino
- A computer with Processing installed

Figure 13.3 shows how to connect the LEDs and resistors to the Arduino to create the equalizer.

This application is simple on the Arduino side: the data from the processed audio file is used to illuminate five LEDs that are attached to the PWM pins of the Arduino. You'll want to attach resistors to those LEDs to ensure that they don't burn out, but nothing else is required to see your song.

13.3.4 Code for the equalizer

You probably have Firmata already included with your Arduino IDE distribution because it's been an included library since Arduino 0012. You should only need to load the StandardFirmata program from Examples > Firmata onto your Arduino (see figure 13.4).

As we mentioned earlier, the Processing library that this example uses to analyze the audio is called Minim, and it comes standard with the Processing library. You just need to import the library into the program using the `import` statement. A library for Firmata, called Arduino, also comes standard with Processing and is imported with the following statement:

```
import cc.arduino.*;
```

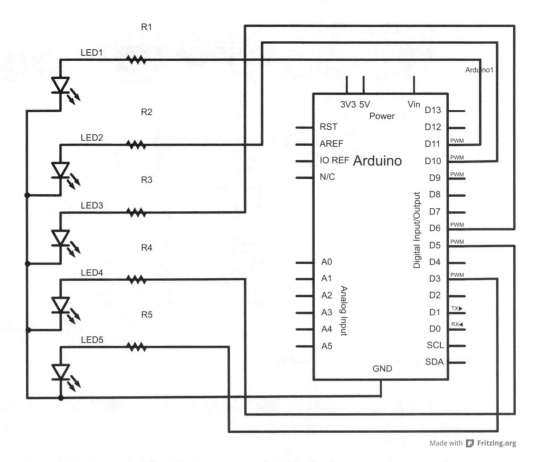

Made with 🟦 **Fritzing.org**

Figure 13.3   Connecting the LEDs to create your Arduino equalizer

This Processing program (see listing 13.3) loads an MP3 file generically called song.mp3 and begins playing it in a loop. (You'll need to name an MP3 file "song.mp3" and add it to the folder for your Processing sketch.) The program then creates an FFT object that can break the audio data from the song into frequency bins.

In the loop() of the application, the FFT forward() method is passed the mixed data from the audio file's left and right channels. The resulting array is then grouped into five frequency ranges—one for each LED that you have attached to the Arduino—and it's then sent to Firmata on the Arduino using the analogWrite() method. This calls the analogWrite() method within the Arduino and brightens or dims the LEDs depending on the strength of the averaged values for the chunk of the frequency spectrum.

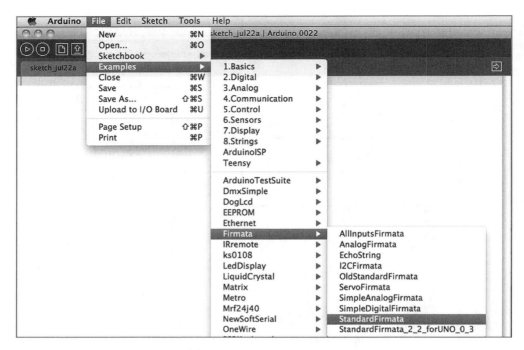

Figure 13.4   Selecting the StandardFirmata program

Listing 13.3   Using Firmata in Processing

```
import processing.serial.*;
import cc.arduino.*;

import ddf.minim.analysis.*;
import ddf.minim.*;

static final int FIRST_LED = 3;
static final int SECOND_LED = 5;
static final int THIRD_LED = 6;
static final int FOURTH_LED = 10;
static final int FIFTH_LED = 11;

float bins[];

Arduino arduino;

FFT fft;
Minim minim;
AudioPlayer player;

void setup()
{
  size( 300, 300 );

  arduino = new Arduino(this, Arduino.list()[0], 57600);

  minim = new Minim(this);
```

```
    player = minim.loadFile("song.mp3");
    player.loop();

    fft = new FFT(player.bufferSize(), player.sampleRate());          ◁───┐  Create FFT
                                                                            object to
    bins = new float[5];                                                    read MP3 file.
}

void draw()
{

    background(0);

    fft.forward(player.mix);

    int bands = fft.specSize() / 5;

    for (int i = 0; i < 5; i++) {
      bins[i] = 0;                                                      ┌──  Sum a section of
      for( int j = 0; j < bands; j++) {                               ◁─┘   values into a bin.

          bins[i] += fft.getBand((i * bands) + j);

      }
      bins[i] /= bands;
      rect( i * 20, 0, 20, bins[i]);
    }

    arduino.analogWrite(FIRST_LED,
      (int) map(bins[0], 0, 10, 0, 255));                              ◁──┐
    arduino.analogWrite(SECOND_LED,
      (int) map(bins[1], 0, 10, 0, 255));                              ◁──┤
    arduino.analogWrite(THIRD_LED,                                            Map each bin
      (int) map(bins[2], 0, 10, 0, 255));                              ◁──┤  and set the LED
    arduino.analogWrite(FOURTH_LED,                                          brightness.
      (int) map(bins[3], 0, 10, 0, 255));                              ◁──┤
    arduino.analogWrite(FIFTH_LED,
      (int) map(bins[4], 0, 10, 0, 255));                              ◁──┘

}

void stop()
{
  player.close();
  minim.stop();
  super.stop();
}
```

That's only the beginning of what Firmata can do. It allows you to easily control an Arduino and keep your control code in the application running on your computer, rather than needing to update your code on the Arduino every time you make a change to your program. For rapid prototyping this is a real advantage, because you can concentrate on your computer program and let your Arduino act like an input or output device. To learn more about Processing I highly recommend *Processing: A Programming Handbook for Visual Designers and Artists* by Ben Fry and Casey Reas (MIT Press, 2007), or *Processing for Visual Artists* by Andrew Glassner (A.K. Peters, 2010).

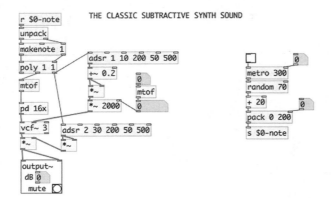

Figure 13.5   A Pd patch

13.4   *Using Pure Data to create a synthesizer*

Pure Data, often referred to as Pd, is a graphical programming environment intended primarily for creating real-time audio and video applications. It's called "real-time" because you can edit your programs as they're running without needing to stop and recompile them as you would need to with Processing or with an Arduino board. Simply making changes in the IDE updates your program as it's running. Pd is completely free software, and there are versions for Windows, Linux, and OS X, as well as other less-common operating systems.

Because Pd is a graphical, patch-based environment rather than a text-based programming environment, completed code looks different than Arduino code. For instance, figure 13.5 shows a program or "patch" that creates the classic additive synth sound. Figure 13.5 shows what subtractive synth looks like in Pd.

Luckily, though, you can paste a patch in text format into the editor and have the editor turn it into the graphical patch layout in figure 13.5.

To bring input from a serial device into your Pd patch, you create an object called a `comport`, which is short for "communication port." Figure 13.6 shows what it looks like.

`comport 9600`   **Figure 13.6   The `comport` object**

The 9600 is a parameter passed to the `comport`, and it sets the baud rate that the patch will be listening at. If you want to use this to read from or write to your Arduino it should match the baud rate that your Arduino is sending or reading at.

There's another object that you need to get access to the serial ports on your computer, though: the `devices` object. Figure 13.7 shows the `devices` object connected to the `comport`.

Clicking on the `devices` object in your PD sketch shows you all of the serial devices that are attached to the computer that Pd can read in. Now it's time to put the power of Pd to work by generating audio in response to tangible input.

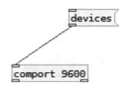

**Figure 13.7
Connecting the
`comport` to the
`devices` object**

13.4.1 *Assembling the synthesizer hardware*

The example you'll explore in this section demonstrates one of the most powerful features of Pd: the ability to easily generate and combine multiple sounds at once with extremely fine-grained control. One of the challenges of making sounds using computers is creating expressive and intuitive interfaces so that people can have both fine-grained control and quick reaction times. A quick survey of some of the favored controls for musical instruments would put the potentiometer somewhere near the top of the list, so in this example we'll use five potentiometers to control four oscillating sine waves. There are much more complex and expressive things you can do with Pd, but this is a good introduction not only to how communication between an Arduino and Pd works, but to some of the components of Pd as well.

For this example, you'll need the following:

- Four potentiometers
- A breadboard
- An Arduino
- A computer with Pd installed

The wiring schematic in figure 13.8 should be quite straightforward.

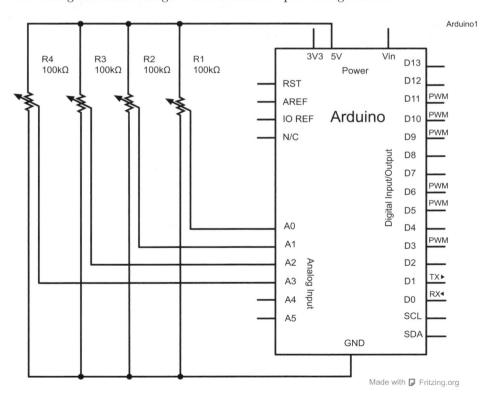

Figure 13.8   Connecting potentiometers for the mixer

13.4.2 Code for the synthesizer

The Pd code is a little strange to look at the first time. You won't see any function declarations, variable types, or curly brackets. But you do have objects, they still have properties, and there is a flow of logic you can follow.

The first thing to realize about Pd is that everything is a flow of data from one component to the next. In our case, the data comes from the Arduino, and it's passed to a parser, then to four oscillators, and finally to the sound card. In the Pd IDE the program looks like figure 13.9.

As text, the program looks like what you see in the following listing.

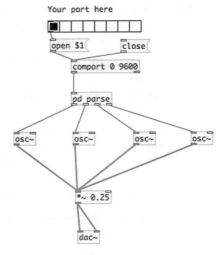

Figure 13.9   The Pd patch in the Pd IDE

Listing 13.4   Pd application as text (AIA13_4.pd)

```
#N canvas 892 52 463 519 10;
#X obj 110 92 comport 0 115200;
#X msg 174 65 close;
#N canvas 194 45 687 494 parse 0;
#X obj 140 122 select 13 10;
#X obj 142 186 repack 22;
#X obj 137 32 inlet;
#X obj 97 390 outlet;
#X obj 142 219 route 48 49 50 51;
#X text 207 47 Comport spits out ASCII strings: potPin id \, val \, carriage
    return \, newline.;
#X text 230 119 strip off return and bang on each newline;
#X text 211 184 repack;
#X text 266 219 route by ID;
#X text 503 296 ASCII to float;
#X obj 213 298 string2any 16;
#X obj 96 299 string2any 16;
#X obj 310 297 string2any 16;
#X obj 405 297 string2any 16;
#X obj 405 389 outlet;
#X obj 310 389 outlet;
#X obj 213 390 outlet;
#X connect 0 0 1 0;
#X connect 0 2 1 0;
#X connect 1 0 4 0;
#X connect 2 0 0 0;
#X connect 4 0 10 0;
#X connect 4 1 11 0;
#X connect 4 2 12 0;
#X connect 4 3 13 0;
#X connect 10 0 16 0;
```

```
#X connect 11 0 3 0;
#X connect 12 0 15 0;
#X connect 13 0 14 0;
#X restore 110 135 pd parse;
#X text 78 16 Your port here;
#X msg 83 64 open \$1;
#X obj 80 40 hradio 15 1 0 8 empty empty empty 0 -8 0 10 -262144 -1
-1 1;
#X obj 118 319 dac~;
#X obj 112 188 osc~;
#X obj 36 188 osc~;
#X obj 190 188 osc~;
#X obj 264 188 osc~;
#X obj 115 266 *~ 0.25;
#X connect 0 0 2 0;
#X connect 1 0 0 0;
#X connect 2 0 8 0;
#X connect 2 1 7 0;
#X connect 2 2 9 0;
#X connect 2 3 10 0;
#X connect 4 0 0 0;
#X connect 5 0 4 0;
#X connect 7 0 11 0;
#X connect 8 0 11 0;
#X connect 9 0 11 0;
#X connect 10 0 11 0;
#X connect 11 0 6 0;
#X connect 11 0 6 1;
```

On the Arduino side we'll attach four potentiometers to control each of the oscillators on the Pd side, and then we'll read the values from each of them, as shown in the next listing.

Listing 13.5 Application to communicate with Pd

```
float val1,val2,val3,val4;

int potPin1 = 0;
int potPin2 = 1;
int potPin3 = 3;
int potPin4 = 4;

void setup()
{
  Serial.begin(115200);
}

void loop()
{
  val1 = analogRead(potPin1);
  Serial.print(potPin1);
  Serial.println(map(val1, 0, 1024, 200, 1000),DEC);

  val2 = analogRead(potPin2);
  Serial.print(potPin2);
  Serial.println(map(val2, 0, 1024, 200, 1000),DEC);
```

```
val3 = analogRead(potPin3);
Serial.print(potPin3);
Serial.println(map(val3, 0, 1024, 200, 1000),DEC);

val4 = analogRead(potPin4);
Serial.print(potPin4);
Serial.println(map(val4, 0, 1024, 200, 1000), DEC);
}
```

There's not much to the Arduino side, but combined with the Pd application it allows you to create a rich range of sounds that can be closely tuned by the Arduino. Note that the data sent over the serial port is mapped between 200 and 1000, which ensures that the frequency of the sine wave is a little more palatable.

Using the Arduino with Pd is powerful because it allows musicians and DJs to create their own tangible interfaces to Pd and to their music. This means that you can not only recreate interfaces that you may be familiar with, but also experiment with new ways of physically inputting data and creating music.

To learn more about Pd I recommend that you look at the Pd tutorial site at www.pd-tutorial.com.

13.5   *Using Python to monitor temperatures*

Python is one of the most popular programming languages—it's flexible, powerful, and accessible. It has a remarkable number of libraries for doing everything from game development to applied mathematics to website development. It's been under constant development since 2001 and has steadily grown in popularity and capability over the years.

The example we'll explore in this section revolves around a simple idea: what is the temperature in discrete parts of a home at any given time? You could walk around with a thermometer and figure this out, but it might be more fun and more practical to place several thermometers around the house and send the temperature data as email messages to your own email account. This example has the Arduino sleep until it's time to wake up (to save on power or battery), and upon waking, send a message to the Python program. Once the Python application has received a message it parses it by room and then emails it off.

One thing to note is that this example assumes for the sake of brevity that you're connecting to an external SMTP server. You can get an SMTP server running on your computer fairly easily, but the steps to do so are a little beyond the scope of this book, so we'll leave it as an exercise for you to complete. Try searching around for "postfix" if you're on OS X or Linux, or "enable smtp iis 7" if you're on Windows.

13.5.1   *The Serial library in Python*

The Python library for serial communication is called pySerial, and you may need to explicitly install it on your computer before beginning to work with serial communication in a Python application. The library, along with installation instructions for your operating system, can be found at http://pyserial.sourceforge.net.

Once you've installed the library you can load it into your program by putting the following line at the beginning of your program:

```
import serial
```

Now it's a matter of creating a serial instance:

```
arduino = serial.Serial(
    port='/dev/ttyUSB1',
    baudrate=9600,
)
```

If you're familiar with Python, the preceding line should look quite familiar. If you're not, you might be wondering where the declaration of the Arduino variable is hidden. The answer is that there isn't one. In Python you don't need to give variables a type before starting to work with them, so the preceding line works fine.

Once you've made a `Serial` instance, given it a port to communicate on and a baud rate, and stored it in the `arduino` variable, the `arduino` variable is now an instance of `Serial`. This is the long way of saying that a variable is only typed after it has been constructed, not before. That might seem a bit bizarre, but it's actually one of the key affordances of Python. If you're interested in learning more about Python and how it works check out http://python.org/. Now we'll discuss more about how to interface Python and the Arduino.

To start the serial communication you issue the following call:

```
arduino.open()
```

Note that this call to `open()` isn't necessary if you haven't closed the connection or reconnected a device.

To read from the serial port call `read()`:

```
message = arduino.read(1)
```

The `read()` method takes an integer that dictates how many bytes you want to read from the serial port. The preceding example reads 1 byte.

You might wonder how you can read everything that's in the serial channel. There's a handy method to determine whether the Arduino has sent anything to the serial port: `inWaiting()`. To get all the data in the serial port, do something like the following:

```
while arduino.inWaiting() > 0:
    message = arduino.read(1)
print message
```

That's all there is to it. To send a message to the Arduino over the serial channel use `write()`:

```
arduino.write('x')
```

Clearing the serial buffer is as easy as calling `flush()`:

```
arduino.flush()
```

When you're all done with the serial communication simply call `close()`:

```
arduino.close()
```

This should all seem a bit familiar from the previous examples; most programming languages implement serial communication in more or less the same way. Now it's time for an example.

13.5.2 *Assembling the thermometer hardware*

For this example you'll need the following:

- Three Texas Instruments LM35 thermometers
- An Arduino
- A computer with Python installed

The temperature sensor we prefer to use is the LM35; you can find more information about it via the manufacturer's site: www.ti.com/lit/ds/symlink/lm35.pdf. It primarily comes in two packages: an 8-pin DIP package and a 3-pin upright plastic package. The 3-pin version has a V+ pin, a GND pin, and a pin that returns the detected temperature as a linearized analog value. The 8-pin package has the same active pins with five no-connect pins, but connecting it is the same. The connections are shown in figure 13.10.

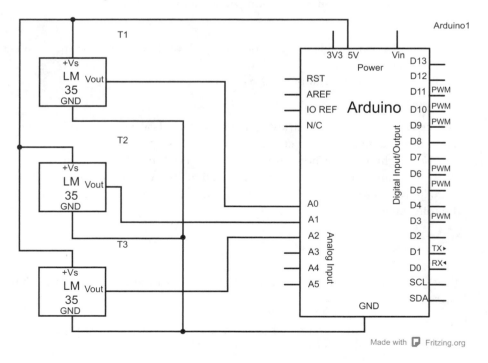

Figure 13.10   Connecting the temperature sensors to the Arduino

13.5.3 *Code for monitoring temperatures*

The Arduino code contains no big surprises, though you do need to convert the voltage returned from the `analogIn()` method to correctly get the temperature in Celsius. That's done in the `convertToCelsius()` method at the end of the following listing. (To convert to Fahrenheit, simply add 32 and multiply by 1.8.)

Listing 13.6 Arduino application to send temperature data to Python

```
const int LIVING_ROOM = 1;
const int BEDROOM = 2;
const int KITCHEN = 3;

void setup()
{
  Serial.begin(57600);
}

void loop()
{
  if(Serial.available() > 0)
  {
    Serial.print(LIVING_ROOM);
    Serial.print(',');
    Serial.print(convertToCelsius (LIVING_ROOM));
    Serial.print(';');
    Serial.print(BEDROOM);
    Serial.print(',');
    Serial.print(convertToCelsius (BEDROOM));
    Serial.print(';');
    Serial.print(KITCHEN);
    Serial.print(',');
    Serial.print(convertToCelsius (KITCHEN));
    Serial.print(';');
  }
}

int convertToCelsius(int pin)
{
  return (5.0 * analogRead(pin) * 100.0)/1024.0;
}
```

The Python application sleeps for 15 minutes and then sends a message to tell the Arduino to query its LM35 sensors and return their values (see the following listing). Once all of the data is read in from the Arduino, an email detailing the detected temperatures is sent to the user's address using the user's mail server to connect to the SMTP server.

Listing 13.7 Python application to receive temperature data

```
import smtplib
import time
import serial

SERVER = "smtp.somemail.com:587"
```

```
FROM = "house@somemail.com"
TO = ["you@somemail.com "] # must be a list

rooms = ["living room", "bedroom", "kitchen"]

def sendMessage(room, value):

    SUBJECT = "Hello! The temperature in the " +
            rooms[room] + " is" + value

    TEXT = "Just thought you might like to know :)"

    message = " From: %s To: %s Subject: %s %s "
    message = message % (FROM, ", ".join(TO), SUBJECT, TEXT)

    # Send the mail
    server = smtplib.SMTP(SERVER)
    server.starttls()
    server.login("house@somemail.com", "password")
    server.sendmail(FROM, TO, message)
    server.quit()

def readArduino():
    room = ''
    temp = ''
    arduino.write("check")
    time.sleep(0.1)
    datastring = ''
    while arduino.inWaiting() > 1:
        datastring += arduino.read(1)

    splitArr = datastring.split(';')
    i = 0
    while(i < len(splitArr)):
        room = splitArr[i].split(',')[0]
        temp = splitArr[i].split(',')[1]
        sendMessage(room, temp)
        i+=1

# here's the actual connection to the Arduino
arduino = serial.Serial(
    port='/dev/tty.usbmodem12341',
    baudrate=57600,
)

arduino.open()

while(true):
    time.sleep(9000)
    readArduino()
```

Login to the server to send the message

Send the message, then stop server

Sleep for 15 minutes, then read the temperature and send an email

In reality you'd probably want to log this data to a service like Cosm or Twitter, but for simplicity in this example we used email. Again, this example is only a start—the advantages and strengths of Python are many. Connecting your Arduino to Python allows you to do more with your Arduino and with Python, and it's great fun as well. To learn more about Python I recommend Zed Shaw's *Learn Python the Hard Way*, available at learnpythonthehardway.org.

13.6 *Summary*

Integrating your Arduino with software allows you to easily create physical input and feedback for an application running on a larger computer, like a desktop or a laptop computer. This means you can extend the functionality of an application into tangible and physical interaction easily, as well as vastly extending the capacity of the Arduino to perform image or audio processing, networked communication, or graphics.

appendix A
Installing
the Arduino IDE

This appendix details how to install the Arduino IDE on the Windows, Mac OS X, and Linux platforms. The Arduino IDE for all platforms is available from the Arduino website (http://arduino.cc/en/Main/Software). Download the IDE package for your platform and continue with the appropriate installation section for your operating system.

A.1   Windows

Arduino for Windows comes packaged as a zip file, so once it's downloaded you must first extract its contents. Browse to where you downloaded the file (typically your User/Downloads folder) and double-click the zip file. As shown in figure A.1, extract or drag the containing folder to somewhere accessible on your hard drive, such as C:\Program Files.

A.1.1   Installing drivers for your board

Now that you have the Arduino package copied to your computer, you're ready to install the drivers for your board. Follow the instructions in the appropriate subsection for the board and version of Windows that you're using.

DRIVER INSTALLATION FOR THE ARDUINO UNO

To begin the driver installation process, connect your Arduino Uno to the computer using a USB cable. The Uno board is USB-powered, so the green ON LED will light up. Once connected, Windows will attempt to install the board's drivers, but it will fail. This is OK!

In the Windows Start menu, select Control Panel > System and Security > System > Device Manager. Next, click and expand Ports (COM & LPT). Your Uno should

Figure A.1 Extracting/copying the Arduino IDE and drivers to your local hard drive on Windows 7

appear in the list as Arduino UNO (COMxx). If Ports (COM & LPT) does not appear in the Device Manager, or your Arduino isn't in the list, your Uno may be recognized as an unknown device. If this is the case, expand the Other Devices menu and your Arduino should appear in the list as an unknown device.

Right-click the Arduino UNO (COMxx) or Unknown Device item and select Update Driver. If you are on Windows XP, the Hardware Update wizard will ask, Can Windows Connect to Windows Update to Search for Software? Select the radio button that says No, Not at This Time, and click Next to continue.

Next, you need to manually instruct the driver installer where your Uno driver file is located. On Windows XP, the wizard should now ask, What Do You Want the Wizard to Do? Select the radio button that says Install From a List or Specified Location (Advanced). On Windows 7, simply select the list item that says Browse My Computer for Driver Software (Locate and Install Driver Software Manually).

Now, on Windows XP, make sure the radio buttons that say Search for the Best Driver in These Locations and Include This Location in the Search are both clicked. Finally, click the Browse button to set your driver path to the Arduino folder you previously extracted, and then to the folder named Drivers. Similarly for Windows 7, under Search for the Best Driver Software in This Location, browse and navigate to the Arduino folder you previously extracted, and then to the folder named Drivers (shown in figure A.2). Make sure the Include Subfolders check box is checked, and click Next.

The Windows driver installer will complete the driver installation process. If a warning message pops up that says Windows Can't Verify the Publisher of This Driver Software, click Install This Driver Software Anyway.

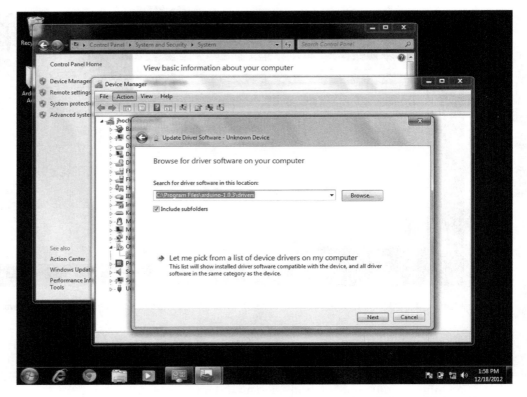

Figure A.2   Setting driver location search path for Arduino Uno driver installation on Windows 7

After the installation process completes your Uno will successfully appear under Ports (COM & LPT). You're all set.

DRIVER INSTALLATION FOR THE ARDUINO DUEMILANOVE, NANO, OR DIECIMILA
Connect your Arduino board to the computer using a USB cable. If this is your first time using the Arduino Windows will automatically begin the driver installation process. The board should be powered via USB and you should see the green PWR LED light.

> **IMPORTANT**   If you are using Windows Vista the driver will automatically be downloaded and installed, and you can skip this section. For Windows 7 and XP users, please continue to read.

If you're on Windows XP the Hardware Update wizard will appear with the prompt Can Windows Connect to Windows Update to Search for Software? Select the radio button that says, No, Not This Time to continue with the manual install. Instead, select the radio button that says Install From a List or Specified Location (Advanced) and click Next. Depending on your version of Windows you'll want to make sure that you uncheck the Search Removable Media check box, but make sure Search for the Best Driver in These Locations and Include This Location in the Search are both checked.

For Windows 7 the prompt will be slightly different. Instead, when asked How Do You Want to Search for the Driver? select the list item that says Browse My Computer for Driver Software (Locate and Install the Driver Software Manually). At the following prompt click the Browse button to set the path in which your drivers are located, making sure to also select the check box to Include Subfolders. Whether you are on Windows XP or Windows 7 (shown in figure A.3), for the driver search path you should browse to your downloaded Arduino folder and browse to the drivers/FTDI USB Drivers directory so that the Windows driver installer will know where to find the driver file.

Click Next and the installation wizard will search for and find the driver, and it'll then notify you that a USB serial converter has been found. Next, the New Hardware Wizard will appear again and it will take you through the process again. Select and set the same options and locations as before, and at the end a USB serial port will be found. You're all set.

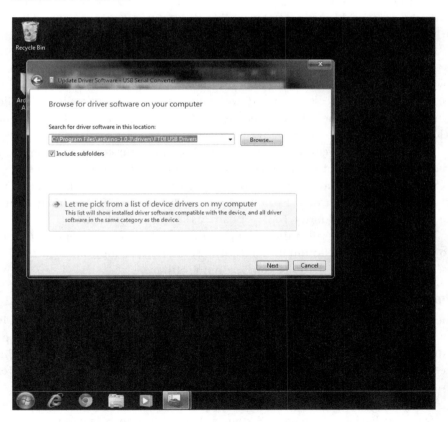

Figure A.3 Setting driver location for FTDI-based Arduino boards (such as the Duemilanove, Nano, and Diecimila) on Windows 7

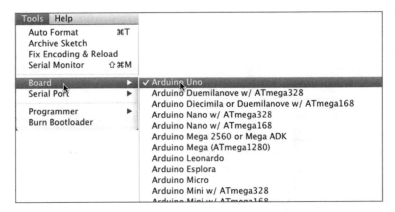

Figure A.4   Select the type of Arduino board

A.2   *Mac OS X*

The Mac OS X Arduino software is packaged as a zip file. Download the latest version. When the download has completed, double-click on the zip file to expand it. Copy the Arduino application to your Applications folder.

If you are using a board older than an Arduino Uno or Mega2560 you'll need to also install FTDI drivers to work with the FTDI on these boards. The drivers can be downloaded from the FTDI website at http://www.ftdichip.com/Drivers/VCP.htm as a disk image (.dmg) file. Once it's downloaded, double-click the file and follow the instructions given. When the drivers are installed you'll need to restart your machine to load them.

The next step is to connect your Arduino board to your computer using an appropriate USB cable. Power to the Arduino board is provided by the USB cable.

Start up the Arduino application by clicking on its icon—this will load the Arduino IDE. To work with your board you'll need to set two settings in the menu. The first is the board type, found under Tools > Board, as shown in figure A.4.

The next step is to select the serial port that connects your computer to the Arduino board. This can be found under Tools > Serial Port, as shown in figure A.5.

That completes the setup of your Arduino software.

A.3   *Linux*

There are many flavors of Linux, each of which comes with slightly different instructions. We're going to outline the instructions for Debian, because that's a very popular distribution, but you can find instructions for other distributions on the Arduino website in the "Getting Started" section. They're fairly similar but have slight differences across versions.

To correctly install Arduino on a Debian-based system you'll want to first start up the Synaptic Package Manager (System > Administration > Synaptic Package Manager) and enter your system administrator password so that you can make changes to

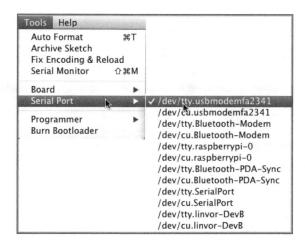

Figure A.5 Select your serial port

your system. Once you have Synaptic up and running, type '`jre`' in the quick search box and find Openjdk-7-jre (Java Runtime Environment). Figure A.6 shows the Synaptic Package Manager.

Now click on Openjdk-7-jre and select the Mark for Installation check box, as shown in figure A.7.

The package manager will want to install a lot of other supporting libraries, as shown in figure A.8, so go ahead and mark all of those for installation as well.

Next you need to install the compiler that Arduino uses, so enter 'gcc-avr' into the quick search box and mark it for installation, just like you did with Openjdk. Finally, you need to install avr-libc, so search for it, mark it, and allow any extra libraries.

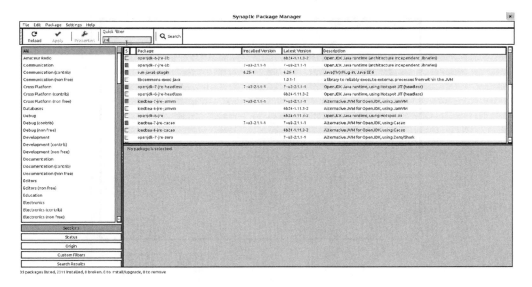

Figure A.6 Using the Synaptic Package Manager to install dependencies for Linux

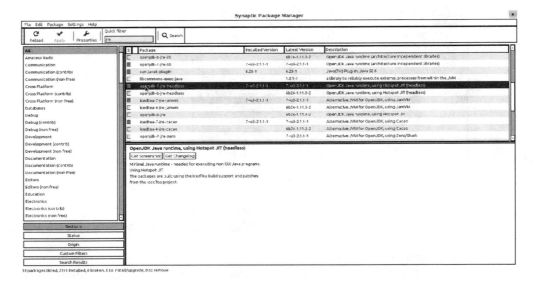

Figure A.7   Marking OpenJDK for installation

Figure A.8   Libraries to be installed for OpenJDK

Now you're done with Synaptic, so you can close it down. You might also need to restart your computer, particularly if you're on Ubuntu, to make sure all the changes you've made have percolated through your system. Even if you're not on Ubuntu restarting is a good idea to ensure that the new libraries you've added can be found.

Now you can go ahead and download the Arduino IDE from the website and unzip it to a friendly location on your computer. You should now be able to run the Arduino IDE and use it to program and communicate with your Arduino boards in the same way as the other operating systems in this appendix.

appendix B
Coding primer

This coding primer is a basic guide to the Arduino language and how it's used to create sketches that can be run on an Arduino. We'll cover the following topics:

- History of the Arduino language
- Using variables
- Using control statements
- Using loops
- Using functions

B.1 The Arduino language

The Arduino language is based on C/C++, and anyone who has previously studied C or C++ will readily be able to read the written code. If you haven't studied C or C++ before, don't worry. The Arduino language was designed to make coding as painless as possible, allowing you to concentrate on what can be done rather than how it's done.

History of the Arduino language

Students at the Interactive Design Institute, Ivrea, the original home of Arduino, were taught to program using a language called Processing. The Processing design philosophy is to teach the fundamentals of programming within a visual context, and the Arduino team, realizing they needed to develop a language that made the prototyping of ideas as simple as possible, adopted a similar philosophy.

The decision was made to use the Processing IDE as the model for the Arduino IDE, because the original Arduino system was aimed at art and design students who were already familiar with Processing. The close links to Processing are still evident today, and any improvements made to the Processing IDE can be directly imported into the Arduino system.

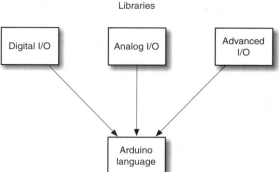

Figure B.1 Additional functionality is added to the language by using libraries.

Arduino makes extensive use of libraries to provide common functions. Figure B.1 shows some of these libraries. The libraries help the language hide much of its complexity and simplify many common tasks, such as setting digital pins as input or output, reading in analog values, controlling servomotors, or switching DC motors on and off. Many of the core libraries used are based on a library called Wiring, which was developed by Hernando Barragan.

Shields that add functionality also often require specialized libraries, and these are normally provided and maintained by the shield developers.

It's now time to move on and investigate the Arduino language in more detail by looking first at variables and their types. Then we'll move on to how code is controlled within a sketch.

B.2   *Variables*

One way to think of variables is to consider them as being like buckets, each containing something. Your code can look in individual buckets and see or change their contents. A variable is the name, or identifier, given to a container holding a piece of data that can be inspected and changed. Figure B.2 shows some typical variables.

The advantages of using variables are twofold: they make code easier to understand, and they also make it easier to maintain. If you had a variable called `pinLED` that denotes pin 13 as a digital output, and at a later stage you decide to use pin 12 instead, you would only need to make one change in your code. The following listing shows this in action.

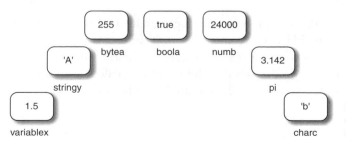

Figure B.2 Typical variables, considered as though they are held in named buckets

Listing B.1   Value of the variable `pinLED`

```
int pinLED = 13;                                         Variable pinLED
                                                         set to 13
void setup(){
    pinMode(pinLED,OUTPUT);
}
void loop(){
    digitalWrite(pinLED,HIGH);
    delay(1000);
    digitalWrite(pinLED,LOW);
    delay(1000);
}
```

The code has four instances of the variable `pinLED`, but it's simple to change them all by changing the value of `pinLED` when it is first declared, from 13 to 12. From then on all instances of `pinLED` will have the value 12.

When naming a variable in your code give it a meaningful, descriptive name that makes your code both easier to read and understand. A variable can be given any name you want, as long as it isn't one of the Arduino keywords. The following are all valid variable names:

- `outputPin`
- `inputPin`
- `leftMotor`
- `rightMotor`
- `pinLED`

You've seen how useful variables can be and how they make code easier to understand and maintain. Now let's have a look at some variable types.

B.2.1   *Variable types*

There are a number of types of variables. The variable type and the variable itself must be declared before you can use them in your code.

Variables don't have to be initialized—given a value—when declared. As a result, the following two statements are both correct:

```
int startIndex;
int startIndex = 0;
```

Nevertheless, it's considered good programming practice to initialize a variable when you declare it as this can aid in debugging—locating code errors.

When declaring numeric variables think carefully about the range of numbers your sketch will need and whether they or the result of a calculation will be whole or decimal numbers, as each is declared differently. Table B.1 outlines the range of variable types.

Table B.1 Variable types

Variable type	Description	Code example
byte	An 8-bit whole number with a range of 0 to 255.	`byte myVariable = 215;`
int	Short for *integer*; a 16-bit whole number with a range of 32,767 to –32,768.	`int myVariable = 32000;`
long	A long integer stored as a 32-bit value with a range of 2,147,483,647 to –2,147,483,648.	`long myVariable = 320000;`
float	A number that has a decimal point, stored as a 32-bit value with a range of 3.4028325E+38 to –3.4028235E+38.	`float myVariable = 3.14;`
unsigned int	An integer without any negative values, stored as a 16-bit value with a range of 0 to 65,545.	`unsigned int myVariable = 45000;`
unsigned long	A long integer without any negative values, stored as a 32-bit value with a range of 0 to 4,294,967,296.	`unsigned long myVariable = 569124;`
word	An unsigned number, stored as a 16-bit value with a range of 0 to 65,545 (the same as an `unsigned int`).	`word myVariable = 53000;`
boolean	A Boolean variable that holds one of two values: `true` or `false`.	`boolean myVariable = true;`
char	A single ASCII character, stored as an 8-bit, or byte, number. This allows characters to have arithmetic functions performed on them. The character `'c'` is stored as number `99`, so you could add 2 to this and get `'e'`.	`Char myVariable = 'c';` `Char myVariable = 99;`

NOTE With the whole number types you can get a situation called *roll over*, where a value that has increased or decreased past the end of the range for that variable type rolls over to the other end of the range. For example, if 1 is added to an int that has a value of 32,767, the value will become –32,768 and not 32,768 as you might think. This is true for all the whole number types.

B.2.2 *Arrays*

Arrays are a collection of variables that are indexed with a number. The array has to be declared before it can be used.

You can declare an initialized array like this:

```
int myVariable[4];
```

Or you can initialize an array like this:

```
int myVariable[4] = {1,2,3,4};
```

The index for an array starts from 0. Using the array name and an index accesses a value in an array.

NOTE Be careful that you don't access data from beyond the end of an array, as it will return meaningless data from memory.

```
int myVariable[4] = {1,2,3,4};
newVariable = myVariable[3];
myVariable[0] = 2;
newVariable = myVariable[0];
```

The preceding code snippet initializes an array with four values: 1, 2, 3, and 4. Then it accesses the fourth value with index 3, which is the end of the array. It then changes the value at the beginning of the array with index 0 and accesses that value by calling it with its index number.

Arrays are commonly used to manipulate values within a for loop, where the increment counter is used as the index for an array. We'll look at for loops in section B.4.

B.2.3   Strings

Text strings can be used in two ways: they can be declared as an array of type char, or you can use the String class. The String class offers a wide range of text manipulation functions that can be performed on text strings; these are discussed in some detail in chapter 7, where we work with LCD displays. Here we'll only consider the simpler array type, char.

When strings are used as an array of char they normally terminate with a null character, ASCII 0. This allows other functions to recognize when they have come to the end of the string, so when calculating the size of an array remember to add 1 to allow for the extra character.

A char array can be declared in a number of ways. All of the following are valid:

```
char myVariable[10];
char myVariable[6] = {'H', 'e', 'l', 'l', 'o'};
char myVariable[6] = {'H', 'e', 'l', 'l', 'o', '\0'};
char myVariable[] = "Hello";
char myVariable[6] = "Hello";
char myVariable[10] = "Hello";
```

The first of the preceding lines of code sets up an uninitialized array, the second line automatically appends '\0' to the end, and the third line includes it. The fourth line automatically splits the characters and auto-sizes the array, the fifth line auto-splits the array, and the sixth line leaves space in the array for a larger string.

B.2.4   Constants

Some variables don't change the values assigned to them at initialization, and in these cases the keyword const can be added to the start of the variable. Typical examples would be assigning PIN numbers or constant values like the value of pi:

```
const int pinLed = 13;
const float pi = 3.142;
```

If you try to assign a value to a constant after it has been initialized the compiler will throw an error.

The Arduino has some reserved words that are constants:

- true, false—true is any value that is not 0; false is the value 0.
- INPUT, OUTPUT—Digital pins can be set as either an INPUT or an OUTPUT using the pinMode() function:

  pinMode(13, OUTPUT)

- HIGH, LOW—You can set the value of a pin to either LOW (logic level 0, 0 volts) or HIGH (logic level 1, 5 volts).

B.2.5 Variable scope

Variables in Arduino also have what is called *scope*; the value of a variable can be referenced from some places within a sketch depending on where it's declared. Variables declared outside the main setup and loop functions are termed *global* variables, because their value is available from anywhere in the sketch. Variables declared within a function are termed *local* variables and they have local scope; their values are only available to the function in which they're declared.

The following listing shows global and local variables in action: pinLedGlobal is available to any function.

Listing B.2 Global and local variables within a sketch

```
int pinLedGlobal = 13;                              <-- Global
void Setup  {                                           variable
    pinMode(pinLedGlobal, OUTPUT);
{
void loop {
    int pinLedLocal = 14;                           <-- Local
    pinMode(pinLedLocal, OUTPUT);                       variable
    digitalWrite(pinLedGlobal, HIGH);
    digitalWrite(pinLedLocal, LOW);
}
```

As your code gets longer and becomes more complex, using local variables can prevent you from inadvertently changing the value of same-named variables that are used in other functions. Figure B.3 shows the scope of variables.

The value of varA is available to functions functionA, functionB, and functionC and in this context has global scope. Both variables varB and varC have local scope: variable varB has its value available to both functionB and functionC, whereas varC has its value only available to functionC.

In this section we've looked at variables and their types, learned about arrays, and investigated a method of dealing with text strings. We've looked at constants, including those already included by Arduino, and we've looked at variable scope. In the next section we'll take a look at some Arduino control structures.

B.3   *Taking control*

Program code, like real life, is based on making decisions, albeit in a simpler sense. Your sketch code makes decisions based on what are called Boolean tests. The results are either `true` or `false`.

Here are a few real-world examples:

- I am tired; true
- It is dark; false
- Carrots are orange; true

In your code, the Boolean test is performed using relational operators:

- 15 < 30; true
- 15 > 6; true
- 17 <= 16; false
- 17 == 16; false

The standard numerical relational operators are shown in table B.2.

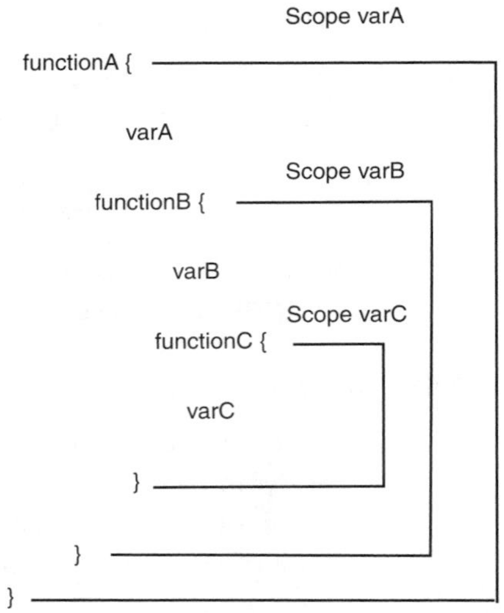

Figure B.3   The scope of variables `varA`, `varB`, and `varC`

Table B.2   Relational operators

Operator	Description	Operator	Description
>	Greater than	<	Less than
>=	Greater than or equal to	<=	Less than or equal to
==	Equality	!=	Inequality

NOTE   == is not the same as =. == tests for equality and returns `true` or `false`.

Control statements control the flow of your code. The statements can perform a number of tasks, and typical examples are reading a value from a sensor, turning an LED on or off, controlling the motors or servos on a robot, or measuring the distance from an object. The results from some tasks can determine what the next action will be.

For example, in the real world, if you went into a room and it was dark you would switch on a light. This sequence of events can be broken down into tasks as represented in figure B.4.

True or false is how computers evaluate an expression.

In the next section we'll look at how the different control structures behave in what are called conditional operators.

B.3.1 *If, else, else if*

The first of the conditional operators we're going to look at is the `if` statement. In the real world the `if` statement would be akin to asking a question with a straight yes (`true`) or no (`false`) answer:

- Am I tired of walking? Yes, then I'll stop.
- Am I hungry? Yes, then I'll eat.

In the real-world examples we're saying that if something is true, we'll perform the action. In code we ask the same questions, and if the statement is `true` we perform the action:

```
if (Boolean expression) {
    // do Action if Boolean expression is
       true
}
```

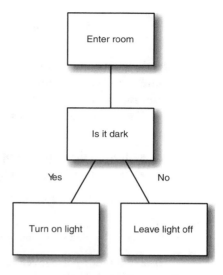

Figure B.4 A simple task: upon entering a room, if it is dark, turn on the light.

The statement preceding the { is evaluated as a Boolean expression. If it's true the code between the curly braces is run:

```
if (indexA < indexB) {
    digitalWrite(pinLed, HIGH);
{
```

In the preceding code, if the value of `indexA` is less than the value of `indexB`, the code statement is run and the pin is switched to `HIGH`.

Now that you understand the `if` statement we can introduce `else`:

- If I am tired, then stop; else carry on.
- If you are hungry, then eat; else pack up.

Here we're saying that if the answer to the question is yes (`true`) we'll perform the first action. Otherwise (`else`), if the answer is no (`false`) we'll perform the second action.

In Boolean expression terms we can think of this as follows:

```
if (Boolean expression) {
      // run this code if Boolean expression is true
{
else {
      // run this code if Boolean expression is false
}
```

If the Boolean expression is `true` the first statement block is run; otherwise the second block is run:

```
if (indexA < indexB) {
    digitalWrite(pinLed, HIGH);
}
```

```
else {
    digitalWrite(pinLed, LOW);
}
```

In the preceding code, if the value of indexA is less than the value of indexB the first statement block is run, switching the pin to HIGH; otherwise the second code block is run, switching the pin to LOW.

We'll now add the last part of the puzzle, else if, where we can ask one or more questions:

- If I am tired, then stop; else, if you are tired, then stop; else let's carry on.
- If you are hungry, then eat; else, if you are thirsty, then drink; else pack up.

In Boolean expression terms, it looks like this:

```
if (Boolean expression A) {
// run this code if Boolean expression A is true
{
else if (Boolean expression B) {
    // run this code if Boolean expression B is true
}
else {
    // run this code if both Boolean expressions are false
```

Here's a code example:

```
if (indexA < indexB) {
    digitalWrite(pinLedA, HIGH);
}
else if (indexA == index B) {
    digitalWrite(pinLedB, High);
}
else {
    digitalWrite(pinLedA, High);
}

}
```

In this case, if the value of indexA is less than the value of indexB the first code block is run; otherwise, if the value of indexA is equivalent to the value indexB the second code block is run; otherwise, if none of the preceding are true the third block is run.

We've now covered the if, else, and else if conditional operators, but if you find you're using a series of else if statements in your code it's worth considering the switch-case statement. We'll look at this next.

B.3.2   *Switch case*

Switch-case statements are a great way of simplifying complicated if, else if statements, and we find them much easier to understand and read. The following listing shows the typical layout for a switch-case statement.

Listing B.3 The `switch-case` statement

```
switch (value){
        case 1:
            // code statements when value == 1
            break;
        case 2:
            // code statements when value == 2
            break;
        case 3:
            //code statements value == 3
            break;
        case 4:
        case 5:
        case 6:
            // code statement when value == 4 or 5 or 6
            break;
        default:
            // code statements run for any other value
            break;
}
```

The `switch-case` statement computes a series of comparisons and the computed `value` is compared with each case. If it's found equivalent the statements are run for that case.

The `break;` statement shown in the listing is optional, but if it's included it ceases further comparisons, which is generally more efficient.

The `default` statement is also optional, but it can be used like the final `else` in a complicated `if`, `else if` series of statements.

This completes our look at `switch-case` statements. We're now going to move on and look at logical operators. These will give us more tools for comparing expressions and will expand our coding abilities.

B.3.3 *Logical operators*

The conditional operator examples we've looked at so far have just considered simple expressions like "if I am tired, then stop." Adding the logical operators AND, OR, and NOT gives us more scope to ask slightly more developed questions:

- If I am tired AND you are tried, then we will stop.
- If I am tired OR you are tired, then we will stop.
- If you are NOT tired, we will carry on.

In code, we don't use the words AND, OR, and NOT but instead represent them in the following manner:

- AND becomes `&&`
- OR becomes `||`
- NOT becomes `!`

Let's look at each in turn.

AND
```
if (indexA > indexB && indexC > indexD) {
     digitalWrite(pinLedA, HIGH);
}
```
If the value of indexA is greater than the value of indexB AND the value of indexC is greater than the value of indexD, then run the code block and switch the pin to HIGH.

OR
```
if (indexA > indexB || indexC > indexD) {
     digitalWrite(pinLedB, HIGH);
}
```
If the value of indexA is greater than the value of indexB OR the value of indexC is greater than the value of indexD, then run the code block and switch the pin to HIGH.

NOT
```
if (!buttonPressed) {
     digitalWrite(pinLedA, HIGH);
}
```
If NOT variable buttonPressed, run the code block and switch the pin to HIGH.

B.4   Going loopy

As we've already discussed, the main part of a sketch typically takes part in the control loop which continues to loop until the Arduino is powered off. But there are other types of loops that can occur within the main loop, designed to be used with repetitive code. These are set so that they loop until a certain condition is met, and if that condition isn't met the loop will continue indefinitely.

We're going to look at three types of loops: for, while, and do while.

B.4.1   The for loop

For loops are used to loop through a block of code a certain number of times. They're normally used with some form of incremental counter that increments until a certain value is reached, which terminates the loop.

The following listing shows a typical for loop that prints the value of i, from 0 to 99, repeatedly until the Arduino is powered off.

Listing B.4   A for loop printing the value of i, from 0 to 99
```
void setup()
{
  Serial.begin(9600);
}

void loop {
 for (int i = 0; i < 100; i++){
     Serial.println(i);
 }
}
```

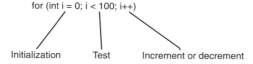

Figure B.5 **A** `for` **loop header showing initialization, test, and increment or decrement**

The variable `i` is initialized with the value `0`. This is incremented by one with the code `i++`, which is a shorthand way of saying

```
i = i + 1
```

The code loops, printing out the value of `i` until `i` equals `100`. At that point the loop terminates that run and starts again from `0`.

The top line or header of a `for` loop consists of three parts, as shown in figure B.5: initialization, test, and the increment or decrement counter.

The initialization only occurs once, at the start of the routine. The second part, the test, is performed each time the loop runs. If the test is `true` the code block is executed and the counter value is incremented (`++`) or decremented (`--`) as specified in the third part of the header. The routine will continue to loop until the test is `false`, which in this case is when the counter reaches 100.

The next type of loop we'll consider is the `while` loop.

B.4.2   *The while loop*

The `while` loop tests an expression contained within parentheses and will continue to loop through a block of code between curly braces until the expression tests `false`:

```
while (expression) {
// do statements
}
```

The previous code for the `for` loop can be written using a `while` loop, as shown in the following listing.

Listing B.5   A `while` **loop that prints out the value of** `i` **from** `0` **to** `99`

```
void setup() {
    Serial.begin(9600);
}
void loop(){
 int i = 0;
 while (i < 100){
   Serial.println(i);
   i++;
 }
}
```

You can consider a `for` loop as a special case of a `while` loop; the `while` loop is used when you are unsure how many times the code will loop. Typical uses for the `while` loop include testing the input from sensors or buttons.

The following snippet tests the value of a sensor:

```
int sensorValue = 0;
while (sensorValue < 2000 {
    sensorValue = analogRead(analogPin);
}
```

This code will continue to loop while the value of sensorValue is less than 2000.

NOTE Make sure the code does change the value of the variable being tested in the expression, or the code will loop indefinitely.

The third and last type of loop is the do while loop, and we'll look at that next.

B.4.3 *The do while loop*

The do while loop is not used as often as the while loop. The difference between it and the while loop is that it tests the expression at the end of the code block, so the code block will always run at least once. The do while loop is typically used for reading data from files:

```
do {
    // code block
} while (expression);
```

Like a while loop, this code block will continue to run until the expression tests false.

B.5 *Functions*

We've already looked at the two main functions or routines that are needed in a sketch: setup() and loop(). Both are declared as type void, which means they don't return a value. Arduino simplifies many tasks by using readily accessible functions to control digital and analog input and output of data, as well as mathematics, trigonometry, and time functions, but we discuss these in the chapters as we come across them.

You can also write your own functions. They are normally used to help with repetitive tasks or calculations. You first need to declare the function type, as you do with a variable, and give it a name—something memorable that indicates what the function does. In parentheses, you place any parameters that you want to pass to the function. Code statements are then contained within curly braces:

```
type functionName(parameters){
// code statements here
}
```

Remember, if the function doesn't return a value you should give it a type of void. Functions of type void can use a return; statement to exit or return from the function; functions that return a value use the keyword return followed by the return value and then a semicolon (;). The following code snippet shows a function that converts a temperature in Fahrenheit to Celsius and returns the Celsius value:

```
float calcTemp(float fahrenheit){
     float celcius;
     celcius = (fahrenheit - 32)/ 1.8;
     return celcius;
}
```

The function is declared as type `float` and it's passed a value for `fahrenheit`. Subtracting 32 from `fahrenheit` and then dividing by 1.8 produces the `celsius` value. The return statement returns the value of `celsius`. This function could be used as part of a system for logging temperature data.

As you can see, functions are an ideal way to simplify code and take care of repetitive tasks.

B.6 *Summary*

In this appendix we looked at some parts of the Arduino language. Variables are a good way to help with our code, and choosing good names for them helps indicate how a code sketch works. We started to come to grips with language constructs such as `if`, `else`, and `else if`, and the `switch-case` statement. We also looked at the logical operators AND, OR and NOT. Finally, we ran through the different loop types, concluding with a look at functions. As you've seen, even if you're completely new to coding these techniques are quick to pick up and master.

appendix C
Libraries

In chapter 4 we covered software libraries and how they're used to extend the basic functionality of the Arduino. Other chapters have provided examples of how using libraries in your own projects can easily extend their functionality.

When you've gained some experience in writing your own sketches there will come a time when you develop a sketch that you could reuse in future projects or that may be useful to the Arduino community. You can either keep the developed code in a sketch or split it out into a library. Splitting the sketch out into a library will probably make it more useful to other users.

This appendix will guide you through the anatomy of a library so that you can see what's involved in writing your own.

C.1 Anatomy of a library

Arduino sketches are coded using C++ (see appendix B for more detail), and much of the complexity and functionality of Arduino programming is hidden from users by the extensive use of software libraries.

A software library is made up of at least one C++ class and maybe many more. A class consists of two files: a header file with a .h extension and a file with a .cpp extension.

The .h (header) file acts as a blueprint for the library, describing the functions of the library and what the class does. The .cpp file contains the fine detail of the library, detailing the functions and variables declared by the header.

Let's start by looking at the makeup of a header file.

C.1.1 The .h (header) file

The header is the blueprint for a library of classes. Imagine that we have a sensor called a *Sabre* that detects the presence of fossils in a patch of ground and counts them. You need to think what functions the library is going to provide. In this example we have two public functions available: one will set up the Sabre and the other will update readings from the Sabre.

We'll define the header in the next listing.

Listing C.1   Sabre.h

```
#ifndef SABRE _H          ◄──❶ Include guard directive
#define SABRE _H
                                          ❷ Include Arduino
#include <Arduino.h>                          library
                                      ◄──┘
class Sabre {             ◄──┘ Start of Sabre class

public:                   ◄──┘ Declare public keyword
                                          ❸ Declare class
Sabre();                                     constructor
void begin();                         ◄──┘
void update();            ◄──┘
                               Declare functions

private:                                                    Declare
    int pollSabre();                                        private
    int countFossils(int inputData);      Declare           keyword
                                      ◄──┘ private
};                        ❹ Mark end of    functions
                             ifndef directive
#endif                    ◄──┘
```

The start of the file is the #ifndef include guard directive. This prevents the code being included multiple times ❶. Including the Arduino library is optional ❷; include it if your code makes use of elements from the Arduino library, such as digitalWrite, delay, pinMode, and so on.

After the public keyword, the library's public functions are included; then the constructor, which is required to set up the library, is included ❸.

After the private keyword are the private functions; these are only accessible to the library. The end of the class is designated with the end of the #ifndef directive ❹.

Having completed the header file, we can now create the .cpp file, which will be the file that carries out the actions identified by the header file.

C.1.2   The .cpp file

The .cpp file contains the meat of the library. It includes the .h (header) file and fleshes out the functions declared in that file. The next listing shows the outline for our .cpp file.

Listing C.2   Sabre.cpp

```
#include "Sabre.h"        ◄──❶ Declare include for class

Sabre::Sabre () {                     ◄──┘ Declare class
                                      ❷ constructor
}
void Sabre::begin(){                                    ◄──┘ Define public
    // perform actions to initialize Sabre sensor here      functions
}
```

```
void Sabre::update(){
    int data = pollSabre();
    int result = countFossils(data);
}

int Sabre::pollSAbre(){                              ◁┐  Define private
    //code to poll Sabre sensor                       │  functions
}

int Sabre::countFosssils(int inputData){
    //code to count number of fossils found
}
```

The class declaration is included at the head of the file ❶ before constructing the class ❷. The public and private functions of the class then complete the library.

NOTE The double colon (::) is the *scope resolution operator*, and it tells the compiler that this function is inside the class.

Once you've finished writing your library you'll want to make it available to your sketches. To do so you need to copy the .h (header) and .cpp files into a subfolder of the Arduino libraries folder with the same name as your library, like this:

```
libraries/Sabre/Sabre.h
libraries/Sabre/Sabre.cpp
```

Let's finish off this section by looking at how to use this library.

C.2   Using a library

Once you've created a library you can use it in your own sketches, and you can also distribute it so others can use it in their sketches. You might consider sharing your code on the Arduino playground, which can be found at http://playground.arduino.cc. The playground is also a good place to find other people's libraries and code examples.

C.2.1   Using a library in a sketch

The following listing shows how the Sabre library would be used in an example sketch, where the Arduino is connected to a Sabre sensor.

Listing C.3   Sabre.ino

```
#include "Sabre.h"            ◁── ❶ Include Sabre library

Sabre mySabre                 ◁─┐  Initialize instance
                               ❷  of Sabre class
void setup(){
    mySabre.begin();          ◁─┐ Initialize
}                                │ Sabre sensor

void loop(){
    mySabre.update()          ◁─┐ Update Sabre
}                                │ sensor
```

You need to include the Sabre library in the sketch ❶ before initializing an instance of the Sabre class ❷. The Sabre sensor is initialized during setup and updated in the main sketch loop.

That's all there is to using a library in a sketch.

C.2.2 Distributing a library

You should consider distributing libraries that you write to the wider Arduino community. By distributing your libraries you give others the benefit of your experience and also invite other people to take what you have written and suggest ideas for future improvements. This sharing of libraries and willingness to help others is what makes the Arduino community so great.

When distributing a library to others, which is normally done as a zip file, you should include one or more example sketches showing how the library should be used. The examples should be placed in their own examples subfolder:

```
Libraries/Sabre/Examples/sabre.ino
```

appendix D
Components list

This appendix lists the components used in the projects for each chapter.

Chapter 1

An Arduino board
One LED

Chapter 2

An Arduino board
A breadboard and a selection of jumpers
Six red LEDs
One green LED
Seven resistors, 180 ohm
One resistor, 10k ohm
A momentary-contact push button

Chapter 3

An Arduino board
A breadboard and a selection of jumpers
A small potentiometer (a trimpot is ideal, as it can easily plug into a breadboard)
Five zener diodes, 0.5 watt 5V1 (we used a BZX55C5V)
Five resistors, 1M ohm
One resistor, 1k ohm
A small speaker, 8 ohm

Chapter 4

Not applicable

Chapter 5

An Arduino board
A breadboard and selection of jumpers
A small DC motor
An external power supply suitable for the motor
An external power supply for the Arduino (9 volts recommended)
A miniature relay DPDT 5 volt coil, rated 2 amps or more
A 2N2222 diode
A 1N4003 diode
A L293D dual H driver
A stepper motor
Two 2-pin screw connectors
A servomotor
A section of 0.1 inch header
A brushless motor
A brushless electronic speed controller (ESC)
A suitable power supply for a brushless motor

Chapter 6

An Arduino board
A breadboard and selection of jumper wires
A parallax ping
A speaker
A sharp GP2D12
One resistor, 10k ohm

Chapter 7

An Arduino board
A Hitachi HD44780-based LCD screen
A potentiometer, 10k ohm, or trimpot
A resistor, value dependent on the backlight of the LCD
A serial LCD (SparkFun compatible 16 x 2 serial LCD recommended)
A DS18B20 temperature sensor
One resistor, 4.7k ohm
A KS0108 graphical LCD
One resistor, 10k ohm
One resistor, 220 ohm

Chapter 8

An Arduino board
An Arduino Ethernet Shield
A momentary contact button

One resistor, 10k ohm
An Arduino Wifi Shield
An accelerometer, such as the ADXL335
A Bluetooth module, such as the SparkFun BlueSMiRF Silver
A AD5206 digital potentiometer from Analog Devices
Four LEDs
Four resistors, 220 ohm
A potentiometer

Chapter 9

An Arduino board
A Wii Nunchuk
Optionally a WiiChuck or NunChucky
An Xbox 360 game controller
A USB Host Shield, version 2.0

Chapter 10

An Arduino board
An iOS device
A breadboard and selection of jumpers
A Mac desktop or laptop computer with Xcode 4.0 or greater
A Redpark serial cable
A RS232-to-TTL adapter
A colored LED
One resistor, 200 ohm
A Sharp GP2D12 IR distance sensor

Chapter 11

Two flex sensors
An Arduino LilyPad
Four LEDs
Three meters of conductive thread
An Arduino Pro Mini
An HMC5883 three-axis digital compass
A 7-segment serial display
Three more meters of conductive thread
A pair of headphones
An Arduino Pro Mini
A QRE1113 reflectance sensor
A 0.25 watt speaker
Ten thin pieces of copper
Five thin pieces of rubber foam
A spool of thread

Chapter 12

An Arduino board
An Adafruit Motor Shield
A 5V stepper motor
Two AA batteries
Two buttons
A small DC motor
A servomotor
A potentiometer
One perfboard (preferably double-sided)
Four female header strips (long pin) or three female header strips and one Arduino offset header
An SD card holder
An SD card
A 74HC4050 level shifter
One resistor, 5k ohm
An SD card shield

Chapter 13

An Arduino board
Two servomotors
A breadboard and selection of jumper wires
A desktop or laptop computer with Processing, Pure Data, and Python installed
A USB webcam
Five LEDs
Five resistors, 4.7k ohm
Four potentiometers
Four resistors, 10k ohm
Three LM35 temperature sensors

appendix E
Useful links

This appendix lists a variety of useful Arduino-related links.

Additional Arduino articles

- *A Tour of Arduino* (http://manning.com/free/green_mevans.html)—An overview and general information about the Arduino, where it comes from, and the development IDE.
- *Adafruit Motor Shield* (http://manning.com/free/excerpt_mevans.html)—Using various motors with the handy Motor Shield by AdaFruit.
- *Introducing the LilyPad* (http://manning.com/free/excerpt_mevans_b.html)—Introducing the Arduino LilyPad, an Arduino designed for use with wearables and textiles.
- *Wi-Fi Communication and Arduino* (http://www.manning.com/free/excerpt_mevans_c.html)—Using the WiFly module for Wi-Fi on your Arduino.

Other useful links and materials

- Arduino home page (www.arduino.cc)—Arduino's main home on the web.
- Arduino foundations (http://arduino.cc/en/Tutorial/Foundations)—Core hardware and software concepts explained by Arduino.
- Arduino examples (http://arduino.cc/en/Tutorial/HomePage)—Additional examples from blinking an LED to other libraries.
- Arduino language reference (http://arduino.cc/en/Reference/HomePage)—The bible for writing Arduino code.
- SparkFun (www.sparkfun.com/)—A popular USA supplier for Arduinos, shields, electronic components, and all things DIY. Lots of information can also be gleaned from the SparkFun message board forum and the product comments.

- Adafruit (www.adafruit.com/)—Another popular USA supplier for Arduinos and DIY electronics. Like SparkFun, Adafruit also has great tutorials and online forums. Highly recommended!

- SK Pang Electronics (www.skpang.co.uk)—UK supplier for Arduinos and DIY electronics.

- Cool Components (www.coolcomponents.co.uk)—UK supplier for Arduinos and DIY electronics. Subscribe to their newsletter for updates.

- Bitsbox (www.bitsbox.co.uk)—UK supplier of a range of electronic components.

- Proto-PIC (www.proto-pic.co.uk)—UK supplier for Arduinos and DIY electronics.

- oomlout (www.oomlout.co.uk)—UK supplier of Arduinos, electronic components, and kits.

index